P9-DYY-417

THE PROF

LORD CHERWELL IN HIS ROOMS IN CHRIST CHURCH

R. F. HARROD

✫

THE PROF

A PERSONAL MEMOIR OF
LORD CHERWELL

LONDON
MACMILLAN & CO LTD
1959

MACMILLAN AND COMPANY LIMITED
London Bombay Calcutta Madras Melbourne

THE MACMILLAN COMPANY OF CANADA LIMITED
Toronto

PREFACE

Lord Birkenhead is now engaged on writing an official biography of the late Lord Cherwell. I can imagine no one better qualified. His father, the first Earl of Birkenhead, was bound to Lord Cherwell by ties of great friendship and mutual esteem. Thus the present Lord Birkenhead knew Lord Cherwell from early days as an intimate friend of the family. And I judge him to have, if I may be permitted to say so, a certain greatness of soul, such as is needed to appreciate the true quality of the late Lord Cherwell.

This volume is, by contrast, a purely personal memoir. I have sat at my desk in the country during the summer months, drawing on my own recollections only. I have resorted to no papers or documents. In the matter of research it has seemed to me that there could be no halfway house. Either one must ransack all the sources of information that the most conscientious historian would consider relevant, as I endeavoured to do when writing the life of Keynes, or one must do no research at all. That renders the status of the work quite clear to the future historian. What I have written down is simply what I claim to remember and is subject to the fallibility of memory.

Where I have written, 'I remember' or 'I recall', this means that I feel absolutely confident that what is stated in fact occurred. In all cases where the memory seemed at all blurred or I had any doubt, I have used such expressions as 'I seem to remember' or 'to the best of my recollection'. For the consolation of the reader I may say that out of the vast mass of memories I have selected only those that stand

out with special vividness in my mind. I believe that he
will infer from these pages that I have a rather good memory
for the kind of episodes described.

There is one exception to my statement that I have done
no research. During the vacation immediately following
Lord Cherwell's death and before I knew that Lord Birkenhead would shortly be writing an official life, I followed the
trail suggested by a chance conversation with the Honourable
Mrs. Reginald Fellowes. I am grateful to the Comtesse de
Pange for being good enough to let me read a series of letters
written to her by Lord Cherwell on varying dates between
1912 and 1957, and a diary kept by her husband, the late Comte
de Pange, and for her permission to publish certain extracts
from the letters, as also from the letters of the late Maurice
de Pange, her son, written when at Westminster School.

Only after this book was completed, and indeed after I
had corrected the galley proofs, did the obituary notice of
Lord Cherwell by Sir George Thomson (*Biographical Memoirs
of Fellows of the Royal Society*, vol. 4, November 1958) come
to hand. This is a sympathetic study and provides much
interesting information. Happily, I did not judge that it required me to make any changes at all in my text ; but I have
referred to it for corroboration in a number of footnotes.
The note by Sir William Farren, which is incorporated in
the obituary notice, supplies valuable information about the
scientific background and the course of aeronautical experiments at Farnborough during the First World War. But it
does not mention the aeronautical spins referred to on the first
page of this book. These were described to me with great
vividness and with circumstantial detail by Lt. Col. O'Gorman,
who, as Superintendent of Farnborough, authorised the spins,
and, along with his assistant superintendent, Mr. Heckstall
Smith, was an eye witness of them. O'Gorman also put down
for me the essentials on a piece of paper, which I still have.

The relevant part of what he wrote was published in my *Life of J. M. Keynes* (p. 589 *n.*), and was seen by Lord Cherwell, who confirmed that it was correct. The spins must have occurred near mid-1916 and were additional to those of mid-1917 narrated by Sir William Farren (op. cit.). The evidence for the earlier spins, which contributed to robbing the spin of much of its terror, is not confined to the testimony of Mervyn O'Gorman, and is, I am confident, quite conclusive.

By reasoning similar to that which made me eschew all research, I deliberately abstained from showing my MS. to Lord Cherwell's closest friends. Those who would first come into the mind, had one thought of doing so, are his brother, Brigadier Lindemann, Mr. Bolton King, Mr. Collie, Mr. Keeley, Sir Donald MacDougall, Mr. Robert Blake, Mr. Harvey and Sir Winston Churchill himself. I feared that if any one of these disagreed with some passage, I should have felt it needful to consult another, and possibly have been confronted with conflicting opinions, which I should then have had to weigh, and so have become involved in the normal process of writing history. And this would have insensibly altered the character of the book. I wished to keep my own personal impressions entirely free of the impressions formed by other minds from other points of view.

Sir Winston Churchill has, however, read the MS., including the foregoing paragraph.

If, in consequence of not consulting close friends, I have left passages in this book which give them offence and might have been removed in consequence of their representations, I am truly sorry for it. None the less I believe that my procedure has been right, and that I should have got into difficulties as soon as I had departed, to however small an extent, from the rigid principle of non-consultation.

When I reflect upon these matters, there is one person the thought of whom perturbs me much more than that of the close friends, namely Lord Cherwell himself. He would have disliked all this sort of thing. He would have disliked biographies, official or unofficial. All through his life he shunned publicity of all kinds, and would not have welcomed the idea of the privacy of his life being invaded after his death. If I could have been quite sure that from this day forward no word would ever be written about Lord Cherwell, I might have deemed the claims of a lifelong friendship to outweigh those of the historic muse. But that cannot be so.

I asked my friend, Mr. John Sparrow, to read this book in typescript, not as an expert in its subject matter, but as the most sage of all literary advisers, who could be relied upon to draw my attention to solecisms, obscurities or errors of taste. I am grateful to him for a number of suggestions for improvement. I am grateful also to Mr. R. H. Dundas for employing his high skill in proof reading upon my galleys.

The reader will find that in the course of the following pages there are some rather long passages that are more autobiographical than biographical. Although the central themes and interests of my own life have lain quite apart from the affairs of Lord Cherwell, yet at times I became personally involved in them, notably during the Second World War. Naturally the matters about which I know most are those with which I was personally concerned. Furthermore, a touch of drama entered into our personal relations, especially in the later years. In places, for instance in relation to my electioneering at Huddersfield, I have entered into my own affairs at some length. The purpose has been to set his successive reactions to my activities in a clear light, and thereby to supplement my general remarks about his character by particular instances of its manifestation.

The consequence is that this book is a somewhat unorthodox amalgam of biography and autobiography, and it contains also passages of general reflection of a philosophical kind. To pause for a time and dwell on such questions seemed appropriate in the endeavour to describe a man whose life was first and foremost a life of thought. I must apologize to the reader if he is put out by the somewhat mixed nature of this volume. I hope that all will be found in the end to bear upon my central theme, which is the attempt to describe what manner of man Lord Cherwell truly was.

Happily there are no rigid canons about what should go to make up the contents of a single book. In looking back upon my literary life, I sometimes wonder whether I have made the mistake — if indeed it was a mistake — attributed to Hilaire Belloc :

> He seems to think that no one minds
> His books being all of different kinds.

The only criterion available for an author is that what he writes should interest himself. This gives him no guarantee, of course, that he will thereby interest his readers. But of this he may be sure, that, if he cannot interest his readers by what interests him, he will not be able to interest them in any way whatever.

R. F. H.

Bayfield Brecks,
Holt, Norfolk,
October 1958

CONTENTS

xiii

ILLUSTRATIONS

CHAPTER I

INTER-WAR YEARS

IT was Colonel Mervyn O'Gorman who gave me an authentic account of 'the Prof.'s' spinning nose-dive. O'Gorman was Superintendent of the Royal Aircraft Factory at Farnborough in the early years of the First World War. Mr. F. A. Lindemann, of half German or French Alsatian extraction, professor at Oxford after 1919, always known to his friends as 'the Prof.', and Viscount Cherwell at his death, was at that time a physicist of foremost quality, engaged at Farnborough on research into problems of signalling between the air and the ground and other scientific matters related to flying.

In the early part of the First World War any pilot who got into a spinning nose-dive crashed, and was lost together with his aeroplane. In his spare time the Prof. converted the aerodynamics of such a situation into algebraic formulae, and convinced himself of how a pilot ought to act; he reported accordingly to O'Gorman. But what then was O'Gorman to do? It was not very nice to ask a pilot on the strength of Mr. Lindemann's formulae to perform an operation of a kind that had so far almost invariably proved fatal; it was clearly impossible to issue directives until the matter had been tried out.

'Why not teach me to fly,' said the Prof., 'and let me do the experiment myself?' Within three weeks of his learning to fly, O'Gorman, albeit with misgiving, entrusted him with an aeroplane, and he flew up alone to a great height.

O'Gorman recalled that, as he watched him, his heart went
into his heels. The Prof. put himself into a spinning nose-
dive, and his recipe worked. To the consternation of
O'Gorman he went up again to a great height. He was
determined, after doing the experiment in a clockwise spin,
to show that it worked equally well in an anti-clockwise
spin ; and he repeated his performance. O'Gorman was there
waiting with his Assistant Superintendent to congratulate him.
But with foresight the Prof. had arranged to take a few days'
leave. He slipped out by a back way, thus eluding their
plaudits, and took the train to London. There he wrote an
elaborate account of the experiment which, on his return, he
routed through the usual office channels to the Superintendent.
So self-effacing was he, that it now appears that his fellow
scientific workers at Farnborough did not know of the event.
He avoided congratulations at that time, and afterwards also.
If in later years anyone broached the subject, he brushed him
aside with an 'Oh, no, it was really quite different'. This
was characteristic. He never courted praise or even recognition ; indeed one might say that he shunned it.

An apt characterization of this exploit might be to say
that he showed the 'courage of his conviction'. The 'courage'
is obvious enough, but the 'conviction' is a necessary complement. On certain topics, scientific or lay, he thought very
deeply, and, when he had satisfied his mind about his conclusion, he stood by it absolutely. He was thoroughly
self-reliant in this regard, and seldom sought outside support.
When he was convinced by his own mental processes, he was
prepared to stand against the opinion of the world. He would
take any risk and face any unpopularity. He was quite calm
and self-assured, sometimes treating those who had reached
opposite views with a measure of contempt. I have never
met anyone who, when once he was convinced by his own
reasonings, was so deeply and unshakably convinced. Al-

though he was peculiar and original in many respects, I believe that to be the characteristic that most clearly singled him out from his fellow mortals.

★

I have searched my mind in an attempt to find some example from the Second World War, when I was working with him, in which the 'courage of his conviction' rendered comparable service to his country. His opinion about the size of the German Air Force in 1940–1 might be taken as an example. In his view the German bomber force was only about two-thirds of the size — I give the figure to the best of my recollection — affirmed by the Air Ministry. The matter was of no little importance in the early months of 1941, not only for the preparations for the defence of these islands, but also in relation to the amount of air strength we could send away from the country with reasonable safety, *e.g.* to North Africa. There were differences of opinion among the various authorities, but the Prof. was away out on the flank, affirming a much lower figure than the others.

His reasoning, reduced to very simple terms, was on these lines. Our little Branch, which was assisting Mr. Winston Churchill, had briefed him in criticizing the Air Ministry on the ground of the very small Battle Array that it seemed able to produce, in relation to the number of aircraft with which it had been supplied from our factories. The reasons came in : the rate of wastage of aircraft was formidably high ; at any one moment there was always a certain proportion of surviving aircraft under repair ; one could not establish a Battle Array without having a certain number in reserve ; front-line aircraft had to be assigned for Operational Training, as one could not send a pilot into the air to fight unless he had some training in the plane that he would have to fly in

3

action. We were not satisfied with all the reasons, and had our ripostes ; but still further reasons were furnished ; and so we had to believe that the final result was due, not to inefficiency, but to the facts of life and warfare. On the basis of this controversy the Prof. argued that it was impossible for the Germans to have a Battle Array that was so much larger than ours in proportion to the planes produced by them. They, too, must have had their wastage, their requirements for Operational Training, etc., etc.

There was a prolonged controversy. The Air Ministry had a vast mass of secret information, which was deployed in successive stages. I watched the Prof.'s face as some new bit of information, adverse to our argument, filtered in from the Air Ministry. He was absolutely unperturbed. He would not yield an inch of ground.

This was not within my particular province in his Branch ; but he asked me to check some of his figures and arguments, and we were all intensely interested in the controversy and discussed it among ourselves. There were moments when the whole world seemed to be against the Prof. ; even the member of our staff who had the best credentials for statistical *expertise*, seemed to be going over to the 'enemy'. The battle raged for a long time. At one point we found that a Christ Church colleague was a subaltern in charge of a pen of German airmen prisoners in London. Through him the Prof., fluent in German, obtained the chance of cross-examining them about the organization of formations, which was germane to our argument. I was told that our colleague got into trouble with his superior officer. 'What right had you to allow the Professor access ? You know that these damned politicians only want to find arguments to do down the Services.'

Day by day the Prof. indoctrinated Churchill with his views. When advocating a case of this sort, he displayed absolute calm and placidity. He spoke *sotto voce*, but with complete self-assurance, as though stating facts that must be obvious to every schoolboy. And what of those who disagreed with him ? They were perfect fools. He dismissed them with little pungent pieces of irony. But his victory was not only behind their backs. He had a super-normal power of quick calculation, so that, when it came to a round-table discussion involving figures, he was able to take them by surprise, by his quick results or by looking at the figures from a different point of view, and to rout them.

I do not know how far Churchill's own view prevailed at this time over those of the Chiefs of Staff ; presumably it counted for something ; I have no doubt that the steady drip, drip of the Prof.'s insistence, his air of certainty, his ability to rebuff all arguments, must have had influence on the Prime Minister's mind.

It might be said that this was an example of conviction, but that courage was not requisite.[1] There was courage in being so self-assured against all the experts. But there was more to it than that. There we were in London, being bombed. Suppose that the Prof. was wrong in his calculations. Suppose that the German Air Force was indeed as big as the Air Ministry claimed. Suppose that, by consequence of a wrong view, too many fighters were sent out to Egypt, so that the home country was left exposed and defeated in a renewed assault. The Prof.'s life was at stake then, just as much as in the spinning nose-dive. More than once he confided to me that, if the worst happened and we were overpowered, he would himself find some means of being

[1] I was intrigued to notice that Sir George Thomson (*op. cit.* in Preface) independently referred to the Prof.'s intervention in this matter as requiring 'intense self-confidence' (page 61). He refers to 'some instinct or fifth' (should it not be sixth ?) 'sense' as having assured the Prof. that the official estimate was wrong. There may have been such an instinct, but the main thing that actuated the Prof., as usual, was a very firm logical inference, namely, from the size of the British Air Force.

killed in the last ditch. He told me that Winston Churchill was of the same mind. I have no doubt that that was the case.[1]

★

The Prof. made notable contributions of his own to the development of quantum physics between 1910 and 1914. However we may assess those, I suppose that, on a broad historic view, they were overshadowed by the part that he played as Churchill's most trusted adviser and intellectual support over many years, including those of the Second World War. I remember turning over the pages of the visitors' book at Chartwell and seeing the Prof.'s name occur repeatedly during the 'twenties ; to the best of my recollection these entries included visits in the weeks immediately before Budget Day.

In the 'twenties Lord Birkenhead (F. E. Smith) and Winston Churchill were both his intimate friends ; they seemed to be co-equal stars in his political firmament. The Prof. was a first-rate tennis player, and during his sojourn in Germany before the First World War he picked up enough silver trophies to fill a large cupboard in his rooms at Oxford. F. E. Smith liked to invite tennis players to his house at Charlton, near Oxford, to give him a good game during the week-end. Mr. J. C. Masterman, also an excellent tennis player, recalls that on an occasion, when they were both taken up to play tennis at Charlton, it was for both of them their first visit. F. E. Smith and Winston Churchill were, of course, great friends. Very soon the Prof. was a great friend of both. Lord Birkenhead died prematurely in 1930. Thereafter Churchill was the Prof.'s sole star.

[1] Sir Winston Churchill has given an account of this episode in *The Second World War*, volume 3, pages 34-38. Appendix D was written by Churchill himself, but his ammunition was supplied by Lord Cherwell.

I remember his telling me how he had discussed with both of them the idea of standing for Parliament. (This was some ten years before his abortive candidature to be member for Oxford University.) Birkenhead strongly dissuaded him, but Churchill was keen that he should do so. Birkenhead had a high, perhaps an idealistic, view of the dignity and importance of Oxford ; he was bred up in it, had even been a don himself (Fellow of Merton), had married the daughter of the Fellow of a College and liked to maintain a close association with the University. He told the Prof. that his professorship gave him a far more worthwhile way of life than he could get by being engaged in the sordid pettinesses of party politics. But Churchill was more buoyant and enthusiastic : the Prof. must join the fray and do battle with the rest of them ; his brains would render vital service to the country.

Churchill had not the same close link with Oxford ; indeed he had not been at a university. But he was not lacking in appreciation of its value. When he was awarded an honorary degree, he had to make a speech at the Christ Church Gaudy. I well recall that, unlike all the other great men thus honoured, he scorned to give any of the ten or fifteen minutes appropriate to an after-dinner speech to pleasing us with jests or anecdotes, but went straight to his serious theme, describing in glorious braided phrases the unique rôle of a university such as Oxford in being able to blend tradition and freedom.

There was another time too when I heard him deploy all the resources of the English language in describing what a university could contribute to a man's life. His son, then my pupil, Randolph, had been offered fees to give lectures in America, which would render him a surtax-payer on earned income at the age of nineteen. It seemed a pity to break his Oxford career in the middle, and I went over to Chartwell, to join forces with his father in dissuading him.

7

Churchill stood in front of his fireplace that evening and let his fancy flow freely. He described the mature wisdom of the dons, only to be obtained by devoting a lifetime to reading and reflection. It was too kind and complimentary to us academics, I fear. But how I wished that I had a notebook in which to put down the golden words, or had been a Boswell to remember them, as phrase followed phrase and sentence followed sentence in glowing and ascending Churchillian oratory. I do not suppose that Oxford has ever had a more splendid and comprehensive tribute than that pronounced just among ourselves at the fireside that evening. He also said, very nicely and modestly, with a look of appeal to Randolph, how much he had felt the lack, at times during his life, for example when in political controversy with such a man as A. J. Balfour, of the weapons with which a period of study under sage university teachers might have furnished him. What was rather touching was that, when it was all over and Randolph had left the room, he turned to me and said, 'Well, we got down to brass tacks'. This hardly seemed a right description of his superb essay in English prose, which, without disrespect for Randolph, I felt sure had flowed like water off his back.

Still, the fact remained that for Churchill the core of life was politics ; to bring things to a successful issue there — and even in the 'twenties he thought that the Prof. might help — transcended everything else in importance. πᾶσαι κοινωνίαι ἀγαθοῦ τινος στοχάζονται, . . . ἡ πασῶν κυριωτάτη καὶ πάσας περιέχουσα τὰς ἄλλας· αὕτη δ᾽ ἐστὶν . . . ἡ κοινωνία ἡ πολιτική.[1] And so the Prof. was to be drawn into the fray. But he was still shy of it.

How did this close alliance between Churchill and the Prof. come about ? In later days it was taken for granted as

[1] All associations aim at some good. The most authoritative of all associations, which embraces all other associations, is the political association. (Aristotle).

a long-established fact and sustained by Churchill's loyalty
to his old familiar friend. But it must have had a beginning.
Why had the friendship started in the first instance ? I would
suggest that it can only be that Churchill, and F. E. Smith
along with him, spotted in the Prof. a brain of original and
outstanding quality. F. E. and Churchill were already in
the front rank of politics during the 'twenties. They had met,
or had had opportunities for meeting, all the distinguished
people. One new professor, one new scientist, even one new
scientist alleged to be of exceptional promise, could in itself
mean nothing to them. The Prof. at that time was already
beginning to be something of a social luminary. But there
was nothing in that for them ; on the whole they only met
social luminaries. Lord Birkenhead had a nodding acquaintance with most of the distinguished people in Oxford. Indeed
the Prof., considered merely as a social entity, was not in any
sense an asset for them. He was already beginning to be regarded in some circles as a rather sinister figure, for reasons
which I shall endeavour to state, anyhow in part. He was
reputedly half-German ; he was someone who needed a little
explaining. One must remember the time sequence and not
suppose he had in their eyes the glamour that long association
with Churchill afterwards gave him in the eyes of other distinguished persons. He had considerable personal charm, but
it was not readily apparent until you got to know him well.
And he had some superficial characteristics which decidedly
put people off him.

One can hardly escape the conclusion that what these two
men, severally and together, saw in him can only have been
his innate quality of mind. That is not to be measured simply
by the position that he had then obtained in his own university, or in his own subject of physics. It was something more
than that, something that raised him above the general run
of the professoriate. It was not his scientific attainment, which

they were not in a position to assess, and about which on inquiry they could have learnt bad as well as good. It was something in the quality of his mind that made anything he had to say worth listening to, on the kind of topics that they themselves were interested in talking over.

Have I made heavy weather about why Churchill first became so close a friend of the Prof. ? I have sought to do so, partly because I believe that it throws an important light on Churchill himself. For the Prof. was not one of those people whose true quality was readily appreciated, even by 'intellectuals'. He had not very good powers of expression. It was quite often impossible to hear what he said. His mind was tortuous and he was apt to express himself in riddles. He also talked quite a good deal of rubbish about matters that were outside his range. It is not enough to say that he was caviare to the general ; he was caviare to a great many people who would regard themselves as on a high intellectual plane. Only a person of considerable intellectual quality would be likely to appreciate the Prof. as being a person of the highest intellectual quality. And thus, as it seems to me, Churchill's selection of the Prof. as his most trusted adviser is important evidence of Churchill's very profound intellectual grasp. I would say that it raises him, and it must raise F. E. Smith along with him, much above other men thrown up into prominence by public life, *on the purely intellectual plane*.

Let us look at the other side. Already at this time, at the beginning of his great friendship with Churchill, the Prof. was moving fairly freely in what might be called high society. In one way or another he was in a position to meet all the prominent politicians of the day. Among all these, F. E. Smith and Churchill were hand-picked by him. He cultivated them, paid them particular attention and sought their favour. And what was it in them that particularly attracted him ? Their brains.

Churchill, we all know, has other great qualities — for instance, his wonderful power of language and his capacity to rise on a great occasion to a sublime level. I do not think that this meant anything to the Prof. He was no judge of oratory, except, possibly, to the extent that it manifested itself in the clear and cogent statement of an argument. Those qualities in public speaking that may appeal to the hearts of hearers he thought of simply as 'sob stuff', and I do not think that he was well able to distinguish a noble passage from claptrap.

Then there was Churchill's abundant and all-pervasive sense of humour. Almost every member of his *entourage*, or even those who have had quite casual contacts with him, have some priceless piece of humour to narrate, whether uttered in a grave moment of crisis or on a trivial occasion. I do not recall the Prof. ever quoting any funny remark by Churchill at all. This must not be held to betoken a lack of sense of humour in the Prof. ; on the contrary, quite a large part of his conversation was shot through with humour ; he was very fond of funny stories or of quoting funny things that had been said. Indeed he often quoted Lord Birkenhead, particularly relishing his devastating ripostes to some unfortunate heckler or impudent interlocutor. This was done with great gusto. Indeed it may be thought that Lord Birkenhead served as a model for the Prof.'s own style of crushing repartee.

Was it Churchill's gift of 'leadership' that drew him — not yet fully proved at that time ? This is a many-sided matter. I have already touched on some aspects, such as his oratory and that sense of humour which has so special an appeal to the British people. There is that part of leadership that, without disrespect, we may call 'showmanship', for which Churchill, mercifully for us, also had some gift. That certainly meant nothing to the Prof. ; indeed it must have tried him. I often recall the occasion when, at about the

time of the fall of France, the first bar of Beethoven's Fifth
Symphony was transposed via the morse code (···——) into
V for Victory, as some kind of secret sign for the underground
movement. I do not know what success it had in that capacity, but most of us, when we now think of the V sign, recall
Churchill sticking up two fingers in response to the greetings
of a crowd. At this early date the Prof. wrote a minute to
Churchill, 'Would it not be a good thing if people, instead
of wasting their time with promoting the V sign, paid
attention to the manufacture of small portable bombs for
placing in the motor cars of German generals?' I remember
Churchill's reply coming into the office. He dwelt on the
question of the small portable bombs, and gave instructions for
suitable directives to be drafted. But then at the end came a
little sentence. 'I am not sure that I can agree with you that
the promotion of the V sign is a complete waste of time.'

The Prof. did not often talk of Churchill in the later
period, but did a good deal more so before the war. The
subject selected for his praise was always the same. It was
Churchill's prodigious brain power. This dates back to the
early days, when Churchill was a prominent British politician
but not a figure of world renown. The Prof. was very
sparing in his intellectual tributes, especially sparing outside
the world of science. From the beginning he was quite
convinced that Churchill was one of the great intellects of
our age. He stressed particularly his capacity for simultaneously grasping the whole wide range of forces bearing
on the world situation at any moment and his capacity to
judge each new event for its influence, not only on the point
of its apparent application, but over the whole scene. He was
tremendously impressed by the skill with which Churchill
was able to assemble his case when in the wilderness, meeting
and overcoming Ministers who had all the advantage of the
Civil Service working on their side and of their secret in-

formation. He was impressed by the unremitting continuity of Churchill's appraisement of the world scene and his comprehension of so many diverse kinds of influence. He was staying with Churchill in North Africa on the occasion when the Stone of Scone was removed from Westminster Abbey, and shortly afterwards some ebullient visitor in the Christ Church Senior Common Room said, 'Oh, Lord Cherwell, do tell us what Churchill said about the loss of the Stone'. The Prof. : 'I am afraid that he said nothing to me ; you know, to be quite frank, he occupies his mind with more important things.'

Such was the Prof.'s testimony. It was directed to Churchill's intellectual greatness, and to that only, and quite consistently so throughout the long period of his close association.

I cannot forbear adding a short corollary. The greatness of Churchill has been so widely recognized and he has been so much idolized, very justly, that it seems absurd to claim at this stage that there is anything more to be added to the universal acclaim. And yet, when all has been said, I cannot escape the feeling that there is a certain deficiency in the general run of comment. The word 'leadership' is used without analysis. While recognizing the sublime passages in some of his wartime utterances, when the situation itself called for sublimity, I would not suppose that, simply as a speaker, Churchill has a unique place. He was no doubt efficient in the handling of affairs, and he had a host of amiable qualities, but these alone did not raise him to the great height at which none the less we wish to place him. I suggest that Churchill's real claim to great pre-eminence, and I believe that the Prof. would have endorsed this from his wide knowledge of Churchill over so long a period, is that he is one of the greatest intellects of the twentieth century and one of the greatest intellects that has ever happened to hold the post of Prime Minister in any country. We speak with respect, and even veneration, of that eminent nineteenth-century Prime Minister, Gladstone. He was no doubt a man of greater erudition than Churchill ; he was a man of meticulous detail and good oratorical power. But for intellectual capacity in its true sense, the power to grasp all the myriad facets of world affairs and assess things in their just proportions, I do not suppose, to judge from the records that Gladstone has left, that he can hold a candle to Churchill. It is this quality of sheer brain power that I believe has not even now been sufficiently appreciated.

Failure to recognize the specifically intellectual quality of Churchill was evinced in discussions people liked to have, to while away the time in the later period of the war, on whether they regarded Churchill or Roosevelt as the greater man ; this might turn on the political complexion of the speaker, Roosevelt appealing more to one of leftward inclination, as being supposed to have a wider vision of world brotherhood. This was, of course, to miss the essential point. Roosevelt was a man of great ability and generous views and an astute politician — perhaps too astute, since he thereby became so much hated by the Republicans ; but no one could suppose that Roosevelt was one of the great *intellects* of our century. Or again, even after the war, it was often said that Churchill was a great war leader, but not so well adapted for the affairs of peace. If that merely meant that it was most needful to have a great brain in the conduct of a war, since, if mistakes were made, the war might be lost, while in peacetime very grave mistakes could be made and yet we should survive and continue to muddle along as usual, the point might be *pro tanto* sound. But I do not think that that was the point that those who made these distinctions had in mind. They failed to do justice to Churchill's most important quality of all.

His works are insufficiently studied for the profound political philosophy which they contain. At the universities, where the young are supposed to be trained to think on political principles, one has found very second-rate writers recommended for study, and, through that, having a great influence in parts of the Commonwealth. How many undergraduates could pass an examination on the thought of Churchill, which is of such far greater value? It is true that Churchill did not write a textbook of political principles ; his wisdom is contained in *obiter dicta* in his speeches and historical writings, or merely implied, or even has to be read between the lines ; thus it needs bringing together by conscientious and discriminating scholarship. Burke gave his political wisdom to the world in the same manner ; it has none the less been carefully studied in the universities for several generations. Yet surely Churchill has been a greater political thinker than Burke.

Thus I believe that the long intimacy of Churchill and the Prof. rested on the firm basis of an appreciation by each of the intellectual qualities of the other. No doubt there are also factors of temperament, which govern the possibilities of friendship. Intellectual affinity is important if the friendship is to be durable.

*

I first saw the Prof. shortly after the First World War at a meeting of the Jowett Society, at which undergraduates discourse on philosophy. He was billed to speak on the Theory of Relativity. I was myself an undergraduate. He had recently been elected as Doctor Lee's Professor in Experimental Philosophy (Physics). At this moment he had a great reputation.

He was born in Sidmouth ; his father was a German or French Alsatian and his mother (Miss Noble) an American.

THE PROF

My former colleague, Major Slessor, the Steward of
Christ Church, a delightful soldier of the old type, yet of
literary sensibility, father of our Air Marshal, recalls seeing
the Prof. being wheeled up and down the parade at Sidmouth
in his perambulator. His father gave a fine telescope to
Sidmouth, which was for many years an object of interest
to tourists, but has since been transferred to the University
of Exeter. The Prof. was sent for his university training
to Germany, and stayed on there to do research. His
brother, Charles, was with him. In the 'thirties I met an
elderly lady, who was a German chemist stationed in Berlin.
I asked her if she had ever known my colleague, Professor
Lindemann, in Berlin in the old days. Her face assumed an
expression of ecstasy and she cast her hands into the air.

'Ah, the Lindemann brothers, the Adlon, tennis !'

It was during his period of research that he won all the
tennis pots that I have already mentioned. He was wealthy,
and could afford to live comfortably at the Adlon ; and it
would be like him to give a good time to colleagues who
might be living an austere life, working on the rock face of
scientific research. It is said that even in those days he did not
get up until between eleven and twelve in the morning. He
was always smartly dressed in a morning coat. None the less
he found time somehow for research. He was in the forefront
of developments in quantum physics before 1914, co-operating
particularly with Nernst.

In 1911 he was made secretary of the Solvay Conference,
a photograph of which is adjoined. I should suppose that
in the whole of human history there can scarcely ever have
been such a constellation of great minds as is there represented. In 1912 he came over to Scotland to give an address
to the British Association for the Advancement of Science at
Dundee. His subject was the atomic heats of solids at very
low temperatures. In this cold region, he was able to show

CONSEIL DE PHYSIQUE SOLVAY, BRUSSELS, 1911

Standing, left to right: Goldschmidt, Planck, Rubens, Sommerfeld, Lindemann, de Broglie, Knudsen, Hasenöhrl, Hostelet, Herzen, Jeans, Rutherford, Kamerlingh Onnes, Einstein, Langevin

Seated, left to right: Nernst, Brillouin, Solvay, Lorentz, Warburg, Perrin, Wien, Mme Curie, Poincaré

that what actually happened could not be accounted for by the classical theory of physics, but fully bore out the theories of quantum physics. This paper was of considerable importance in the development of physics, since it contributed to the accumulation of evidence for the universal application of the principles of quantum physics. It was partly through this paper that his reputation in his own country was established. Thus when, after the war, Oxford University appointed him to this important Chair in physics, it was taking a bold and progressive measure ; he was still a young man, but he had an international reputation ; he was in close contact with the intellectual giants who had been making the physics of the twentieth century ; he had made notable contributions himself ; if all went well, given his youthful energy, he might well make his Clarendon Laboratory a co-equal with the Cavendish Laboratory at Cambridge. Meanwhile rumours had filtered through to Oxford of his splendid acts of dauntless courage in flying experiments, of which I have given but one example in the opening of this book. Thus, in the eyes of the undergraduates waiting to hear him in the Jowett Society he was quite a tremendous person.

Its meeting was held in an ordinary set of residential rooms in college, such as is commonly used for meetings of small societies to which learned papers are read. The rooms were filled to overflowing. People were sitting on the arms of chairs, on the floor and on top of one another. Not only were there the regular undergraduate members, but many of the philosophy dons had also turned up. There were scientists too. And there were also men of general culture, who were interested to hear about what was then a brand new scientific development. Mr. R. H. Dundas (ancient historian) remembers being there.[1]

[1] And has given a very brief account of the meeting in his obituary notice in the annual history of the works of Christ Church (1957).

When the protagonist of the proceedings of the evening entered, he gave us a great surprise. He was exceedingly *bien soigné*, dressed in a dinner jacket and boiled shirt. (The boiled shirt he affected until his dying day.) He was well built, tall, upright and slim. (In his middle-age he became rather stout.) He had a black well-groomed moustache. His rather pallid face did not appear, on first inspection, to be notably intellectual. The features were well formed, but heavy. He was essentially an elegant figure. One might take him for a man about town, perhaps a Guards officer. Owing to the crowding of the room, he was placed in an upright chair with his back to the wall; he seemed to be a prisoner in our midst, and rather cramped. But he was not put off. The Theory of Relativity is not an easy subject. He treated it as though it were. He had a most natural and extremely self-assured style of speaking. His manner was as though he were explaining to an audience, which would readily pick it up, how to work some new gadget. He knew his subject exceedingly well, having been over the whole ground many times with the greatest masters of thought in the world. He spoke in short, clipped sentences, not always quite audible. He took the attitude that, as we were presumably highly intellectual people, if he gave us an essential point lucidly, we would grasp it quickly and appreciate its bearings. Sometimes he adorned his discourse by an illuminating example or analogy. The whole thing was stimulating in a high degree. We were put on our mettle. We felt that we ought to be able to follow it all. If anything could make this difficult theory plain, the short, staccato sentences and the brilliant illustrations should have done so. We certainly felt that we had been given our fill, although those who were not scientists may, if honest with themselves, have realized that they had not understood the matter to its depths.

Professor J. A. Smith, Waynflete Professor of Metaphysical

Philosophy in the University of Oxford, had been invited to open the discussion. Although Professor Lindemann had sat in a cramped position, Professor Smith took up his stand in front of the fireplace. He had abundant snow-white locks and a drooping white moustache, and he had a hint of the venerable about him. He was not the most highly esteemed of Oxford philosophers at that time, but he was in the tradition and had formerly been a tutor at the great College of Balliol. He had a gift of mellifluous speech, learned, courteous, polished. No one could better phrase a gracious expression of welcome to a distinguished visitor. In his lectures he sometimes became like one inspired ; there was a touch of purple in his beautiful scholarly presentation and deep philosophy. He was modern, by Oxford standards, in one sense, since he subscribed to the philosophy of Gentile. This philosophy was in the vanguard of modern idealism, but destined soon to be rubbed out by quite different developments. The Theory of Relativity, constituting from a high intellectual point of view a mighty revolution, was a truly momentous subject for philosophical consideration. I always remember how, on the morrow of the ascertainment in 1919 that the light rays from a star bent in the vicinity of the sun, J. B. S. Haldane came round among the undergraduates of New College and announced that Kant had been proved right. That was not an acceptable view ; but it was tending in the right direction, in indicating that the Relativity Theory was of the most profound interest in relation to the historic arguments of philosophy.

The allocution of Professor Smith, when he had got over his preliminaries, proved rather surprising. In the first place he was bent on showing that the Theory of Relativity was 'wrong'. More surprising was the fact that he did not seem to be about to deal with it on a high philosophical plane, on that of Gentile for instance, at all. On the contrary, he soon became immersed with the theory at its technical level. He discussed certain mathematical equations and certain assumptions. Then, as he droned on, he stated an assumption that he seemed to think important ; indeed it was this assumption that, on his view, showed that the Theory of Relativity was not self-consistent. When he came to this particular assumption, someone from the room interposed an objection. He repeated the assumption, which was, so to speak, within the realm of physics itself, rather than within that of philosophy. On this repetition there was a sort of chorus from the floor of the house — quite a number of scientists were present — that this assumption was wrong. Professor Smith protested violently ; I cannot remember whether he claimed that it had been explained personally to him by Professor Einstein or only that he had read it in a work of that scientist. (Einstein visited Oxford shortly after the war, and I have an idea that Professor Smith took a walk with him round Christ Church Meadow.) But then there was renewed vociferation ; Smith had got it wrong ; no such assumption was required by the Theory of Relativity ; indeed it was inconsistent with that theory ; there was a babel of voices. It became clear that the sense of the meeting would not let him get away with this one. He looked extremely vexed. He knocked out his pipe abruptly in the fireplace and sat down. That was the end of the contribution of Professor Smith.

This episode made me feel extremely uneasy. Professor Smith had formerly been a Greats tutor at Balliol. We had been told much about the wonderful generation of Greats men at that College before the war. Balliol apart, it was the current idea that the course of Greats at Oxford was the highest intellectual training, apart from the specialisms of mathematics and science, to be found in England, perhaps even in the world. In this course were trained the most

brilliant of our young men, destined to play their part as
civil servants and possibly as statesmen in the management
of our affairs. Even a democracy must have an *élite*, and
Greats was deemed to provide an *élite* of the *élite*. How
came it that this distinguished purveyor of Greats wisdom,
himself neither a mathematician nor a physicist, supposed
that he could find, not on the plane of philosophy, but on
the plane of physics itself, a technical error in the assumptions
behind a theory that had been minutely scrutinized for some
time by the greatest minds in the world ? We may recall
those men who surrounded Professor Lindemann in the
photograph that I have supplied of the Solvay Conference.
Had there been a technical error, would all these men of
great genius have missed it ? Was it left for an unmathe-
matical, unscientific don at Magdalen College (where he
now was) to detect a technical error ? This idea seemed to
argue an attitude of mind totally remote from the world of
reality, utterly provincial and parochial and incredibly com-
placent. Did he not know that science was being carried
forward by men of great intellectual acumen, that it was
international, that each published finding was subject to the
most severe checks ? And if he did not know that, if he
was living remote in some fastness of Greats, was he, or
others like him, really capable of giving a first-rate intellectual education to those destined to be responsible for the
intelligent management of the affairs of the great British
Empire ? What was this Greats ? If in this centre, an arsenal
of British thought, there could be such inspissated parochialism
and complacency, were we not indeed in a rather parlous
position ? These thoughts disturbed me at the time.

And did not our position in the inter-war period in fact
deteriorate precisely because of the prevalence of parochialism
and complacency ?

So much for Smith. The meeting, however, was not

stranded at that point, because the kindly undergraduates had
prudently provided a second respondent to the main subject.
And there he was now, sitting plump in the middle of a sofa
facing the fireplace. He was a somewhat shaggy individual,
with greying locks, not altogether tidy, and a rather bushy
greying moustache. I knew him well already ; he was my
tutor, Mr. H. W. B. Joseph, with whom I had had some
painful verbal contests. His general appearance was not that
of a thoughtful savant ; his shagginess did indeed make him
look more like an intellectual than Professor Lindemann.
But his face was not distinguished : rather full and convex,
it was marked by no expressive traits of thoughtfulness. He
had come into the room, a stocky figure, with a schoolboy's
satchel slung across his shoulders ; to judge from its dila-
pidated appearance, it might well have been his own schoolboy
satchel.

Now he had it at his side in the middle of the sofa, from
which, unlike J. A. Smith, he was evidently prepared to
speak sitting. To the dismay of the audience he proceeded
to extract from the satchel a thick wad of manuscript. Balancing a pair of *pince-nez* on the lower end of his nose, he made
ready to read from his papers. We steeled ourselves to a
long session.

In one respect Joseph was at one with J. A. Smith ; it
appeared from an early stage that he was setting out to prove
that the Theory of Relativity was 'wrong'. But he did not,
like Smith, proceed at a technical level ; what he had to offer
was, in its own way, genuine philosophy. Joseph had a most
remarkable style, which will always be remembered by, and
indeed sometimes had an important influence on, those who
heard him. His philosophy was influenced by that of the
already deceased J. Cook Wilson ; it was a philosophy in
which a rather crude realism had been grafted on the doctrines
of the ancient Greek philosophers, especially Plato. What

was peculiar was, not the corpus of the doctrine, but the manner of its elucidation. It was a tradition of this school, a very sound and excellent tradition, that one should eschew polysyllables and all technical philosophical jargon, and confine oneself to short English, preferably Anglo-Saxon, words, the meaning of which was plain from their habitual use in ordinary discourse. These philosophers were careful also to keep their sentences, in so far as the subject allowed, crisp and clear. Thus, if one listened to one sentence, one had the idea that this was a most beautifully lucid exposition and expressed a thought that commended itself to plain common sense. But Joseph had a certain cleverness, which prevented his remaining quite in the austere Cook Wilson tradition. He was very fluent ; and he had learnt the trick, which was a truly remarkable one, of running his sentences together into a discourse of interminable length. Thus, although each sentence seemed all right by itself, it was exceedingly difficult to grasp the meaning of the totality. He achieved what was almost an acrobatic trick. He rushed on and on ; one could not complain that any single word was of obscure meaning, or even that any single clause was. None the less the whole was difficult to follow, and some-times one could not help having the feeling, as sentence succeeded sentence, that he had cheated somehow in the process of leading us up to his clear and well-defined con-clusion.

Professor Joad, in his wireless talks in the Brains Trust, has habituated large British audiences to the idea that a philosopher is apt to say, 'It all depends on what you mean by that'. Joad's technique was a feeble caricature of Joseph's. The latter chose his ground carefully, and when he turned to you and gave you a piercing look and said, 'What do you mean by that ?', your heart sank ; you thought hastily how to explain your meaning ; you realized that you could not explain it ; you realized finally that you had meant just nothing at all.

Joseph had the idea that certain words that are commonly used express some genuine apprehension by the mind. On this particular evening he was much concerned with such words as 'greater than', 'less than', 'before', 'after', 'simultaneously', 'moving relatively to'. What was meant by these words was based on a definite intellectual apprehension. One must not import different meanings, which violated these original apprehensions, into them. There they were, tokens of the mind's power of grasping certain things. And so he proceeded forward, in a lengthy and elaborate demonstration, to show that among the mind's original powers to grasp certain things, powers indicated by the use of words, powers which you could only challenge by using words in senses that were manifestly improper, was the mind's knowledge that space was Euclidean in character. Therefore the Theory of Relativity must be wrong.

Undergraduates, hand-picked although they are for the great seats of learning, do not always get things quite right. There was current in New College a limerick about Joseph :

> There was an old person called Joseph
> Whom nobody knows if he knows if
>   He knows what he knows, which accounts I suppose
> For the mental condition of Joseph.

They were right in thinking that the question of what he knew or did not know was quite essential to the inner personality of Joseph. But the whole point about him was quite the opposite to that suggested by the limerick. What was peculiar was his very great degree of assurance that he *did* know certain things. For instance, he knew, absolutely and unshakably, that the space in which we live is in fact Euclidean.

At long last his discourse ended. One felt, as he proceeded, that the smooth polished surface of his phrases ought really to be interminable ; and yet they did in fact terminate, no one quite knew why. All eyes were turned upon Professor Lindemann. What on earth was he to say ? He had had lengthy discussions with Einstein, Max Planck, Broglie and other great men of thought. But I do not suppose that he had ever heard anything like this before. It was a hot-house Oxford product. He had been fairly and squarely challenged. He had been told that the Theory of Relativity was quite wrong, and this great chain of argument had been furnished.

There is a further point that must be made about Joseph. His paper against Relativity must have caused him much arduous work and taken much time to compose. But he did not show the slightest sign of his ever having seriously tried to understand either what the theoretical considerations were, or what the experimental results had been, that had led these distinguished physicists to feel the need to expound these tiresome theories of the relativity of space and time. It was evident that, in the ordinary sense of language, he knew nothing whatever about the Theory of Relativity. Since it was so evident to him that the conclusion reached was untrue, on quite different and sufficient philosophical grounds, there was no need for him to bother with the reasons why certain persons had been induced to frame such a theory. Indeed, I would go further. I have doubts myself as to whether Joseph, who had very limited intellectual capacity, despite his quite extraordinary linguistic acrobatics, would ever have been capable of understanding the Theory of Relativity.

So what was Professor Lindemann to do about it ? He resumed, in his previous style of brief staccato sentences. He reiterated certain points. He gave some further illustrations. Then, with the corners of his lips turned down and an ironic expression on his face, he said, 'Well, if you really suppose that you have private inspiration enabling you to know that. . . .' But that was precisely what Joseph claimed.

When there was a pause in Professor Lindemann's utterances, Joseph began unwinding again. And so each time. The Prof. really never got to grips with his argument; he did not know how to do so; none of the real points of interest in relation to relativity had been touched on; the whole game must have seemed to him to be perfectly futile. None the less there was this distinguished audience listening, and he was by no means winning in debate.

I suppose that some others among the learned persons present must have contributed something to the discussion. If so, that is entirely effaced from my memory. The spotlight was upon the Lindemann-Joseph interaction.

I mingled among the audience as they finally left the room. The Wykehamist Greats men were jubilant; a scientific professor had been torn to pieces; the Theory of Relativity had been shown to be untrue. But I was reluctant to join in their jubilation. I had already had unhappy experience with Joseph. Unlike those Wykehamists, I had read a great deal of philosophy at my school (Westminster), and had come up to Oxford full of theories and of earnestness to learn more. My arguments with Joseph had led to nothing but frustration. He had successfully shown that I was unable to express my thoughts in clear English and that sometimes what I had written for him meant nothing at all. But he seemed to be totally indifferent to what I had *tried* to mean, of the thought behind my words, just as he had been totally indifferent to the question of what were the theoretical considerations and the empirical facts that had led to the Theory of Relativity. Thus I had a certain fellow feeling with the unfortunate Professor Lindemann. I remember that I turned to an old friend, N. A. Beechman, a Balliol Greats man, afterwards President of the Union, and still later Minister of the Crown. He had a certain worldly shrewdness such as is necessary to those who interest themselves in politics. I asked him, 'Which was right?' He answered at once, 'Of course Professor Lindemann was right'. That little bit of worldly wisdom saved him from the illusions of the Wyke-hamists. In retrospect it is easy enough to perceive that Professor Lindemann was indeed right. But many of these young men were genuinely thinking otherwise ; they believed then, in 1920, or whenever precisely it was, that relativity had been disproved by these verbal tricks. I had given up classics for history in my last two years at school and won a history scholarship for New College ; but New College insisted on my doing Greats, the crown of all humane studies, before reverting to history. But what was this Greats ? What was the significance, in relation to the pressing problems thrown up by science on the one hand and by the evolution of social affairs on the other, of this linguistic dialectic purveyed by Greats ? Professor Lindemann remained in my mind after that evening as a sort of symbol of the free advance of the human spirit. I did not suppose that I should ever see him again.

*

But some time after that meeting I took the trouble to go to a course of lectures by him on 'science for philosophers', or 'the philosophy of science', or words to that effect. In these lectures he dealt with the Theory of Relativity, but with other questions also. He propounded perplexing matters arising out of the quantum theory, also 'statistical laws', cosmological questions, the nature of entropy and the im-probability of the existence of the Universe in which we find ourselves. Again there were the short, clipped sentences, the difficulty — but one had to acknowledge that the subject was difficult, and I for one had had no proper training — the brilliantly illuminating illustrations, the humour, the excitement, the glimpses that he gave of problems of real fundamental significance, problems still to be solved, even by philosophical thinking as well as by further experimentation. They were inspiring lectures ; yet they were also depressing, because beyond one's range, which seemed unduly restricted by the narrowness of one's own education.

I once asked Vivian Jackson what the Prof.'s regular lectures in his course on physics were like. He gave a typically Jacksonian answer : 'Too difficult, and obsolete'. 'Oh, Vivian,' I said, 'how can you be so disloyal ?' He then modified his aspersion a little. Both Vivian and Derek Jackson were great admirers of the Prof., as he was of them. He often used to bring one or other to dine in Christ Church ; I remember one occasion when he brought them both ; they were placed at either end of the table, and one could not hear oneself talk for the noise. He admired them for the highly distinguished physicists that they were — but Derek is still with us ; he admired them also particularly for devoting themselves to physics, although rich. He argued that one could not be sure that a young physicist without independent means did not persevere in his study, more for the sake of his wife and family, as the best means of keeping things going, than out of a pure devotion to physics as such. The Jacksons could have devoted their whole lives to fun and games and still prospered. There is something in the argument, but I would add that the Prof. himself had the highest respect for all really good scientists, whatever their origins, whatever their means and whatever their worldly circumstances. Perhaps in this reference that he made more than once to the Jacksons' riches, he had a hindthought for himself. He need never have done anything for science.

*

The next time that I met him was when I was at dinner

at Christ Church High Table, being vetted for an appointment there. I was on the opposite side of the table and was introduced to him across it. 'I have been to your lectures on the philosophy of science', I said. 'Unlucky man,' he replied immediately. But, as he went on eating his peculiar food, I thought I detected an expression of pleasure on his face ; I was a candidate for being his colleague, and I believe that there were no other rivals in the field for this particular appointment. There had not been many unscientific undergraduates at his lectures.

It was his invariable rule to refer to any public or other performance by himself in terms of self-depreciation. This might be regarded as a suitable conversational trope, showing due modesty and gracefully terminating the topic. But it also represented something deeper, as I was in due course to learn. He was not in his own heart a humble man ; on the contrary very proud, and also very sensitive to any slight. He regarded himself as of foremost intellectual calibre and the vast majority of his fellow men as abysmally 'stupid'. We have already seen that he did not wish for any parade of his gifts or seek public recognition — very much the opposite. But, although proud, he also had a deep abiding sense that there was something about himself that was unacceptable to others. Some years earlier he wrote to the Comtesse de Pange two days before he was to give the lecture in Dundee (1912) that made his name in this country : 'On Monday I have to give a lecture. I pity the audience.' The simple 'a lecture' is characteristic.

If he had a sense of being unpopular, he was quite right. I hasten to add that few people were more dearly loved by their own circle of friends. Those who got to know him really well acquired a deep affection for him, even a kind of protective attitude ; for there was something in the Prof., despite his array of formidable powers and his fighting spirit, that suggested that he did not really know how to manage his life and that he needed friends to sustain him. They were glad to fulfil that rôle ; he was very loyal to his friends and they were loyal to him. But outside the narrow circle he was intensely unpopular for a number of years. Those who came to know him, or of him, only after he had risen to some measure of fame through being Churchill's right-hand man during the Second World War, and after he had become a manifestly important personage through his Peerage and membership of the Cabinet, may not appreciate the degree of his unpopularity in the inter-war period. The fact of his unpopularity may not have fully accounted for his self-depreciatory attitude ; there was something deeper there, to explain which one might need a psychological probing into his infantile history. After all he had scarcely had time to begin to be unpopular with a British audience at Dundee. He had indeed a slight touch of persecution mania. There is always a vicious circle in these matters. His sense of being unloved led him to adopt defensive attitudes, and even to entertain suspicions, unjustified on the first round, which caused others in their turn to feel an estrangement from, and suspicion of, him ; that gave a just cause for his own sense of persecution ; and so the thing proceeded.

One could hardly have a long conversation with him without some reference cropping up to him being unpopular. I remember in the early days going to collect him in his rooms so that we might proceed together in his large Mercedes, to a meeting of Congregation where it was needful for us both to cast our votes — probably against some measure that he deemed to be hostile to the interests of science in the University. It was a lovely day of spring or early summer. He put up his arm to take his heavy greatcoat off its peg — his greatcoats were always very heavy — when I said to him, 'My dear Prof., it's a lovely day ; you do not need a greatcoat'. Recognizing the force of my observation, he desisted. But after some fleeting moments he had second thoughts, and put his arm up again. 'I had better have this in case someone throws a rotten egg at me.' An unlikely event, you will think, and words not to be taken seriously. No doubt it was a joke ; but it is not thereby to be reckoned as meaningless ; it had that characteristic twist. There really was no need for a greatcoat. He had a psychological impulsion to arm himself against the attack of the enemy.

All through his life, anyhow from my first knowledge of him until the end, he wore a bowler hat. This became quite a famous feature. There were stories current in the old days, which I have not checked, that there was a special place for his bowler hat in his aeroplane when he was a pilot at Farnborough, so that, when he emerged from it, he might be properly equipped for pedestrian life. Why did he always wear a bowler ? The simple explanation is that he liked to be as conventional as possible in sartorial matters and in all the ordinary business of life. He took an amused interest in the most novel fashions in society, but for himself he preferred to err on the side of being old-fashioned, proper and correct. But there was another side to this question of the bowler hat that cannot have been so congenial to him. It became a notorious feature, and in the case of anyone else in the world one would have said that it was just a little harmless piece of showmanship ; it is the sort of thing that the press photographer likes to catch or that the gossip paragraphist likes to refer to for lack of anything more profound to say.[1]

But these were precisely the things that the Prof. hated. He genuinely detested publicity in any form whatever ; one might say that he had a morbid dislike for it ; with him this

---

[1] Bowler hats have rather returned to fashion in London since the Second World War ; but there was a period in the 'thirties when they became quite rare even there ; they were certainly so in Oxford.

was certainly not the case of an indirect approach to publicity in the rôle of a mystery figure, as with such a person as T. E. Lawrence. During the Second World War, should there be a perfectly innocuous paragraph about him, he became quite furious, and wrote to the editor with dire threats of prosecution under the Official Secrets Act, if anything similar should occur again. I can testify, as a result of numerous experiences, to the sincerity of his dislike of public attention. The showmanship aspect of his bowler hat, of which he must have been aware, would in itself have been a weighty reason for abandoning it. Here again I am convinced that there was a deeper psychological reason. He retained it as a helmet.

In his last years the unpopularity had largely died out, anyhow had ceased to be a thing of any importance. But his sense of being unacceptable remained. A few weeks before his death he went to a little cocktail party given by his great friend, Molly Mure, wife of the Warden of Merton, to view the bust of her husband executed by the sculptor, Nemon. During the party Nemon went up to the Prof. and asked him when someone would commission a bust of him. 'Oh no, there is no danger of that,' the Prof. replied ; 'people do not like me enough, you know.'

*

So it happened that in the following summer I found myself installed as his colleague at Christ Church, and for the next thirty-four years I saw him fairly continuously. He had a great love of the Christ Church Common Room. He came in every evening, when not on a visit to one of the distinguished hostesses whose invitations were recurrent ; even when he was in the Cabinet after the war, he tried to get up to us on as many nights as possible.

Before the war he dined in Hall. When we adjourned to

the Common Room to drink port, in which he did not par-
take — he was a total abstainer — most of us, save for the
acting chairman, took up our places at random, varying them
according to the convenience of ourselves or guests. But
he always sat in the same place with his back to the fire, one
or two places from the bottom end of the table. This too
no doubt needs its psychological explanation ; he liked a
rather rigid routine, which also served him for defensive
purposes.

The kitchen had to provide him with a special dinner.
As well as being a teetotaller and non-smoker, he was a
vegetarian with an extraordinarily narrow range of food that
he was prepared to eat. Certainly nothing animal ; the
whites of egg but not the yolk, a little stewed apple, rice
croquettes, salad with an ample supply of mayonnaise, Port
Salut cheese, but no other variety, seemed to be the main
ingredients of his diet. It looked woefully inadequate for a
man of large frame, tennis champion, and of a reasonably
active life. Although so austere himself, he had no element
of the spoilsport. He liked to see his colleagues eating and
drinking their fill. He positively approved of pleasure of
all kinds, and wished to see his friends enjoy themselves.
Furthermore, he was in no sense a conscientious objector to
eating meat.[1]

His brother, Brigadier Charles Lindemann, gave me an

---

[1] I have never admitted that there is any valid argument from the premise
of kindness to animals for vegetarianism. If everyone became a vegetarian,
that would entail the final extermination of many millions of animals, which
may be presumed to have a reasonably happy life. I would support any
movement for humane treatment and slaughter. It is not to be thought that,
in the absence of any commercial demand, mankind would continue to sustain
and pay for the upkeep of all these millions of animals. Thus, if it has to
be admitted that the meat eater is in a sense guilty of the murder of individual
animals, the vegetarian would commit the far greater crime of exterminating
all these species in perpetuity. I once tried to explain this to Lady Mary
Murray, a fervent vegetarian, but she merely thought that I was being 'clever'
at her expense.

account of how it happened. When they were both infants, their parents became convinced by some current dietetic theory, and decided to apply it to their children. Both were brought up as vegetarians. When they were young boys they stayed with an uncle who said : 'Now, come along, boys, I am going to give you a really good dinner'. They both felt unwell after the sudden change of diet, but reacted differently. Charles decided that the pleasures of the table were worth while and that he would doubtless get adjusted to them. But the Prof. resented the discomfort, and decided that he would never put up with it again. He was an obstinate man.

Here again I believe that a psychologist should be called upon for an explanation. I recall entertaining him to lunch in Oxford with my mother, who was a violent advocate of a meat diet. She attacked him with the full force of her eloquence, which was quite animated in those days. What was wrong with meat ? He said that he did not like putting animal matter into his body, since there might be little creatures that would turn to attack him. Incidentally Charles told me that he once discovered something animate in the yolk of his egg, and that that incident ruled out yolks for the rest of his life.

He carried this practice forward at some cost to his own convenience. Charles told me that when they were young men in Germany, highly eligible no doubt, but not yet intrinsically very important, distinguished hostesses just could not be bothered with special culinary arrangements, and that attractive opportunities were missed. By the 'twenties already, distinguished English hostesses evidently thought him worth the trouble entailed, for he was a very frequent guest.

In 1938, still before the Prof.'s rise to power and fame in the land, I got married, and gave a bachelor party in a private room at the Savoy. I arrived a few minutes early, in order to place cards upon the table. Guests began to arrive, and, when I saw the Prof.'s figure fill the doorway, I had a horrible shock ; I had entirely forgotten to tell the butler about his special food, and rushed off, doubtless with a flustered expression, to explain what had to be done. 'Don't worry, sir,' he replied, 'I have already seen the Professor's name on your card ; we know quite well here what food he likes.' So even then he had attained V.I.P. status at the Savoy in his quiet way.

The Second World War gave considerable trouble.[1] He took to keeping chickens, and we supplied him with all our garbage for their sustenance. It was my belief at that time, although I studiously did not seek to confirm it, that for rationing purposes the Prof. was counted as resident with the Churchills, with whom indeed he frequently stayed for weekends and at other times. And so I liked to nurse the strictly secret thought that my garbage was indirectly serving an even higher purpose.

One of the most important ingredients for keeping the Prof.'s body and soul together was olive oil, of which he consumed an inordinate amount. This went off the British shopping list during the Second World War and something had to be done about it for the Prof. It seemed that within his exceedingly narrow range there was no substitute for it. After the fall of France, his brother Charles became scientific adviser to the British Embassy in Washington, and among his duties — others will be mentioned hereafter — was that of seeing that a case of olive oil was periodically despatched by air to England in the Foreign Office bag. I was told that this was a perennial headache in the Embassy. For someone had to remember who was

[1] Lord Adrian has lately informed me that, as Medical Officer at Farnborough during the First World War, he signed a certificate to say that the Prof. required extra rations of butter and eggs, in order to sustain him in sufficiently good health for flying.

going over each week, to whom this important trust could be consigned.

I became involved, owing to two visits that I paid to Washington, in something that came very near to being a quarrel between the two brothers. To the best of my knowledge they were lifelong friends. They worked together in Berlin, and played tennis together ; Charles too had scientific attainments, and I believe that certain scientific papers were published over their joint names. Charles often stayed with the Prof. in Christ Church and dined with us ; unlike the Prof. he drank our port. In due course he became a familiar figure and those of us who had got to know him over so many years became fond of him. Immediately before the Prof.'s death, the two brothers had a very happy time together.

But towards the end of the war there was a little friction. The Prof. thought that his brother was stinting him of olive oil. He sent me out with fierce messages. 'Tell Charles that I can only suppose that he attaches no value to what I am trying to do in the war effort, that he would as soon have me go to bed. And that is what I shall have to do unless he sends me more olive oil.' But Charles, I found, looked at the matter in a different way. Though a rich man, his ration of dollars for spending was severely restricted. He took the view that the case of oil, as despatched from Washington, went to Chequers, where it was avidly seized upon by the Churchill cook and used to garnish such food as the austerity of war allowed to be set before the Prime Minister's enormous weekend parties. What could possibly be more acceptable to a chef, hard pressed by wartime shortage ? 'Perfect nonsense,' replied the Prof. on my return ; 'nothing of the sort happens ; Harvey looks after my oil supply most strictly.' Calculations were made of gallons, cubic feet, etc. ; Charles made counter calculations, and the battle waxed furiously.

There was a change of arrangements in the final phase. Olive oil was despatched from Canada. For some obscure, although no doubt profound, reason, it was sent to my name and address, and I had to stagger under heavy packing cases, transferring them from my house to the Prof.'s rooms in Christ Church.

During the war he judged that it was giving our kitchen too much trouble for him to dine at High Table, and got the faithful Harvey to supervise the cooking of his dinner in his own rooms. He did not resume the habit of dining after the war, but came round regularly to us, after listening to the nine o'clock news. If we had some interesting guest dining, our eyes strayed over to the door at about 9.15, hoping that he would appear and add new life to our party. We were usually not disappointed. The door opened slowly, and his well-known figure appeared. He walked with measured tread, for he was already ailing. He took off that heavy greatcoat, and placed it methodically on the table and the bowler hat on top of it. Then he came forward to join us, ready and anxious to be interested in the affairs of whoever was there, attentive, quite unassuming, and full of jests and anecdotes appropriate to the person. Or, if there was no one who especially wanted to talk with him and a bridge table was out, he liked to stand behind and watch the game. He knew all about it, but only very rarely interjected a comment. Over and over again we tried to persuade him to play himself, but he declined to do so on the ground that, if he made a mistake, that would cause him to lie awake all night replaying the hand. Our mistakes, although he watched and noted them, did not apparently arouse any disposition to lie awake replaying our hands. Here, again, the psychologist must come forward.

The only occasion on which I recall seeing the Prof. sitting at a card table was when I came in late one night and found that our golfing champion colleague, Barrington-Ward, had brought in a number of other golfing champions to the Common Room after some great event in Oxford. The Prof. had been roped in, in order to complete a second four. Barrington-Ward had been so lavish in honouring these athletic pundits with a supply of Christ Church wines and spirits, that they were in an uproarious condition, and, as the two bridge games proceeded, sang loudly in chorus. I have never seen the Prof. look more unhappy or out of place. But it was like him to feel that, although he was absolutely rigid in refusing to make up a four just for us, he must support our good repute for hospitality by making life happy for the golfing champions.

Although a layman in such matters, I could never escape the idea that the Prof.'s feeble diet was inadequate to sustain him and would be the cause of trouble in the end. Even during the war there was an occasion which made me think that all was not well. Mr. Francis Hemming, with whom we had many dealings, suddenly chose to move to the top storey of the new Scotland Yard building, which as yet had no lift. The Prof. and I went along to see him. When the geography was explained, he looked very gloomy and stood for several minutes before embarking on the ascent ; and he paused a little on each storey. It is sad to think, but hard to resist doing so, that his death at the age of seventy-two may have been hastened by that piece of obstinacy after his good meal with his uncle.

*

But I must return to 1923. The Prof. had not yet mellowed then, nor become the 'great man' of whom we were later justly proud. He was a distinguished physicist, but we had other men in our Common Room, such as J. D. Beazley, who were even more eminent in their own lines. The Prof.

was very much on the warpath. There was a crackling atmosphere of controversy. He resorted freely to F. E. Smith-like repartees of great rudeness. He had disputes with our Governing Body (of which he was not a member), which involved the taking of Counsel's opinion by both sides on one occasion. 'Intolerably litigious person', he was dubbed; and he was suspect in a number of ways. I am afraid that I allowed him in due course to say very unkind things about my esteemed colleagues behind their backs. 'I should like to castrate him,' I remember his snarling out about one of them, and then adding in a discouraged tone, 'not that it would make any difference.'

He did indeed have a sense that the traditions at Oxford required him to become more gentle in his modes of speech, and he made many jokes about how he was adapting himself to his new environment. He had a story about some undergraduates in Wadham College, where he lived during his first two or three years in Oxford, who were making a noise on the stairs outside his room. He opened his door and strafed them and, when they fled downstairs, he heard one say to the other, 'the professor has evidently been in the Army'.

Despite these untoward circumstances we very soon became fast friends. One may wonder why. We had different subjects and our centres of interest and business in Oxford lay widely apart. In those days we had few friends in common, except for our Christ Church colleagues. We differed profoundly in our political opinions. We could not talk on literary matters, since he knew nothing about them. He read for information only — save possibly some second-rate fiction, of which there seemed to be a good stock in his bedroom. Pictorial art was a subject to be avoided at all costs. So what was the affinity? The explanation is really quite simple.

I was brought up in a literary and artistic home in which

the tradition was that conversation was by far the greatest pleasure, if not the prime object, of life. At Westminster School, after being for a year in the Classical Seventh, I migrated to the history form. There a don from University College, London, came to lecture to us for one hour each morning ; after that we were left free without supervision ; only when we had exhausted every possible subject of conversation among ourselves, did we revert to our reading ; none the less in those two years I seem to have read more good books than at any other time in my life. At New College the gospel of conversation was also to be found ; one has only to mention the name of Maurice Bowra ; he had a sort of salon there. I also at that time had a great friend in Douglas Woodruff, who was the most inveterate talker of all. Maurice Bowra and I once went together to work in a vacation to Llanthony Abbey and managed to maintain a reasonable division of the day between work and talk ; but half-way through the time Douglas Woodruff appeared, and discipline was completely subverted, to the detriment, I fear, of the 'collections' that we had to face in New College. I also had a group of old Westminster friends, who were at Christ Church, and I frequently resorted to them.

I have always felt that the central educational feature of Oxford and Cambridge [1] — and one hopes that this is a target for other universities also — is the unrivalled opportunity that the colleges provide for extensive conversation among undergraduates, who have an intense interest, appropriate to their time of life, in the central questions confronting mankind. In the gospel of conversation there are two strands. On the one hand one may regard it as a good thing for its own sake, the most satisfying pleasure known to man. The

[1] That the state of affairs at Cambridge was not different from that at Oxford, I inferred from the evidence provided in the undergraduate letters of J. M. Keynes, and I endeavoured to convey this in my *Life* of him.

40

highest praise that Aristotle gives to contemplation is that it is an end in itself ; οὐδὲν γὰρ ἀπ' αὐτῆς γίνεται παρὰ τὸ θεωρῆσαι.[1] This may apply to conversation also. But it also has its usefulness. By its give and take, by the interplay of minds, one may go deeper and further and come nearer to wisdom than by reading the best book in the world. After all a book cannot be cross-examined ; it cannot answer back.

Dons have always struck me, lifelong don although I have been myself, as playing a subsidiary rôle in Oxford and Cambridge. They provide a certain background of quiet culture, and they supply standards of precision and self-discipline in research, so that the young man can get a glimpse, an inkling, of the exacting nature of the pursuit of truth. I dissent violently from the view that the main service of the University is in the provision of courses and examinations, and in the insistence on the desirability of obtaining high classes ; I frankly view the tendency of the dons to encroach upon the life and time and energy of the undergraduates with suspicion.

When I myself became a don, I was much disappointed in one respect. In the Senior Common Rooms I found a lack of that probing, ardent, even feverish, quest for solutions to the fundamental problems. The dons have their own conversation, but it is of a different kind. They are apt to concern themselves with points of fact, the derivation of words, or their proper use, or with the careers of particular people, or with questions in history or in geography, or with matters of local gossip — who is to succeed to the Headship of a House or to some Chair. In fine the conversation, although scholarly and polished, tends to be conventional and placid ; this may be needed to give a rest after a day of intellectual toil.

I was so much put out by this change that it made me wonder if I had chosen the right profession. I had supposed

[1] It produces no result beyond the act of contemplation.

that a university, being essentially a home of intellectual endeavour, was the one place where the supreme intellectual pleasure of conversation about serious subjects could be continued all one's days. Perhaps it was an illusion of youth to suppose that that could be so.

It is fair to add that, despite what I have said, Christ Church was a place where we did have many evenings of lively general conversation. After the port was removed, we made a semicircle around a large old-fashioned coal fire and, especially if any guests were present, we were stimulated to proceed until a late hour. The Prof. used to be a protagonist ; Dundas also. Some years ago Sir David Pye paid us a compliment by saying that a night in Christ Church in the 'twenties, when the Prof. was in active form and Dundas had brought in Reggie Coupland as his guest, stood out in his mind as an evening of the most scintillating conversation he had ever heard.

In my early days at Christ Church I still spent much time with undergraduates, and was lucky enough to become intimate with the brilliant circle that centred on Harold Acton, many of whom became lifelong friends. But still, although they were kind to me, there was inevitably some division between us ; they had their own fun and frolics ; there was a limit to the amount of time that a don could spend with them. Of my old friends, Maurice Bowra was already beginning to be less accessible. He had on his hands a threefold task : he had to run Wadham College ; he was beginning to write a tremendous series of volumes of scholarship and criticism ; and he laid himself out to influence the minds of almost all the literary undergraduates who passed through Oxford in the 'twenties, many of whom have become famous. Thus he was very fully occupied. David Cecil was indeed an apostle of our creed, and was always entirely accessible. So much so that, when in those young days I had a free morning and some *Weltschmerz* made the sight of a printed page repellent, I used to go and see him. I might arrive at ten o'clock and, if he happened to have no pupil, I settled down on his sofa for a prolonged conversation. He took this as the most natural thing in the world. My Christ Church colleagues would have thought that I must be demented, had I invaded their rooms at such a time.

Then a great surprise occurred. It turned out that one, but only one, of my colleagues was of my creed in the matter of conversation. Who should it be but this austere, remote professor, propounder of the Theory of Relativity, which one would suppose not to be a conversational subject. Often at the end of the evening, when we had had good general conversation round the fire for three or four hours, he was not satisfied. As the diners dispersed and Tom struck twelve, 'Do come over to my rooms', he would say in a pleading voice, and so I went back with him, and we chatted away until three o'clock in the morning. That happened night after night. There was no refreshment of any kind ; sometimes a thin glass of *cointreau* was produced, more often nothing.

I sometimes thought selfishly that these repeated evening sessions were exhausting me, undermining my constitution even. I had a very active life as a young tutor. On most days I had to be fresh and brisk for my first pupil at 9 A.M. In due course when Censor, I had to be ready in cap and gown at 8.20 A.M. for our matutinal discussion with the Dean on the events of the previous day ; indeed when Censor in Course I had to be in cap and gown at 7.45, and take the roll of the College. I knew perfectly well that the Prof. did not rise from his bed until after 11 A.M., and then would be thoroughly well valeted. I remember one morning going across to his rooms to speak with him on some matter of business between eleven and twelve. One man showed me in ; when I reached his bedroom I found two others. One of these was taking down in shorthand to his dictation, the other was tying up his shoe laces while he himself was putting on his tie. Then he quietly went downstairs and drove round in his large Mercedes to the Clarendon Laboratory, perhaps to be in time for a twelve o'clock lecture.

I have since sometimes wondered whether this anxiety about getting over-tired, which occasionally flitted across my mind, was not altogether egocentric. Ought I not to have looked at the matter the other way round ? Might not these conversations, which it must be admitted were not strictly necessary, have held the Prof. back from his scientific work? Sometimes in those days indeed, instead of taking me back to his rooms, he invited me to go round with him to the Clarendon Laboratory. There we found in their dimly lit cubby holes such figures as Griffith, C. H. Bosanquet, Bolton King, Atkinson, working away at mysterious tasks among extraordinarily makeshift contraptions reminiscent of Heath Robinson. He tried to explain to me what they were doing ; usually they seemed to be taking photographs, a slow process. I was shown plates, showing only thin vertical lines. Very often they stayed up working all through the night ; I was impressed by the arduous life of these scientific researchers.

But ought not the Prof. to have stayed up all night in among them ? I think I can honestly say, without bias in my own favour, that, even if I had not been there with my willingness to converse with him, he would not have gone to the Laboratory any more frequently.

*

It is for others to speak with authority about the Prof.'s contributions to science. It seems to be agreed that in his Berlin days he was in the forefront of the exciting develop-

ments then proceeding in the Quantum Theory. Then came
the interruption of the First World War. It was precisely
in the 'twenties that he ought to have forged ahead, made
his further contributions and established a secure claim to
being one of our greatest physicists. That he had the intellectual power I have no doubt, but I fear that he was lazy.[1]

He was loud in complaint during that period at the
obstructiveness and tiresome interferences on the side of the
administrative authorities of the University. All his time
was taken up, so he pleaded, in counteracting their manœuvres,
instead of getting on with his own scientific work. I could
not help feeling that he was making excuses for himself. I
have no doubt that he did encounter many difficulties. The
Clarendon Laboratory had, before his day, fallen into gross
neglect. He had much work to do in reconstituting research
and organizing his staff. It may be the case that Oxford
really does owe a great deal to him for the work that he did,
during the thirty-five years in which he was head of the
Clarendon Laboratory, in reorganizing it, planning and super-
vising the erection of a completely new building, and bringing
it up to its present high pitch of efficiency. That is for others
to assess.[2]

Could he not have proceeded with this and at the same
time made more personal contributions of his own ? His
reputation did not go from strength to strength. In Oxford
it seemed, on the contrary, to be rather on the downward
curve in the 'twenties, in consequence of what we were able
to glean about him from the outside world. Perhaps he
fussed too much about the interferences of the authorities ;

[1] Sir George Thomson (*op. cit.*) gives an account of the Prof.'s pre-war
work in physics, and refers also to some post-war work, which may suggest
that I have done less than justice to his work in physics in his early days at
Oxford.

[2] Professor Thomson pays a substantial tribute to what the Prof. did for
the Clarendon Library (*op. cit.* pages 55 and 56).

I remember that I used to try to persuade him in this sense. He was very belligerent. He resented fiercely anything that he deemed an encroachment on his proper rights, even although it was in fact trivial and would make no practical difference, and he spent his time fighting back accordingly. If only he could have acquiesced and accepted small things that he did not like for the time being, and have proceeded vigorously with his own work, so that his reputation grew, the University would have been willing to do more for him. If the Clarendon had grown strongly in reputation in the 'twenties, those fusty old dug-in members of the Hebdomadal Council would probably have sought to help, rather than hinder, him. They were not as unenlightened as they might appear on first inspection ; they had their hunches ; they had their devious methods of assessing the facts of the case ; they would have been proud of the Clarendon, if it was rising in reputation, and have wished to further its progress. But what was felt was that the Prof. was becoming ever more truculent and tiresome and yet all the while not doing his stuff.

I have suggested that he was lazy. But this may be a superficial verdict. He occupied himself fully during the Second World War ; not only did he sit up to the early hours, whether to comply with the hours of Churchill, or to con over his papers and thrash out the daily problems when we spent our evenings at Marlow, but also he appeared at a proper hour at his office in the morning, to face his daily round of committees and conferences. He had a sense of duty and spared no pains to achieve what that dictated to him. Furthermore, all through his life his mind was incessantly occupied.

There may be another explanation of his not devoting himself more arduously to laboratory research in the 'twenties. Great although his powers were in science, he may have had some deep inner feeling that it was not that realm that would give him the best opportunity of deploying all his gifts fully. He was not a politician in any ordinary sense, but already in those 'twenties he was spending much of his time in the company of our leading statesmen. On July 1st, 1929, he wrote to Madame de Pange, 'I am not really a serious politician though I move a great deal in political circles'. He may have had some dim sense of his own destiny. Others were available to further physics. It was a more rare combination of qualities, perhaps not assembled in any other person, that enabled him to fulfil the rôle, of no little importance to us all, of being the prime intellectual support of Winston Churchill during the Second World War.

On two successive summers (1931 and 1932) we had Einstein living with us in Christ Church and he dined on most evenings. He was a charming person, and we entered into relations of easy intimacy with him. He divided his time between his mathematics and playing the violin ; as one crossed the quad, one was privileged to hear the strains coming from his rooms. In our Governing Body I sat next to him ; we had a green baize table-cloth ; under cover of this he held a wad of paper on his knee, and I observed that all through our meetings his pencil was in incessant progress, covering sheet after sheet with equations. His general conversation was not stimulating, like that of the Prof. I am afraid I did not have the sense that, so far as human affairs were concerned, I was in the presence of a wise man or a deep thinker. Rather I had the idea that he was a very good man, a simple soul and rather naïve about worldly matters. He had his little fund of amusing stories on an unsophisticated level. Victor Cazalet was dining with us on one occasion during the first summer, and happened to return during the second. He had a proper respect for great people, and on the second occasion he drew from his pocket a little diary. 'Oh, Dr. Einstein,' he said, 'will you be very kind and tell us that story again that you told us last year about the bank director and the cow.' Einstein too had his public debate with Joseph. At this (later) time Joseph did not quite venture to combat the Theory of Relativity itself, dwelling rather on some peripheral, philosophical points. When he began to unwind rather too much, Einstein fobbed him off in a genial manner : 'Well, that is just a matter of taste'. By that time the audience was inclined to believe that on the high plane of physico-philosophical theory, Einstein's taste was likely to be the better of the two.

An easy, intimate relationship having been established, our younger physicists got Einstein into a corner one evening and sought his frank opinion about the Prof. I regret that I was not present on that occasion, but listened avidly to the report. The Prof., so it went, was essentially an amateur ; he had ideas, which he never worked out properly ; but he had a thorough comprehension of physics. If something new came up, he could rapidly assess its significance for physics as a whole, and there were very few people still in the world who could do that. Such was the Einstein summary.

That seems to accord with what an unscientific person might judge of the Prof.'s mental qualities in other fields. As well as these intellectual powers of the higher kind, the Prof. had the more humdrum attainment of lightning speed of thought. He could always out-distance others in his rapidity of making complicated calculations ; it is true that he carried a little aid in his pocket, in the form of a small slide-rule which he brought out on frequent occasions. But, even allowing for that, his speed was very great. And this speed operated too in more subtle and abstruse fields. Einstein happened to mention at High Table some mathematical proposition which he took to be well established but for which he had never been able to furnish himself with the proof.

The Prof. returned the next day, claiming to have thought of the proof in his bath ; Einstein was satisfied with it.

Some years before that I had sat next to J. J. Thomson at a luncheon given by the Headmaster of Westminster School. I thought it suitable to refer to my colleague, the Prof., but did not get so satisfactory a verdict. 'He seems to think that he can run his Laboratory by the methods of a Prussian dictator ; but that is impossible.' I could not squeeze a word of praise out of him.

I thought that I might strike a more charitable feeling by referring to a Cambridge man, namely my great friend J. M. Keynes. 'We blackballed him at the Royal Society for his bad conduct in attacking the government that he had served, in *The Economic Consequences of the Peace*.' (Keynes was eventually made a Fellow of the Royal Society, but that was many years later.) I spoke up vehemently in support of my friend. 'But surely the great good that this book did in the world should outweigh any technical irregularity ?' 'Not at all,' J. J. replied. 'What he said in that book was only what every sensible person knew already. He merely got easy publicity by mentioning things that he could have known only by being in the public service, such as Clemenceau's wearing mittens.'

I was certainly having bad luck with J. J. The conversation took another turn and he made a notable remark. 'The best American society is the only one into which you cannot buy your way with money.' This was striking, and, deeming J. J. a high authority, I remember that, in order, no doubt, to gain some spurious reputation for my profound social knowledge, I used to repeat his dictum in casual conversation. I found that it seemed to cut no ice ; I was viewed with looks of scepticism ; indeed by repeating it I seemed to be losing rather than gaining reputation ; and so I dropped this conversational gambit.

I have often wondered what J. J. meant by it. Was he thinking of some dim Bostonian circle ? Some forty years before that, my mother, then Frances Forbes-Robertson, had been invited to pour out tea by Mrs. Jack Gardner.[1] She was poverty-stricken all through her life, and I like to think that she was then accorded an honour that billions of dollars could not have bought.

My youthful enthusiasm for this luminary of science was so great, that I did not allow this adverse experience to topple the pedestal on which he stood in my mind. I had merely had a piece of bad luck. The only moral is that one must not judge a man by the experience of one lunch party — a moral that many have not learnt. Keynes once told me that he had sat next to Marcel Proust at a dinner party in Paris on one of his visits after the First World War. 'Oh,' I said excitedly, 'how fascinating ! What did you make of him ? What transpired ?' 'Nothing,' he answered. 'We did not speak to each other.'

Over many years I have made a point of asking distinguished scientists about the true prowess of the Prof. in physics. I have had many tributes on general lines similar to that by Einstein, as well as criticisms like that of J. J.[2]

Quite recently I acquired a little volume entitled *Les Premiers Congrès de Physique Solvay*,[3] which contains a brief note on the Prof. by the Duc de Broglie and a photograph of the fragment of a letter from him given below.

1. If in stable equilibrium all the energy is in the ether and none in matter, how can the fact that matter

---

[1] In those days in the United States the greatest honour one could confer on a guest was to ask her to pour out tea for the party.

[2] Sir George Thomson's appreciation (*op. cit.* page 55) resembles that of Einstein more than that given me by his father. But J. J.'s severity at that particular luncheon may well have been due to grounds for displeasure that he may have happened to have at that time.

[3] Albin Michel, Paris, 1951.

Mr Lindemann. 34

1) If in stable equilibrium all the
energy is in the ether and none
in matter, how can the fact
that matter may be heated
by radiation be explained?

2) Prof. Jeans suggests that
the specific heat may be
due to the free electrons.
                    would
This hardly seems to be in
accord with the fact that
metalloids such as S, J etc
and for the matter of that
salts suchas KCl, AgCl
have the same atomic heats
as metals at corresponding
temperatures.

PAGE OF A LETTER IN LORD CHERWELL'S HANDWRITING

may be heated by radiation be explained ?

2. Prof. Jeans suggests that the specific heat may be due to the free electrons. This would hardly seem to be in accord with the fact that metalloids such as S, J etc. and for the matter of that salts such as KCL, AgCl have the same atomic heats as metals at corresponding temperatures.

I showed this to Professor Wilkinson. He said that it was characteristic, and added that it often happened that one thought that the Prof. had merely run a little pin into one, but soon realized that it was a long thin stiletto that pierced right to the heart. How often have I had that experience.

*

It may help in my attempt to fill out this sketch of the Prof., if I say something of our subjects of discourse during those many night sessions in the 'twenties. The list that I have given of topics where we could find no common ground may seem rather comprehensive. What was there left ? In fact there always seemed too much rather than too little matter ; I had to tear myself away, in order to get to my bed.

There was certainly a wide gulf between us on political questions. I was a Liberal, rather to the left wing, who favoured in those days, and indeed until the middle 'thirties, a working accommodation, if only that were possible, with the Labour Party. Only in the late 'forties, when my contacts with the Prof. were rather infrequent, did I decide that the Conservative Party, as it had then evolved, represented my own opinions more closely. I would claim that I have been fairly steady through life in my subscription to certain views, anyhow since coming of age ; but if, as is commonly supposed, increasing years produce some tendency to greater Conservatism, I do not think that there is anything to be ashamed of in that. The Prof. by contrast was a very strong Conservative, even one might say in some respects a reactionary, although he liked to represent himself in conversation, by his tart remarks, as more right wing than he proved to be when practical responsibility put the matter to the test. His bark was worse than his bite. We had an implicit agreement to differ, and seldom mentioned topics of party politics in those days. Occasionally he would make an agreeable remark such as : 'When are you going to detach yourself from that putrefying corpse?' meaning thereby the Liberal Party. But he did not often tease me ; he respected my private judgement and we kept off that ground. There was, however, no bar to the quite different exercise, always a pleasant one, of discussing the personal qualities of prominent politicians.

At the humdrum level of day-to-day affairs, there was much talk of the neglect of science by Oxford in those days. Here my Victorian radicalism made me completely sympathetic to the Prof.'s point of view ; I earnestly believed — and still do — that the progress of science and the progress of man were intimately linked together, and that in England, on the whole, science was not taken sufficiently seriously. I was as keen as he that there should be a great increase in the attention paid to science in Oxford. In all those matters I do not suppose that his views differed much from those of other scientists. But he was more belligerent than most, and the prospect of a great fight for this worthy cause was stimulating for a young man. In those far-off days I too had a certain tendency to belligerency, but I had doubts about the Prof.'s strategy.

He felt that among the humanists of Oxford there was great complacency and a profound ignorance about the intellectual status of science. He liked to tell the story of one of his first dinner parties in Oxford. He had been bidden, as a new professor, by the Warden of All Souls, and, finding himself sitting next to his wife, Mrs. Pember, expressed his misgivings about the status of science in Oxford. 'You need not worry,' she assured him, 'a man who has got a First in Greats could get up science in a fortnight.'

When he told this story in later years, he credited himself with replying, 'What a pity it is that your husband has never had a fortnight to spare.' But I believe that this retort, although characteristic and by no means beyond his capacity for rudeness, was a subsequent gloss. I do not recall it from the earlier days. There was a sea-change in his tone of narration of this episode. Later the story was told to amuse, in a spirit of mellow retrospection. At the time he was hotly indignant ; although Mrs. Pember's dictum was obviously not to be taken at its face value, he judged that it represented, albeit in fantastic caricature, what the humanists really thought. They believed that the kind of mental discipline provided by Greats, and exemplified by the polished discourse of Joseph, armed the mind with weapons that would be sufficient for dealing with scientific problems. In other words, he read into the humanists' point of view a very great complacency. They did not understand the very different qualities required, mathematical, logical and imaginative, or the patience needed for framing hypotheses, tracing their implications and confronting them with the results of experiments, in the construction of which also imagination was required.

The Prof.'s argument was not only concerned with the insufficiency of the kind of mental training provided by Greats for scientific research ; there was more to it than that. He held strongly that in the modern world the habits of thought engendered by science were needful for statesmen and civil servants also, if they were to reach correct decisions on the problems before them. He wanted to see a sprinkling

of men with a really professional scientific training in the
Cabinet and the higher ranks of the Civil Service. Skill in
analysis and dialectic were not sufficient to cope with all the
complex problems of the modern world ; one needed also
that aliveness to the quantitive aspects of things and that
awareness that generalities must be put to empirical tests,
which scientific training alone can deeply implant in the
mind. Thus he wanted to train more scientists, not only
for the pursuit of science, but to produce men who would
bring their special point of view into co-operation with those
who had been trained in the arts.

I may refer forward here to the long-sustained campaign
which the Prof. waged in later life for the establishment of
Technological Institutes. The very urgent need, as shown
during the Second World War, for a greater number of
technologists of high scientific standing, made this his primary
objective ; and his wider aim of working scientists into the
liberal professions then fell into the background. I also have
an uncomfortable feeling that in the interval certain experiences
made him somewhat sceptical of the wisdom of scientists when
they apply their minds to political or social affairs.

He was very keen that we should establish Technological
Institutions of standing not inferior to the M.I.T. On the
one hand, he argued that the task of teaching Technology,
even at the highest level, could not be undertaken by the
universities ; for its needs would throw the universities out
of balance. One required, say, fifty or a hundred Professors
of Engineering alone for the adequate handling of that
subject. On the other hand, he also argued that these Institutions should be of the highest standing ; professorial
appointments to them should have a status and prestige value
equal to those at universities. One needed to attract men
of first-rate scientific attainments. Furthermore, these institutions should have their own Arts departments, as subsidiary

branches, so that the technologists trained there should not be lacking in culture or in knowledge of social questions.

I believe that it was through his efforts that the Barlow Committee was set up at the end of the war, to assess and establish the need for a greater output of scientists. He continued his campaign unremittingly, and what has actually been achieved in this direction owes much to his efforts ; but he was by no means satisfied with their results at the time of his death.

In 1923 the laboratory equipment in Oxford was inadequate ; and there were too few positions. Among those that existed, too few were associated with Fellowships of Colleges. I was to get into great hot water in fighting his battles on this subject later. He used to count up how many physics Fellowships there were ; and, to the best of my recollection, it turned out that there really were only three or four in the whole University.

He was very strong on this question of Fellowships ; he rightly perceived that it was a Fellowship, conjoined with membership of the Governing Body of a College, that carried prestige and power in the University. Even a well-paid appointment in a laboratory did not raise you above the helot class unless a Fellowship was attached.

The Prof. had a keen sense of the importance of the social hierarchy. The absence of a Fellowship would diminish the incentive, whatever the money awards might be — and they too were low —, to men of scientific promise to devote their lives to research in Oxford. He was acutely conscious too of a more subtle factor. There remained some tendency among the humanists, in the ordinary give and take of conversation, to refer in a slighting way to science. I do not assert that the old-fashioned word 'stinks' could still be heard, but there were relics of that attitude ; scientists were an inferior breed of man, not quite civilized. There were even traces of a social stigma, to which the Prof. was exceptionally alive. I do not quite know how that had come about ; it was not so in eighteenth-century England. The Prof. became rather hard of hearing at a fairly early stage ; but, like others with that failing, he always seemed to manage to hear anything detrimental from the other end of the room. He became less quarrelsome on this point as the years passed. But I remember all the old anger returning when he came up for one of his infrequent week-ends during the Second World War, and overheard a remark of that type. He had come from a London harassed by bombing ; there we were trying to bend the enemy's beam, and there he had been watching a fierce battle of strokes and counter-strokes, all within the domain of science, on the success of which our survival depended. His position gave him some knowledge of all the different fronts on which scientific warfare was being waged ; in the background was the atomic bomb itself. And here were these Oxford humanists, such of them at least as remained in position, living a relatively comfortable, although austere, life — but even the austerity was mitigated by a cellar full of old wine — and making derogatory remarks about those who devoted their lives to 'stinks'.

He resented the idea that scientists tended to be people of limited general culture. His own range of knowledge, especially in history, was extensive. It is fair to add that his inspissated philistinism, which he paraded, in all matters pertaining to literature and art, somewhat militated against the idea that he could, in his own person, demonstrate that a scientist might be a man of wide general culture. He had a favourite conversational trope for teasing the humanists, claiming that scientists had normally a very good general knowledge of humane matters, but pointing out some appalling item of ignorance on the part of the humanist on a most elementary scientific point. 'You do not realize,' he said, 'what abysmal ignorance that shows; it would be as though a scientist did not know. . . .' At this point his discourse took one of two lines. To a general audience he might refer to some well-known fact like the date of William the Conqueror, about which it would be absurd to suppose a scientist ignorant. In more sophisticated company he would say, 'it would be as though a scientist did not know the significance of the battle of Tours'. No doubt he had it in mind that the humanist himself might not be so sure about that battle.

Often passing beyond these day-to-day controversies, he talked to me of science itself, endeavouring to expound Relativity and the latest findings of the Quantum Theory. These were not easy matters. Sometimes under his instruction, I thought I had a thorough grasp of Relativity Theory ; but then afterwards my hold on it seemed to slip. The Prof. often said that, if only scientists had had their wits about them, they ought to have been able to reach the Relativity Theory by pure logic soon after Isaac Newton, and not to have had to wait for the stimulus given to them by certain empirical observations that were inconsistent with the classical theory.

The problems of philosophy came into our conversation. We had common ground in deploring Joseph's point of view. This also made him indignant. Later, when the indignation had worn off, he developed a conversational gambit, implying a more lenient view of Joseph. 'I know that Joseph is quite an able man really ; if I had an afternoon with him, I could easily disabuse him of the idea that he has *a priori* knowledge that space is Euclidean ; but I am afraid that it would give him a nervous breakdown, and I should not like to do that.'

When I heard him deliver this utterance, so different in tone from his earlier, and, in my judgement, correct view that Joseph was of limited mental powers,[1] I often wondered whether he merely made this comment, which was harmless enough, irresponsibly, because he thought it sounded well. I had to admit to myself, however, that it was not impossible that he believed it to be true. His misjudgement of people could sometimes be very bad indeed. To begin with, it is not easy to envisage the stocky, tough, plodding, imperturbable, methodical and utterly self-assured Joseph having a nervous breakdown at all. Still more unreal was the idea that the Prof. could, by some patient explanation, have persuaded him of his errors.

Although much opposed to, and even contemptuous of, the philosophical views that he found prevalent in Oxford, he did not share the philistinism of some eminent scientists in relation to philosophy. On the contrary he was deeply interested. Furthermore, he had the positive belief that a philosophical approach could be of collateral assistance to science in the coming times. He was anxious that there should be people of genuine philosophical training who knew physics in a professional way ; it was not good enough that a physicist should have a smattering of philosophy or a philosopher a mere smattering of physics. There was a scheme in the early 'twenties to establish a Science 'Greats' ; this was killed by a speech by Joseph in Congregation, who pointed out that it would be impossible to find people well qualified to give instruction in the course. That was no doubt correct. But did it not involve arguing in a circle ? How would suitable people for teaching ever be trained up, if a beginning was not made ? A beginning could be made only by producing men who were well trained in both disciplines. The philosophy of science was still a thing of the

[1] This was also the view of Whitehead, who told me that he had advised Keynes not to reply to the attack made by Joseph on his *Treatise on Probability* on that ground. Cp. R. F. Harrod, *Life of J. M. Keynes*, page 138.

future, which this new generation would have to create. But I daresay that Joseph was profoundly sceptical about this 'philosophy of science'.

The Prof. believed that philosophy could make a significant contribution, always providing that the philosophers had themselves a deep understanding of physics. Although he did not accept the facile conclusions that some laymen were prepared to infer from the 'principle of indeterminacy', he did believe that there was something there needing philosophical interpretation. At a deeper level, he believed that there were profound questions about the relation of evidence to the construction placed upon it, about the meaning and purport of scientific laws or hypotheses, and about the limitations of knowledge, with which it should not be impossible for our understanding ultimately to get to grips.

When expounding these matters in his heyday (the 'twenties), he struck my youthful mind as extraordinarily impressive and exciting. There were various qualities. One felt that his thought was actively and continuously engaged. He was ceaselessly turning the problems over and going at them afresh. He was open-minded. He knew quite well that he had reached no satisfactory conclusions and was not content, like some 'great' men, to clothe the problems in some provisional formulations, and let the matter rest at that. Then he struck me as very penetrating ; he seemed to take one right to the core and essence of a problem ; he gave one a glimpse of it, only a momentary and fleeting one, so difficult is it for a man to focus in this subtle and abstruse field of thought. Again on these serious and central problems he seemed very modest and very sincere. That contradicts the impression that he often gave when discoursing on less important matters.

His mind was in incessant play. In later years, for good or ill, it was directed rather to other subjects. Of all the

THE PROF

people with whom I have had more than superficial contact,
I would say that he most completely fulfilled one's idea of
an 'intellectual'. It is a paradox so to describe this strange
figure with his motor-cars, his riches, his philistine attitude
in regard to many matters, and his frequent excursions into,
and preoccupation with, high society ; but we have to regard
the essential man. Thought was his meat and drink. All
the time he was turning the matter over. Pascal described
man as 'a thinking reed' ; poor man does not always quite
live up to that. The Prof. was a thinking reed, totally and
absolutely ; the rest was frilling.

Those 'twenties were times when physics was making
rapid progress. Some scientists, like Eddington, made attempts
at philosophizing about the new developments. It is proper
to be quite open about this ; the Prof. had a very low opinion
of their attempts. When, many years later, Miss Susan
Stebbing's critique appeared,[1] he enjoyed it immensely, and
recommended it as good reading.

Changing the subject somewhat, I more than once sought
his opinion about Bertrand Russell's thought as expressed in
Principia Mathematica. The Prof. tended to brush it aside as
being concerned with trivial problems. I was shocked by
this at the time, still having a starry-eyed view about Bertrand
Russell. Already at school, where I had studied my J. S. Mill
thoroughly, I was excited by the idea that Russell and Whitehead had put the logic of mathematics on a better foundation
than did Mill. I do not think that the Prof. disagreed that
the certainty that we get in mathematics was due to its being,
in some sense or other, tautological ; indeed he often expounded this himself. What he regarded as of minor importance was the construction of a symbolic language to escape
the contradictions and paradoxes of ordinary speech. It
irritated him that an allegedly able mind should be side-tracked

[1] Philosophy and the Physicists.

60

into doing arduous work on such an undertaking, when far more important problems were crying out for attention. In retrospect I am no longer shocked by the Prof.'s attitude, but, on the contrary, believe it to be correct.

I do not recall ever discussing Wittgenstein with him, and I do not think that he had read him. If I ever thought of suggesting that he should read this author, I was probably deterred by the sense that he would be exceedingly irritated by him. He was modest himself about such matters, and intensely disliked anything in the nature of showing off by others. To describe someone as 'talking for effect' was one of his strongest terms of vilification.

I cannot refrain from a rueful reflection at this point. I believe that there are some members of the intelligentsia for whom Wittgenstein has, by his essays in private asceticism, gained prestige as a sort of saint of philosophy, while they regard the Prof. as having rendered himself disreputable by his worldliness.

He had a story against himself. He and Edward Marjoribanks had entered a provincial town and drawn up beside a policeman. Edward asked if he could inform them of the best hotel. The policeman extended his chest and said solemnly, 'Now, sir, that all depends : when you say the best hotel, do you mean the best hotel or the most expensive hotel ?' 'The most expensive hotel,' the Prof. chipped in before Edward had time to reply, much to Edward's disgust.

If we are to be serious, how totally irrelevant are such things. In intellectual matters what counts is intellectual virtue and that only. There must be no thought of reputation and fame or of creating an impression on others ; the quest for truth is paramount ; that little ego, which is apt to perk up, must have no place. When I compare the beautiful modesty and integrity of the Prof. with the showmanship of Wittgenstein, I cannot help feeling uneasy about the power of contemporaries, I mean of able intellectual contemporaries, to distinguish true virtue from the specious. No doubt posterity usually sorts these things out. But the man who publishes little is in danger of not getting his due.

When A. J. Ayer appeared on the Oxford scene, the Prof. was delighted. He had a personal regard for him and ranked his abilities high ; and of course he was immensely pleased by his onslaughts on the established school of Oxford philosophy. Although Ayer had very difficult going at first, it was only a question of time before victory was gained. Ayer was vociferous enough in all conscience, and used all his resources of quick thinking and fluency to win victory in debate. His talk certainly had effect, but this was by no means the sort of thing that the Prof. condemned when using the expression 'talking for effect'. For in the talk of Ayer, his absolute integrity shone out ; it was plain that he was straining every nerve and using every muscle to make the point that he had in mind and convince his interlocutor. What the Prof. disliked was the use of adventitious methods, of paradox or queerness, to startle or surprise, or to make some impression irrelevant to the sheer force of the argument. He said to me more than once, 'I do hope that Ayer will make himself acquainted with the problems of physics'. Neither he nor Ayer supposed that this could be done in a fortnight !

I do not think that the Prof. followed those developments in linguistic analysis which have recently become so prominent in Oxford and elsewhere. If one may judge from his views about the triviality of Russell's work, one may doubt if he would have cared for them. They are indeed far removed from those absorbing topics that we used to discuss in the 'twenties. From my contacts with him in later years, which were less frequent, I gained the impression that the life had gone out of his thinking about such matters. He concen-

trated his mental energy, which seemed to have ebbed somewhat, perhaps owing to his inadequate diet, upon the problems
presented to him by Winston Churchill, upon those arising
out of the existence of the atomic bomb and upon other
political developments at home and abroad. I ought to
record, however, that the Comte de Pange's diary refers to
the Prof. as talking about time, causality and probability in
August 1955. I have an idea that by then his remarks on
these subjects may have become a little stereotyped.

It may be in place here to mention my own disappoint-
ment at philosophical developments in Oxford. One gets
an interesting side-light by sitting as an examiner in economics
at the same table as philosophical colleagues in joint judgement
on candidates presenting themselves for the *viva voce* examination for honours. Before the Second World War it was
extremely difficult — perhaps even impossible — for a follower
of Russell or Wittgenstein, or even a plain empiricist, to get
a First Class on his (or her) philosophical attainment. Ayer
himself, so I was informed at the time, was awarded a First
only because of his excellence in ancient history, his philosophical work not seeming to the examiners to be meritorious ;
and I believe the examiners for the John Locke (philosophical)
prize told Christ Church that they saw no distinction in his
work. This was not, I think, due to any conscious intolerance
on the part of the examiners, or a wish to penalize 'heretics' ;
it was simply that they were so convinced themselves of the
validity of their own modes of thought, that those who did
not accept that validity, and held other modes to be valid,
genuinely struck them as deficient in intellectual calibre.
After the war the scene had entirely changed. An adept in
Plato, or in Kant, could still get his First ; but philosophy of
the Wittgenstein type now had an established respectability.
The observing economist was sometimes presented with a
strange spectacle. When a certain question was put across

the *viva voce* table, an adept in Wittgenstein's philosophy assumed an expression of consternation ; he might perhaps utter a groan, or bury his head in his hands in a gesture of despair. All turned, of course, on whether he made these gestures at the *right* moment, *i.e.* whether the question contained some element that, according to Wittgensteinian principles, justified these kind of reactions. Not much had actually to be said. If the performance was judged appropriate, the First was gladly awarded. But still an ordinary empiricist, so it seemed to me, had as dim a chance of a First Class as ever before.

It may seem odd after all these years, and after all the heat that the Prof. and I worked up in our discussions together, to say a word in praise of Joseph. Although his philosophy was intellectually defective and may even have set up in his pupils habits of incorrect thinking about practical matters, at least he was concerned with the ultimate problems confronting mankind, and the mere fact that undergraduates had been induced to dwell upon these problems, gave them a sort of moral stuffing and a sense of purpose in life thereafter.

I remember going to a lecture by Gilbert Murray in a series given by various luminaries as an introductory course for those starting upon Greats. Murray used some such words as that what a young man learnt in the study of philosophy, ancient and modern, could serve him through life as, in some sense, a substitute for a religious creed. Douglas Woodruff, who happened to be a Roman Catholic, left this lecture in the middle, not as a vulgar protest, for he could slip out without being seen, but because he was so furious inside at the affront to religion implicit in Murray's observation. But there was truth in it. Linguistic analysis, although it requires and elicits mental subtlety and precision, touches the great problems only in a peripheral manner — by showing that they are not really problems at all. But then there are real problems. There are, for instance, the kind of problems in which the Prof. was interested.

If philosophy is reduced to mental gymnastic only, the case for according it an important place in the syllabus is much weakened. There are other different kinds of mental gymnastics, as in mathematics and science itself, that may be more relevant. I am not sure that the particular kind of gymnastic required by linguistic analysis is helpful in strengthening the mind for other tasks. By an intense concentration on the anomalies and contradictions in our ordinary language, it neglects the logic actually used in science and everyday life, which is no less subtle, but is different in character and requires a different kind of training.

Thus the total story is rather one of frustration. There were these obsolete modes of thought that the Prof. found on arrival. In the 'thirties there were prospects of an invigorating revolution, of which Ayer made himself a symbol, and the Prof. returned to the idea of somehow getting a fusing between the thought of philosophy and that of science ; but he was no longer then concerned to press his point very much, leaving the battle to others. In the post-war period attention has not been given to these central subjects, and there has been much pre-occupation with the arid and the trivial. Linguistic analysis had originally a striking contribution to make, but it has spread its domain too widely. I believe that in the very latest phase there are signs of a hopeful reaction from it.

*

It is time to return to science itself. About this I am not qualified to speak. None the less it may be useful to record a layman's impression of the Prof.'s point of view. As various theories were developed during the 'twenties, the Prof.

regarded it as of prime importance that one should retain a grip on their 'physical significance'. He held that things would eventually go wrong if physicists lost this grip and were content with mathematical formulations, which did indeed comply with the new phenomena, but could not be given a physical meaning. He often referred contemptuously to the mathematical formulae as 'mere squiggles on paper'. He thought that one might carry on for a time, when divorced from the anchorage of real physical significance, but would get into trouble in the end. He was also quite unsympathetic to what one might regard as a conceptual and mathematical rehash of existing findings, such as the work of Professor Milne. When a young mathematical physicist of promise devoted himself to that line of thinking, he was disappointed and cross.

What did he mean by 'physical significance'? He did not go so far as to mean that a physicist must describe the universe in terms that could be visualized. Physical meaning was something betwixt and between visualizability and abstract mathematical formulation. I tried to probe him to define this, but he could not do so — not unnaturally ! None the less he seemed to be able to apply his criterion very decisively to new theories as they came out, as between those that still had their roots in physical significance and those that were merely floating mathematical formulations. He was not altogether content with the way things were shaping. I think he had the idea that our power of intellectual synthesis was not keeping pace with the results of experiment. The recent multiplication of ultimate entities that has been occurring in physics must leave its practitioners rather uneasy, going against the great historic trend of science, which has been to reduce the number of ultimate entities. Perhaps the Prof. was not altogether wrong in his disquiet at the contemporary failure of the intellectual power of physicists to keep pace with their experimental results.

In the late 'twenties he wrote a book entitled *The Physical Significance of the Quantum Theory.* I am not qualified to judge whether this book has lasting value, or even if it had any great value at the time when it appeared. From what I have said it can be surmized that the title is a key to what he wished to stress. It might be objected that this book was in its own way itself but a conceptual re-hash showing how the established theorems of quantum physics could be reached by an alternative approach. But the re-hash, if such it may be called, was not an end in itself ; it had an ulterior motive ; he feared that, if the theoretical physics drifted too far away from the moorings of physical significance, it would in due course get into increasing difficulties.

It is to be noted that he expressed indebtedness to Mr. Harvey, who had succeeded his valet, Mr. Thorpe, and later became his factotum, his private secretary, aide in all things, and his friend.

The Prof. gave me the galley proofs to be read one morning when I was about to journey to London to the wedding of Frank Pakenham. I read them in the train, and still had them in my hands when I spotted an empty seat in church next to the beautiful and radiant Diana Guinness, as she then was. I told her that this was the Prof.'s book and proceeded with my reading. 'Put that away at once,' she said rather severely. 'Why should I?' I replied, 'I have heard this service many times, but I have never read this book before.' However, she insisted strongly, and, as she was unconventional and daring in her generation, I felt that, if even she was shocked, I must comply, and managed to stuff the snaky galleys into a pocket of my morning coat.

*

We had a great deal of discussion on economic questions. Here I was the propounder and the Prof., so to speak, the learner. In those days (the 'twenties) I had scarcely begun to have original thoughts of my own, but spent my time conveying the ideas of Keynes. The Prof. never became deeply interested in the subtler points of economic theory, but in due course developed his views on a number of economic topics ; it is interesting accordingly to note that his grounding, such as it was, was thoroughly Keynesian.

The most outstanding event of those days was the return by Britain to the gold standard at the pre-war parity (1925). I developed every twist and turn of the argument against that course. The Prof. was then entering deeply into the confidence of Winston Churchill, and he informed me, at some time after the event, that Churchill had told him that all the official advice he got from the Treasury, Bank of England, etc., and all the unofficial advice from the persons whom, as Chancellor of the Exchequer, he had had the opportunity of consulting, was unanimous in favour of the return, with one exception only — that of Lord Beaverbrook. Among the quite different circle whose views were accessible to me, mainly those who published their views, the same was true. Even those whom we regarded as of us, the monetary reformers like Reginald McKenna, successively left our camp and took the line that we had better after all return to the gold standard and then try to 'manage' it. But Keynes never compromised, and by the beginning of 1925 was a lone voice among economists warning against the return. It is not likely that Churchill was in contact with him at that time.

This was one of the very few major decisions in his life, the wisdom of which Churchill came subsequently to doubt. The unique advice of Lord Beaverbrook may well have had the effect of increasing the weight that Churchill subsequently attached to his opinions on that kind of topic. I like to think that my intensive indoctrination of the Prof. in regard to this matter — and the Prof. seemed quite a willing disciple — may have been one of the causes of Churchill's subsequently coming to have doubts about the wisdom of his policy.

*

Although we seldom spoke of political matters in those days, it is proper that I should add something about the Prof.'s political views, since in the end the part that he played in the political scene proved to be his most important contribution to our affairs. He professed a right wing Conservatism. Strangers sometimes expressed surprise, expecting an up-to-date scientist to incline rather to radical views. He used to shake his head, and, putting on a slightly disdainful expression, say, 'I have regard to essentials'. He often remarked in a deprecatory way, even to those of moderate or conservative views, 'I am afraid that I am much too conservative to suit you'. He made many tart observations, at which one could hardly take offence, since they were often amusing, having his own peculiar slant or being almost a caricature of what an old-fashioned person might say.

At the centre of his political views was a very strong and genuine patriotism. Although not English, he had thoroughly identified himself with England. In the post-war period he was very pro-American. In the inter-war period, when the Americans were isolationists in foreign policy, his chief sympathies were with the French. He made it plain that he was deeply suspicious of the Germans long before Hitler. He professed himself, although speaking with a slight self-deprecatory sneer which made people suspect him, as wanting, above all things, *peace*. In the 'twenties the desire for peace was taken for granted ; but the Prof., when he said that he wanted peace, professed to be singling himself out and contrasting himself with us others ; he wanted peace, while we others were relatively indifferent to that great aim, so he claimed. None the less he did not have much sympathy in the early days with the League of Nations, referring to it commonly as 'a home from home for cranks'. He constantly insisted on the precariousness of that peace, which we were apt to take for granted. He was most anxious to retain the existing balance of power, with the preponderance of strength on the side of Britain and France. 'No one can say', he repeated over and over again, 'that the French have any aggressive intent likely to engender war.' Nor had the British. Therefore if they stood together and retained a great superiority over everyone else, the world would be safe. All through the 'twenties he was acutely anxious lest that position be undermined.

He held that the Germans, if allowed any rope, would seek revenge for their defeat in the First World War and subsequent humiliations. That was the danger against which we must be constantly on our guard. He had no patience with those who pleaded that the Germans had been unfairly treated, because he feared that such pleas might give our thoughts a wrong turn. Compared with the great issue of whether we were to have peace or war in future, this question of the precise merits of the existing settlement with Germany was secondary. He made the mistake, however, of over-stating his case. So concerned was he at the danger of people becoming sentimental about the Germans, that he used to make out that they had been having a wonderful time ever since the end of the war, and that all the hardship stories, for instance about there having been a shortage of food there, were the greatest nonsense.

I have spoken of his superb integrity in his attitude to those deeper questions that we used to discuss. But on political topics he allowed himself to exaggerate under the influence of the idea that the end justifies the means. Taking the prevention of another war as a thing of paramount importance, I suspect that he allowed himself to belittle German hardships more than would have been justified by his own objective estimate. This tendency cropped up in many connections. The trouble was that he overplayed his hand. He did not seem to appreciate that his saying that the Germans had not suffered would not avail, nor quash the general belief that they had suffered ; on the contrary it merely made people suspicious of him and think that he was twisting the truth for his own purposes. And that in turn deflected their attention from his main case, which was that, human nature being what it is and German nature being what it was, the policy of allowing the Germans to regain military strength was fraught with danger for us all. He did not win my assent in those days ; but what subsequently happened compels us to treat his main contention with respect.

The Prof.'s wrath was especially roused by the disarmament conferences held shortly before the rise of the Nazis to power. He thought that they were a great mistake, often repeating that they served to reopen old wounds. The right thing was for Britain and France to jog on quietly, doing what they could to keep their defences more or less up to date, and trying to create an atmosphere in which other peoples forgot this painful and expensive subject — no government likes to have to spend money. Turning the spotlight on to international disarmament conferences was gratuitously to rekindle German resentment at the unilateral disarmament imposed on her by the Treaty of Versailles. This was an occasion when he would inveigh against the stupidity of mankind. If the conferences succeeded in their objective — which they seemed unlikely to do — what should we gain thereby, except the saving of a few pounds spent upon arms ? What a trivial aim for the sake of which to jeopardize the peace of the world.

Behind political principles are moral principles. I recall how in general conversation someone asked for a definition of morality. The Prof. assumed his cynical expression, turning down the corners of his lips, and gave utterance. 'I define a moral action as one that brings advantage to my friends.' Mrs. Winston Churchill, who happened to be sitting next to me, touched me lightly and whispered, 'Doesn't the Prof. sometimes say *dreadful* things ?'

How dreadful was it ? His principle did not imply a selfish attitude in theory or in practice. It allowed an unlimited scope for altruistic conduct. That cynical expression that he assumed, which was an expression of his standing belief that his points of view were unacceptable to the majority, made the remark sound more cynical than it really was. No doubt his principle is not ultimately acceptable ; yet I often find myself vexed with those who scorned the Prof. for his lack of a wider humanitarianism. The Prof. showed much altruism in his private life, and perhaps more than many of his critics who were apostles of a wider creed. Is there not a real problem about where one draws the line exactly ? I have noticed that some advocates of the universal brotherhood of man were quite indifferent to the widespread massacre of rabbits through myxomatosis. In the last resort, when man has achieved greater control of the whole environment than he yet possesses, our moral code will surely have to embrace the animal world also, and we shall have to weigh pain incurred there against the 'benefit' to our particular circle of 'friends', even if we define that as conterminous with the human race.

It must be granted that the Prof.'s narrow definition of the proper scope for altruism represented something special to him. There were two strands in this. One was his sense of being cut off from the main mass of humanity ; he felt that they were, or would be, suspicious of him, and this was true, and he was accordingly suspicious of them. He was indeed lacking in the bond of human sympathy for every chance person who was not brought into a personal relationship with him. This may have been due to the simple fact that he was actually an alien in the community where he lived, and that this set up awkwardnesses in his relations with people with whom a status of friendship had not been achieved, or whom he had not met in a friendly environment. Or it may have been due to something deeper in him.

The other strand was a quite genuine belief in his own superiority and in that of his circle of friends. Primarily it was a belief in the superiority of their intelligence. He had an abiding and strong conviction that the great mass of people were 'very stupid'. He also held that intelligence was highly necessary, if the human race was to be saved from disorder, disintegration and ruin. And the corollary to that was that it was highly needful to sustain the position and secure all possible advantages for this 'circle of friends'. He would not have had that expression taken too literally. Unless the circle of intelligent people was maintained in a position in which they had the power to bring their intelligence to bear, everything in the world would go very much amiss.

For himself he sometimes claimed that he subscribed to the moral code of an elephant — unremitting loyalty to his friends and implacable hostility to enemies. (Is this a correct description of the elephant?) In speech he was very fierce against his alleged enemies, full of dire threats and prognostications of the evil that he would wreak upon them. While he never spared himself pains to help his friends, I do not recall any case, over a stretch of some thirty-four years, in which he did a serious injury to an 'enemy'. About his goodness and kindness in private life, Mr. Harvey, who had without exception the best knowledge of him and of all his private affairs and machinations, wrote a beautiful tribute in the *Daily Telegraph* a few days after his death. Harvey's testimony counts for more than all the rest put together.

The Prof. did, it must be admitted, on the lines of the doctrine of the elephant, maintain the most violent prejudices over long periods against those who had given offence. In the 'twenties he had conversation with an economic colleague of mine about the value of British exports. In those far-off days one would not necessarily expect an academic teacher to be well versed in current statistics. The Prof. by contrast was acutely interested in quantities, and did not venture a comment in the economic sphere without having first ascertained the orders of magnitude involved. He was already, at that time, beginning to advise Mr. Churchill, then Chancellor of the Exchequer. My economic colleague named a figure of what he thought the value of our exports might be, and the Prof. named another figure. The matter was subsequently looked up, and my colleague wrote to the Prof. to acknowledge the fact that his, the Prof.'s, *guess* had been nearer than his own. This word 'guess' was quite fatal ; the Prof. never forgave him. I remember that many years later the Prof. had to consider a proposal put forward, and objected to it. 'Why did you object, Prof. ?' I said. 'The proposal seems a very reasonable one.' He made some specious criticisms which struck me as quite unconvincing. Then it suddenly flashed across my mind that the proposal was associated with the name of my unfortunate colleague, who had accused the Prof. of 'guessing' some twenty years before.

In the later period of the Second World War he wrote a memorandum that gained him a reputation of ruthlessness. I was no longer in his office and only heard the rumours of it. He recommended as the primary objective for our bombing sorties the rendering of as many German civilians homeless as possible. I find it hard to judge this. Already in the early days of the war it seemed that civilians on both sides were to be 'in the front line'; the distinction between military and civilian elements in the citizen body seemed already to have become blurred, so far as the moral code of war was concerned.

Talk apart, when endowed with actual responsibility, it by no means appeared that the Prof. took an illiberal line in relation to such matters as social questions. Immediately after the war his 'branch' in the Prime Minister's office gave the Prof. a little dinner, and very kindly asked me to come along, although I had left the office some time before. Sir Donald MacDougall made a speech in which, by piecing together the Prof.'s views on a variety of topics, all of which were thoroughly well known to us, since we had been serving him in intimate familiarity all through the war, he advanced the thesis that, if one wanted to give the most accurate possible designation of the Prof.'s position in politics, one ought to call him a Liberal. MacDougall had said nothing that struck us — and we were the greatest experts on the subject — as incorrect, and the Prof. made no protest at his conclusion.

While the Prof. was merciless in his verbal castigation of Socialists and used language implying the inference 'because he is a Socialist, therefore he must be a very bad man', there again the furnace of events brought to the surface his power of just appraisal. On many occasions I heard him stress how much the country owed to the ability and brains of the Labour members of the War Cabinet.

Complementing his rather restricted view of the proper sphere of benevolence, was his opinion that we should do wrong to expect a high standard of virtue in most people. 'You must not expect that everyone will behave like St. Francis of Assisi', was a dictum that he was fond of repeating. One may call this a realist view, or perhaps even a cynical view. But it is as well to be alive to human failings, if one is to form a correct assessment of the probable course of events.

His cynicism, if we should so call it, was no doubt a valuable corrective to an excess of hopefulness in international affairs. When applied to individuals it sometimes led to shrewd and penetrating perceptions. But on the whole I would say that his judgement erred on the harsh side and that his pessimism in regard to the prevalence of bad motives led him into mistakes. He was, it has to be admitted, a very poor judge of character.

It must have been in the very early days of my donship at Christ Church that I read a paper on Punishment to the Christ Church Essay Society, to which the Prof. came along. This was a paper previously read, when I was still an undergraduate, to the Jowett Society, which specialized in philosophy. Its rather narrow dialectical approach was not quite suitable for the less specialist audience of the Essay Society, and I recall that Dr. Rawlinson (Bishop of Derby), who was asked to respond to the paper, developed more general themes and thereby held the attention of the audience for the rest of the evening. The Prof., however, deigned to make some observations on my paper. This approached the problem of punishment from a utilitarian point of view : punishment was justified mainly as a deterrent ; one might allow just a little to the 'reformatory' view of it, to the extent that the view that punishment had a reforming influence was based on sound psychology ; to the retributive view one allowed nothing at all ; punishment merely as retribution should be completely excluded. The Prof. objected that this principle ignored the pleasure that many derived from the knowledge that a malefactor was to be punished for his misdeed. I strongly deprecated this in a shocked tone. 'Oh,' the Prof. quickly replied, 'you must not suppose that I am passing any judgement myself, or defending such a view of punishment ; I am simply temporarily assessing the matter on the ground you yourself have put forward ; the basis of your paper is that the ultimate test of an arrangement is whether it tends to increase the sum of pleasure and diminish the sum of pain ; and on that basis surely no one can deny that, as a matter of hard fact, the amount of pleasure derived by other people from the knowledge that a malefactor is being punished far exceeds in sum total the amount of pain inflicted on a malefactor by his punishment.' I had no ready answer to this argument ; of course it rested on the premise that the emotional make-up of the other people had not the fine charitable quality of St. Francis. I suppose that this might be called a cynical view.

I do not think that the Prof. was greatly impressed by my paper on Punishment. But some ten years later he came to a paper on ethics which I read to the Philosophical Society and subsequently published in *Mind*.[1] He told me afterwards that it was the first time that he had ever heard a paper at the Philosophical Society containing *eine wesentlich neue Idee*.[2] Note the German ; it would have embarrassed him too much to pay so striking a compliment in English.

I recall an absurd example of overdone cynicism, which may be worth quoting because its tortuousness was typical and contributed to the suspicion with which the Prof. was regarded. It was at the time when Stanley Baldwin suddenly and unexpectedly soared into great prominence in the political scene. The Prof. announced that he had heard that Margot Asquith and Maynard Keynes were both saying that Baldwin was a very good man ; these clever Liberals would never give currency to such a judgement, unless they had it in mind that he was a worthless individual and that his elevation would injure the Conservative cause. The Prof. persisted in this little propaganda campaign against Baldwin for some time. Its psychology was deplorable ; anyone who knew Margot

[1] " Utilitarianism Revised," *Mind*, April, 1936.
[2] A genuinely original idea.

Asquith or Maynard Keynes would know that they both, in their different ways, attached value to their repute as good judges of people, and would not jeopardize that repute for the sake of undermining the Conservative Party by this Machiavellian method. But, even apart from this special knowledge of these two characters, this line of thought was not likely to appeal in the slightest degree to the Oxford dons to whom it was propounded. It was a ludicrous method of seeking to reduce their regard for Stanley Baldwin ; but it did reduce their regard for the Prof. 'If that is the sort of way in which your mind works,' they thought, 'we will know what to think next time we hear you singing the praises of an eminent Labour or Liberal statesman.'

He was asked from time to time to give an address to one of the undergraduate Conservative Clubs and, for this purpose, he prepared a discourse. 'I am afraid that it will shock them', he said, assuming a gloomy expression ; and after he had read it, he said, 'I am afraid that they were shocked'. And indeed they were shocked. But this did not prevent his reading it again. I never heard the paper, but he told me the gist, which was as follows.

All the world's dreary work had to be done — ploughing and reaping and fabricating ; it was a wretched, tedious and painful manner for our fellow mortals to have to spend their livelong days. It had been suggested that science might eventually succeed in getting all the sordid toil of humanity done by robots ; but, from a scientific point of view it would be easier, so he claimed, to dehumanize people. You could take human bodies and strip them of all emotional content, so that all the hard labour became neutral to them and would not appear to be onerous. I must confess that I had a certain sympathy — but was it unreasonable ? — with the undergraduates who were shocked by this interesting proposal.

If one could cast aside all prejudice, one could perceive

that it was well meant. It was a sincere attempt to relieve the human kind of its load of toil and suffering. The victims of the dehumanization would experience no grief, while the remainder would be able to lead happy and interesting lives, all the beastly work being done for them. Other considerations apart, this essay by the Prof. is of interest as illustrating his extreme remoteness from ordinary people. Apart from his excursions into spinning nose-dives, he did lead a very pampered life, moving from his valeting into his expensive cars, and having everything clean and comfortable and to his taste. He was free in his own cloistered régime to devote his mind to fascinating thought and his emotions to the pleasures of friendship. His imagination in human affairs was defective ; he just could not imagine that the horny-handed son of toil could, in his own way, be leading a happy life, and indeed taste pleasures that were unknown to him, the Prof.

> Let not ambition mock their useful toil,
> Their homely joys, . . .

He could not enter into the spirit of that at all. It frightened him. There was his own cultured circle ; then there were rough people who threw rotten eggs. There was this deep-seated alienation that divided him from sympathy with the ordinary man. Yet, in fact, when the psychological gulf was bridged, he was as kindly as anyone. He had many natural impulses of warm feeling, and these found vent among his friends ; but there were more abundant sources of warmth and kindness within him, which were frustrated.

It was our custom on Friday evenings to entertain some undergraduates from another College to dinner at High Table. This was regarded as a mark of attention, and we hoped that they had a pleasant evening. One evening I had Evan Durbin along, then still an undergraduate, an ardent

THE PROF

Socialist, of non-conformist background, a lovable person, a friend of Lord Pakenham and Mr. Hugh Gaitskell and personal assistant to Lord Attlee during the Second World War. He was a man of great integrity, who never feared, when his principles required it, to take a line that might be unpopular with his Socialist associates ; he embodied some of the finest elements in the British character and his tragic death when swimming to the rescue of his children was a real loss to the nation. Well, I thought that he was the kind of undergraduate whom it would be nice to have to dinner, and, when we moved down to the Common Room, I thought it would do him good to sit him next to the Prof. The conversation turned to the value of hereditary stock — Durbin was a keen egalitarian — and the importance of ensuring that those of the best stocks were given every chance to play their part in the more responsible positions in our national life. The fact that a man's ancestors had done well should be considered as a *prima facie* recommendation and we must not carry death duties to an extreme. Durbin was prepared to concede something to the idea that some stocks within the nation were abler than others, but was hot and strong in favour of death duties. When the Prof. suggested that this was contradictory, Durbin challenged him on why he supposed that the mere fact of success in money-making was a proof of general ability. The Prof. : 'Those who succeed in getting what everyone else wants must be the ablest'.

I have never seen a more pained expression on any face. Durbin took the matter up with me afterwards. He had had no idea that anyone existed in the world who had such a debased view of human nature. Was it possible that the Prof. could really have meant what he said ?

I cannot remember how far I went in my endeavour to appease him, for, on this point, despite my Victorian radicalism, I had some sympathy with the Prof. I was a great believer then, as I still am, in the importance of the varieties of stock. The fact that there are many valuable members of the community who scorn the quest for money, does not invalidate the maxim that success in acquiring it is one, and not an unimportant one, among the criteria of general usefulness. This affects the question of death duties and also that of our educational set-up. The Prof. himself was all in favour of the widest possible ladders for advancement through the educational system, which means essentially through the examination system. There is no doubt that by scholastic examination it is possible to select intellectual ability from the main mass of people and give those selected the benefit of a more elaborate education, such as cannot by definition be available for all. But as one who has taken part in every kind of examinership, from the highest to the humblest, I would testify that even in relation to purely intellectual ability, it is somewhat chancy, and, in relation to many characteristics of importance for the more responsible positions, impotent. It would be very bad if we had to rely on scholastic examinations alone for the selection of those who are to have those positions. Some indeed have sufficient innate qualities of a practical kind to raise themselves despite a total lack of advantages ; but these are rare. The only known principle by which we can supplement the examination system is to give advantages to those whose forbears have proved themselves. It is thus important that we should retain the system, now threatened, by which parents can buy their children a better education, and not at the top level only.[1] Thus, *pace* the spirit of Durbin, I had more sympathy with the Prof. in that fearful clash of sentiment.

I may refer here to certain views of the Prof. about examinations. He had no tendency to belittle the important

[1] I have expressed my views on this subject in my submission to the Royal Commission on Population (1944) reprinted in *Economic Essays. Essay 1.*

part that they can play in our society by providing ladders for advancement through scholastic prowess. But he did not value intelligence tests as a supplementary method of ascertaining merit, and in later life he often inveighed strongly against them. This may be deemed 'big' of him, since he was himself so exceedingly efficient in exercises of that kind that, had he submitted himself to the ordeal, he might well have proved to be the British champion. He was scornful of the claims made by their advocates that they could provide a final assessment of intellectual qualities. He did not think that they could reveal the more important qualities. These, he often said, usually came into effective operation only in a man's middle age ; in youth they were still dormant. Conventional examinations might at least yield some hints of future promise ; the intelligence tests could not do so. He was scornful also of the 'weekend parties', arranged as an alternative form of competition for admission to the Civil Service, and had much sparring with Sir Percival Waterfield, who was a member of our Common Room and had sponsored this alternative mode of competition during the Second World War.

*

It was the Prof.'s habit to sit very quietly in his chair when he talked. During those night sessions he used to sit for hours on end without moving in his hideous, but comfortable, armchair, upholstered in grey plush. One had the idea that physical placidity was needful for the play of his mind. He had minor fidgets, including a trick of adjusting his collar. When he had important interviews during the war, he possessed himself of a paper-cutter which he ran up and down the crease in his trousers, and then touched gently with his fingers, presumably to feel the electric current. His quest for an easy position in his chair was rather deliberate.

It was not like some loose-limbed person casting himself into an armchair in an obvious position of relaxation. He settled himself in very deliberately, as though the quest for a comfortable position was a matter requiring careful attention. And so in his life generally. He sought to obtain ease and comfort, but they did not seem to come to him naturally. Sometimes, as I watched him sitting quietly, I wondered if he was as much at ease as he purported to be. Even when he sat talking in the Common Room with his legs crossed, his free foot was drawn up, which suggests tension. People who were presented to him often felt a certain awkwardness, and that not entirely because they were alarmed by his reputation. There was, on his side, some lack of perfect naturalness, although an ease of manner was studiously cultivated. I recall a remark which Bob Boothby made, after the Prof. had left the room where the company had admittedly not been entirely congenial to him. 'I could not go on living, if I were as uneasy as that.'

At this point it may be fitting to remark that all his conversation was strongly laced with his sense of humour. Indeed if one was to do full justice to that, one would devote half this volume to it, for it was a very prominent feature. But, alas, humour is notoriously illusive and unsusceptible to the written record. He could not be regarded as a wit ; when he made deliberate essays in that direction, the results were usually rather crude. Nor is it really relevant to his humour to remark that he had a vast fund of funny stories, including improper ones. In the early days he used sometimes to shock the Common Room with these. He had an even greater fund of stories that might more accurately be described as *risqué*, suitable for the *débutantes*, in whose society he delighted ; they were always *convenables*. For he was intensely conventional.

His special form of humour, however, arose out of the

way in which he saw things ; through his vision the sundry stupidities of mankind became droll, ridiculous, laughable. It was part of his idea of the way in which life should be conducted that in conversation there should be a constant by-play with fun and jokes. Indeed his attitude was a sort of challenge to oneself. If one had some ponderous point to make to him, one thought it a good plan to dress it up in an amusing guise. Thus everything was kept gay and light. He was appreciative of jokes ; he sometimes gave a little chirrup, sometimes a loud guffaw, followed perhaps by a 'No ; not really ?' His laughter was monosyllabic ; it did not ripple on. One cannot imagine the Prof., even as a schoolboy, ever having had a fit of the giggles. But he was smiling, and amused, and amusing. This was an essential part of his charm ; he was in every respect the opposite of a bore. The Prof. is no longer with us ; I often catch myself thinking, when something is said or done, 'that would amuse the Prof.' And then one has a rueful thought that one cannot think of anyone else whom that particular slant, that particular aspect, would amuse. I suppose that the funny in things is just as objective as those qualities that produce sensations of warmth or colour ; but like those it requires a percipient mind. The Prof. made one see all sorts of funny things in the world which, without his guidance, we are unable to see. Do they still have a real existence ? Or has all that gay spangle ceased to exist along with him ?

He had a quiet manner of talking. Occasionally he flared up, as when someone slighted science or made a political observation that he regarded as exceptionally stupid, or harmful to our interests ; then he had an ugly rasping tone, which could strike his interlocutor as offensive. In controversy his quiet flow of speech could be quite devastating. 'How can it be that . . .?' 'Your view evidently is that . . .' Bit by bit his adversary's position would be

reduced to ruins. It was the greatest fun when some personage, such as a member of the German Embassy before the
war, or some scientist with whose views he was known to
disagree, appeared in Common Room, and one prepared
oneself for the spectacle of the total demolition of his position.
I cannot, at this moment, recall an occasion of defeat of the
Prof. on any subject when he had a well-thought-out position. He was very quick, very logical, very resourceful. No
matter how distinguished a visitor might be, a gold medallist,
member of all the academies of Europe, one would have
complete faith in the Prof. winning, should debate break
out ; and so he did. Sometimes, if one met a scientist elsewhere who spoke disparagingly of the Prof.'s current work,
one had no ready defence ; but if he went on to speak slight-
ingly of the Prof.'s general powers, then one could not help
thinking, 'Let me get you into the Christ Church Common
Room, you old scientist, and we shall soon see who is the abler
man'.

He had a lightning speed of riposte, fully equal to that
of Keynes. I do not recall ever seeing these two men in a
serious controversy together. I had a near miss at one time.
Keynes was staying with me (in 1930) and had only just
retired to bed, when, to my amazement, the Prof. came into
my room. In all our long intimacy it was almost always I
who went to his rooms — I suppose it was because he was
considerably my senior — and he very rarely came to mine.
But he had got wind of the fact that Keynes was staying
with me, and now here he was. I had given a dinner for
Keynes, to meet economists, and taken him on to a meeting
at Rhodes House, which had proved to be a large one, and
he had had to answer many questions. By about eleven
o'clock he had been ready for bed.

'Go and fetch him down again', said the Prof. This was
not as exorbitant as it sounds, for he himself would have

been quite ready to resume his clothes for the sake of entering into conversation with an interesting visitor. I went up ; Keynes had moved quickly for he was already lying in bed. 'I have got this extraordinarily interesting man, Professor Lindemann, downstairs.'

'Well, you cannot expect me to get up.'

'No, I do not think that I can.' I had to confess defeat to the Prof.[1]

It is not within my knowledge that they ever did clash. It was during the Second World War that they had most occasion to see one another. Then anyhow they had a basis of agreement on the need to defeat Hitler. There was one occasion when there might have been trouble, at the meeting in Washington for Stage 2 negotiations (1944). But through tact on both sides, conflict was avoided.[2]

It is tempting to compare these two men of supernormal mental power, and may be helpful also for defining the Prof.'s strength and limitations. Keynes' range was far greater. Within it fell the whole world of art and letters. Mr. Clive Bell would have us believe that his views about the visual arts were not of value, but at least he could talk about them in a fascinating way and in one that was acceptable to intelligent people. From this whole world the Prof. was excluded ; if he ventured a view, which he did but rarely, it would bring a blush to one's cheek. Keynes was by no means impeccable in his judgement of character, which, after all, provides the largest scope for conversation, but was always interesting ; in this field too the Prof. was quite hopeless. Very occasionally he hit off a shrewd observation ; far more often he talked the greatest nonsense.

His experience of men was very limited. One might gain

[1] That was many years after I had got Keynes out of bed at a, for him, inordinately early hour in order to have breakfast with none other than H. W. B. Joseph. See *Life of J. M. Keynes*, p. 138.

[2] See *Life of J. M. Keynes*, pp. 588-9.

the impression, and he himself perhaps believed, that he knew everyone who was anyone. But his acquaintance really only extended to a thin top crust — prominent people in politics, diplomacy and London society. He had certain connections with foreign society also ; he was a little more cosmopolitan than Keynes. But he was not at all in touch with the main mass of intelligentsia, with the writers and thinkers and those people of the upper middle class, who embody the spirit of the age and determine its trend more effectively than the top crust. He was quite out of touch with the course of contemporary thought, and this considerably cramped his style. Keynes, aspiring less to the flights of high society, none the less had far greater knowledge of the world. Keynes had another advantage. He had a superb command of the English language and whatever he wanted to say was embellished with his wit and his fancy. He could dress all his thoughts in the most attractive possible guise. The Prof.'s command of the spoken word was very limited. His vocabulary was minute. He worked certain words, themselves inelegant, to death — 'carting', 'bull-dozing', 'four-flushing'. Furthermore, he mumbled inaudibly. It was difficult to hear what he said ; he, on his side, could not hear what one said, as he was rather deaf. Sometimes he seemed to understand what one was thinking without hearing. At other times he just pretended to understand. Yet, despite these appalling handicaps, no intelligent person could talk to him for more than a few minutes on subjects within the Prof.'s range without realizing that he was in the presence of a most powerful and distinguished mind.

At this point I should make one exception to the general charge of illiteracy, which is implied in the foregoing account. He had a supreme, perhaps even unique, power of expressing an argument succinctly and lucidly in writing. This surprised me considerably when, after knowing him for nearly twenty years, I found myself serving him in Churchill's office. Churchill had made it a rule that, if we possibly could, we should confine our memoranda to one quarto double-spaced page. Our office contained a number of people of considerable educational attainments. But in the power of succinct statement the Prof. far outclassed us. He could take three pages and compress them into one without losing a point in the argument, and yet the resultant composition never appeared crabbed or compressed. It retained an easy style, and of course the most perfect lucidity. So we cannot deny him a literary gift.

Although his conversation was so lacking in grace and verbal resource, it had a certain raciness. As an instrument for persuading worldly and unbookish people, this had its effectiveness. Despite Keynes' marvellous powers of persuasiveness, I am not sure that I should not have chosen the Prof. if it was a question of convincing some thoroughly low-brow man of business or affairs. So far as the question of not missing any logical point in the argument was concerned, Keynes and the Prof. would run neck and neck. But to the ordinary man Keynes might seem too academic and high flown, while the Prof. was thoroughly earthy. His very lack of vocabulary would bring him into closer affinity with his interlocutor.

Within their own fields of thought Keynes' achievement was much more important than that of the Prof. Keynes revolutionized economics. All that the Prof. had to his credit were some minor contributions in the early days of the Quantum Theory. Of course it could be argued that physics requires stronger intellectual fibre than economics. I am not sure that I am prepared to concede that.[1]

Of the Prof. it can be said that he had a highly original

[1] For a discussion of this point in connection with Max Planck, Bertrand Russell and Lowes Dickinson, see my *Life of J. M. Keynes*, p. 137.

mind. Keynes had that too. The Prof. seemed to be original in a deeper way, perhaps because Keynes' outlook was more coloured by contemporary thought and feeling; he took much for granted as being axiomatic for an enlightened twentieth-century man; the Prof. took nothing for granted. The Prof. had great depth and what one might call solidity. Within his range he thought everything through very fully; he did not take up a position unless it had deep foundations. Keynes could be carried away by the fascination of some new train of thought and he expounded it so beautifully that you were carried away also. But then you might have an afterthought. Had you been seduced by the convincing flow of words? Had you been glamorized? Keynes himself could have an afterthought also and might make a concession on the next day. The Prof. was quite as devastating as Keynes in argument, but not so convincing; the seduction was not so great. But then your afterthought went the other way. Although perhaps not quite convinced at the time, the more you thought about the Prof.'s argument, the stronger it seemed. And as for the next day, it was as likely that the sun would not rise as that the Prof. would climb down an inch from the position previously taken up.

Keynes might be described as, of all his generation, the greatest apostle of sweet reason. The Prof. was an apostle of remorseless reason. Keynes convinced you that, if only we could get people to be just a little more sensible and to show just a little more goodwill, then, with the aid of his own ingenious ideas, one could get things moving in the right way. The Prof. was more conscious of the crass stupidity of all around him. He felt that there would have to be such a vast shift in people's preconceptions, such a revolution in current modes of thought, such a mighty conversion, that the position was fairly hopeless. Keynes was more attuned to the temper of his age ; the Prof. ploughed his lonely furrow. And so it was perhaps necessary that his original, deep, and often true, ideas, too potent and different to be assimilated by the ordinary man, had to be distilled through the more widely comprehending mind of Churchill, to become practically effective.

*

The Prof. moved between the Common Room and his rooms in College and the Clarendon Laboratory. Where else did he go ? He gave up tennis, at which he was so proficient, fairly early. I never saw him play, although I recall seeing him go off with a tennis racquet in his hand and a look of determination in his eye. He took up golf. He went off on his travels occasionally, preferably towards the south in search of the sun. In the later period he usually went with Churchill. I recall his complaining in Common Room of the Golden Arrow on the ground that it had no second class. There was a chorus of voices, 'Oh, but, Prof., you surely never travel second class'. 'No, but I mean that one has to have one's servant in with one.' (That was in the days of Thorpe and before the days of Harvey, who should be rightly ranked as his friend.) He was fond of photography. Mr. Bolton King, a fervent supporter and ally in many connections, has pleasant memories of joint excursions with the camera. He acquired each new type, as it came along, for coloured photographs, for motion pictures and for coloured motion pictures. He took a splendid coloured motion picture of Sir Winston Churchill wedging himself into and descending the chute into the water at Maxine Elliott's villa, the Château d'Horizon. His pleasures were not costly in sum total. He did not spare himself in cars and cameras. But his intake of food was negligible ; he neither drank nor smoked. He never acquired a home of his own, living always very simply in his rooms in College. When he had friends to luncheon he entertained them lavishly, but my impression is that he did not do this frequently. Foremost among his recreations was that of guest. Already in the 'twenties one was conscious that he was frequently taking to the road to stay in the great country houses of England. There were a number of ducal homes which he visited regularly ; famous hostesses sought him. Then he went to his political friends, the Birkenheads and the Churchills; sometimes just to his own particular friends. It was to rich houses that he resorted, such as would expect him to come with his valet as a matter of course. He went down to London frequently to distinguished dinner parties. It was observed that even a cocktail party in London of the right kind could draw him from Oxford. He loved society and was regarded as an eminently eligible member of it.

The word 'snob' rises rapidly to the lips, and was frequently applied to the Prof. It is a word of many fluctuating and ill-defined meanings. It is a case where Joseph's technique of 'what do you mean by that ?' could be applied more appropriately than to the Theory of Relativity. There is no doubt that he took trouble to court people of the world ; such a great and rapid proliferation of social connections can hardly come without a little care and effort. What did he seek ? He was a man very proud of his own inherent qualities. He thought no one his superior, or indeed even his equal, save only for two or three individuals — the Churchill, the Einstein.

I have the idea that what he sought more than anything else was an assuagement of his own interior malaise, of which he showed so many symptoms. There, in high society, if anywhere in the world, one finds consideration ; all runs smoothly and nothing can go amiss. These people have been bred through many generations to make those they favour comfortable and happy and, yes, above all, at ease. It is to be remembered that the suspicion and hostility to which the Prof. became progressively more the victim right up to the outbreak of the Second World War, originated among the professional classes, the scientists, the dons, the civil servants. But these other more aristocratic people had no such suspicions and were not interested in the matters that gave rise to them. They accepted the Prof. simply for what he seemed to be and liked him for it. Of course nothing can be said without exception. I was told of one lady who would have no truck with him, and summed him up in very simple terms — 'a German spy'.

An unkind cynic might allege that, whereas the professionals knew that he was not making good in science, he passed himself off in those other circles as a great scientist. That would be an utterly wrong idea. They did not ask him again and again because he was a great scientist. Great scientists can be great bores. They asked him because they were amused by him, because they enjoyed his tart remarks, his quiet effervescence, his very special flavour.

There are some young ladies talking together on the terrace which is in view of the drive. 'Who else is coming for the weekend?' 'Didn't someone say the Prof. was coming?' '"The Prof.", what does that mean?' '"Prof." is for "professor".' 'What, not an actual professor, you don't mean?' Even as late as the 'twenties a professor was apt to evoke the image of a white beard and someone a little scruffy. 'Oh, yes, he really is a professor — at Oxford I believe.' 'But he's rather different, you know.' 'What, have you never met the Prof.?' Thus would arise a certain flutter of expectancy. Ought one to try to think of some serious book that one had read?

Then there purred up the drive a large glistening Rolls Royce. The driver stepped out, an active, youthful figure, elegant and conventionally dressed, except for a bowler hat. The car also disgorged a man-servant, who began handling heavy valises. The Prof. was soon in among them, with a flow of banter for his friends, perhaps a touch of gallantry. Then you were introduced. He was ready with some funny stories and chaff; he seemed to know quite a lot of your friends ; he was anxious for gossip. He was anxious too to know what *you* had been doing ; he mentioned a theatre, a night club. All this question of serious books had evidently been utterly irrelevant.

He reserved the grimmer side for his host and some wise heads over the port, which he did not share. He would discourse on politics, tell them the latest thing that F. E. Smith had said about India, or that Winston Churchill had said about our finances, adding a pungent, and probably pessimistic, comment of his own. He had lately been staying with the Duc de Broglie and could give an account of how French politics were shaping. If he were a guest for the first time, his host would be impressed with his up-to-the-minute information on current affairs, all coming from authoritative sources. He was obviously an interesting man to have to stay ; his conversation was most illuminating ; and he seemed to be quite a *persona grata* with the ladies.

I do not say that the Prof. never tried to dazzle the younger people by the 'wonders' of science. He might explain how, if you collected all the atoms that there were in the Atlantic Ocean and made a pile of them, the pile would still be too small for you to see with the naked eye ; and yet, if you could split the nucleus of only one of these atoms, you would have enough power to . . .

He would be in luck if some scientific item had entered the newspaper headlines that morning, because there is usually something a little phoney, from a scientific point of view, in such reports. If it was also the case that a scientist, of name known to the public, had been doing a little showmanship, then he would pour out the vials of his scorn and ridicule, but in a voice of quiet sarcasm, as though the matter was hardly worth exposing. It was really rather impressive to be talking to someone who was so easily able, apparently with complete authority, to debunk the famous scientist, Professor X.

But I have not yet come to the essence. The thing was that these great hostesses or distinguished ladies, who asked him regularly, became very fond of him ; there was truly something lovable about the Prof. that underlay his strangeness and pugnacity. Perhaps that is often so with those who do not achieve the normal satisfactions of love in their own domestic life. There is some residue in the emotional make-up which seems to ask for and evoke affection. Fear kills love. Among those whom one might call the Prof.'s 'equals', he was feared for his sharp controversial manners, his formidable powers and his inclination to intrigue. The figures in the great social world were not involved in all that ; they had no grounds to fear the Prof. and were thus ready to be attracted by what was lovable in him. That analysis applies to the Christ Church Common Room also in the final phase. By no stretch of words can he be said to have been a loved figure there in the inter-war period ; but after he had achieved power and fame in the political world his belligerency in University circles ceased, and most members of the Common Room came to love him.

If he found himself the object of affection in the great world, he valued that, naturally enough. And so, finally, if we ask why he took so much trouble to cultivate these hostesses and allowed himself to be drawn away on visits so often, I judge that the word 'snobbery' is superficial and gives a wrong idea. There was a genuine warmth of feeling between him and his aristocratic friends, which arose in a perfectly natural way. In their society he was able to assuage his inner anxieties and he found an affection that was reciprocated.

It was noted that he always took much trouble with the children in a family of which he had become a friend. There was a young French boy, Maurice de Pange, descended from the long Broglie line, which played so great a part in French history and in this century produced two physicists of the top rank, and from Madame de Staël ; he was full of charm and intellectual promise, and, when he was fourteen, spent a year at Westminster School. Because unhappily he died a year later, his engaging letters, conscientiously written in English, since he was temporarily at an English school, were printed.

9.11.1924

Who do you think came to see me on Thursday evening while I was doing my homework ? Mr. Lindemann ! He heard from Uncle Maurice that I was here, and spent a whole hour looking for the house ! He too invites me and Papa to go to lunch with him at Oxford one Sunday.

27.2.1925

I received an answer-paid telegram at school to-day from Mr. Lindemann, to spend a weekend in Oxford. It would not be convenient this time but I will arrange for next week.

6.3.1925

Just as the Corps parade was ending this afternoon, Mr. Lindemann walked into the school yard ! I ran to stop him, and we spoke longly, and I showed him the 'Up school', the cloisters etc. . . . in fact the whole school. He was very interested and told me that he would be in Paris towards Easter. Then he invited me to spend this weekend at Oxford with him, and I accepted and intend to go to-morrow evening.

9.3.1925

I have spent a lovely weekend at Oxford. On Saturday evening I dined in Christ Church Hall at the High Table with all the dons, which is considered to be a very great honour. . . . Mr. Lindemann was very kind to me, showed me the different Colleges, his big new Laboratory, etc. In the afternoon we had a long motor drive and dropped to tea at some of his friends. I went back in the evening greatly pleased, with a big box of chocolates.

Thus I may have met this charming young boy, but I do not recall him. But we all remembered his bringing in Randolph Churchill on several occasions, also when very young and an exceedingly good-looking schoolboy. In that case, too, so Randolph has since told me, there was a large box of chocolates for him to take away.

There was always a tendency to think the unkind thing about the Prof., and in these cases it was alleged that he was merely courting favour with the parents. This was partly his own fault, because he was so apt to read sinister motives into what others did ; this came back as a boomerang upon himself. I am sure that he found genuine pleasure in doing a good turn to the children of his friends — he took immense pains about placing them in a college, and so forth. It was just a little outflow, in substitution for parental feeling. I may be allowed to mention an instance, where he had no axe to grind. Our relations had cooled a trifle in the final period, for reasons presently to be explained — although not, I like to think, at the deepest level. He left my elder son, his godson, a legacy of £500.

Sir Geoffrey Faber has recently endeavoured to enforce the view upon us that, even in the case of such a man as Benjamin Jowett, the question of sex is all important and must receive lengthy treatment by a biographer. I feel, on the contrary, that in a case where there is, in fact, little to be

said, it can be left to the reader's imagination to do all the
hard work. There were one or two ladies whom the Prof.
courted, but I cannot judge with what zest ; one at least was
not, strictly speaking, available. When I first got to know
him he was a comparatively young man, and eminently eligible
from a material point of view. It never occurred to me
that he had any thoughts of matrimony ; of course I may
have taken quite a wrong view, owing to the absurd gulf
that sixteen years of difference in age interpose for a young
man in the early twenties. Thus the Prof. struck me as a
comparatively elderly person, in whom all thoughts of marriage, had they ever existed, must have long since passed !
Be that as it may, there did not in fact appear to be the slightest
symptom of his being in quest for a wife. Or did he think
that he would find one among the lovely debs whom he met
at the great houses ?

He was not at all prudish. He was racy, even smutty
sometimes, in his talk. Furthermore, he was full of schemes
and hopes for his friends. One could hardly mention the
name of a lady, however innocently, without his thinking, or
at least pretending to think, that there must be some desperate
intrigue. That was engaging. It made one's own life seem
so much more romantic and interesting than in fact it was.

The Prof. was extremely susceptible to good looks in both
sexes. Perhaps one should stress the other side a little more,
and say that he could not bear an ugly person. If he found
a face displeasing to him, that set up a violent prejudice,
which only the most supreme intellectual merits could counter-
weigh. I have given much thought to the question of homosexuality in relation to him ; I would say that, although
there is probably some slight streak of it in everyone, the
Prof. should be regarded as 'normal'. He greatly enjoyed
the society of women ; he sought them out ; he became
happy, and almost radiant, in their company. All that being

so, there is something that needs explaining, something that Sir Geoffrey Faber would insist that a biographer must explain, in the Prof.'s not appearing to be in more active quest at that very time when I first got to know him. Perhaps he was all the time. He was highly secretive, keeping the various sides of his life rigidly apart.

All that I can contribute is this. I can only revert to his deep sense, which showed itself in so many ways, that he was unacceptable to other people. Reference to this recurred again and again ; it was not a mere pose. He thought that he was generally disliked ; he may have thought that he was physically unattractive ; his friends had to work quite hard to persuade him that they were fond of him. At the same time he was intensely proud. He firmly believed that he was a great man ; he was equally convinced that everything about him was displeasing to other people. The slightest rebuff hurt him deeply ; he would be only too ready to believe that he was repellent to the other party ; he was probably just not tough enough to endure the ups and downs of a courtship. He had some lack of normal animal spirits, such as serve the ordinary man in good stead ; he was altogether too sensitive and touchy, too despondent about his own charms and too ready to be put off. One thinks of that first, and only, meat meal ; the discomfort encountered rendered him a vegetarian for life. One has heard much of the evils of repression ; he certainly showed many outward symptoms of a highly repressed person. At heart he was certainly a man of feeling, of deep feeling. But at some point he had made up his mind that the normal pleasures of life were not for him. And so he turned inwards, and established a fixed routine, allowing himself in substitution all personal comforts, such as his wealth could make readily available, fussing too much about the 'expensive hotel', unduly fearful lest, the main consolations of life having been denied him, his own minor and cherished comforts should be in the slightest degree disturbed.

And those young ladies on the terrace ? Some repressed persons create for themselves a world of pure fantasy. This was something betwixt and between. Those young people were not the figments of his imagination ; they were alive and fond of him. At the same time I think that they belonged for him to a kind of fairyland. He had no serious intention of even beginning to try to marry any one of them. But his romantic feelings achieved a partial satisfaction.

*

He did not talk much about his social life in college, partly through tact, partly through secretiveness. Although my colleagues knew about his dabbling in high politics, I doubt if they realized in the early days how wide his social ramifications were. He hardly ever mentioned them to me, although I had so much intimate talk with him. I gradually discovered about them from other sources of information. Occasionally one felt a whiff of the great world, especially when we reassembled at the beginning of term. And if one's ears were open, one could detect tell-tale phrases in his conversation. The name of Venetia Montague happened to come up, I do not recall why. 'She is one of the cleverest women in London', he remarked. The form of this assertion implied that he regarded London society as a unity, which one can only do at its top level, and that he was moving freely and widely enough to form a judgement of the intellectual merits of the various women in it ; he might indeed be merely repeating the verdict of others — although he seldom accepted such verdicts for himself ; but even that would imply wide acquaintance, in order to be so sure what the verdict was.

99

The political side was necessarily more evident. F. E. Smith came to dine with him in Christ Church quite often. I only remember Churchill coming into Common Room on one occasion, although there may have been more. I was due that evening to read a paper on the 'Measurement of Pleasure'. Churchill was most anxious to come and hear it, and immediately went off into some superbly embroidered phrases. I cannot recall his actual words but they were on these lines. 'I suppose,' he said, 'that every particle of pleasure, every scintilla of emotion, can be weighed and measured with meticulous precision on the finely adjusted scales of science.'

I was still very young ; this was an early essay on the great cardinalist-ordinalist controversy in which I came down on the cardinalist side ; it was written for a philosophical society. As I listened to Churchill I felt that my dialectic would be too narrow, crabbed and parochial, to interest this man, who was evidently preparing himself to bring his active mind to bear upon the issue. I passionately dissuaded him from coming. At first he persisted ; but, when he saw that I really did not want him to, he deferred to my wishes. I am sorry now.

Our society is in the continuous process of change as regards social stratification. Whatever the ideal of a classless society may be, so long as people have differences in certain defined respects in their manners, habits of mind and ways of talking, one has to admit that, on a strictly objective assessment, social classes exist. From a psychological point of view, especially if one is dealing with a person where there is lack of ease, and anxiety, the question of social class may be hardly less important than that of sex itself.

It was very difficult to place the Prof. socially. He had a thoroughly respectable, solid and wealthy background. And yet, from a social point of view, he seemed deracinated ; this may have been because he was by birth a foreigner, who was anxious to assimilate himself completely to England. But he never succeeded in becoming in the least like an ordinary Englishman.

One peculiar thing about him in this connection was that, despite his own excursions into the upper class world, he seemed quite unable to judge the social standing of other people. If there were some external mark, such as a title or a high position held in politics or diplomacy, well and good ; if he recognized a face that he had seen in a distinguished drawing-room, again he knew where he was ; but those ordinary signs of intonation or manners, whereby a person of good breeding can commonly be distinguished, meant nothing to him ; he must have had to proceed in his social calendar by the method of 'complete enumeration'. He always behaved with perfect correctness to any academic guest ; but if someone arrived in Common Room from the outer world, you had to give the Prof. a little more briefing than would have been needed by some of our other colleagues.

I remember being struck when Miss Helen Makower, economist and sturdy democrat, pointed out to me, as a mere matter of sociological interest, that the Prof. was totally incapable of making social discrimination within our little staff that was working for the Prime Minister during the Second World War. In the humblest part of our establishment, where people were simply engaged in draughtsmanship, there might be an artisan whom the Treasury had collected for us from some storekeeper's office and there might be a well-educated man of cultured background, who had happened to find this humble part to play in the national effort to defeat Hitler. It would have been nice if the Prof. had given some little recognition, the smallest token in the world would have sufficed, that this man would in peacetime be in a somewhat higher sphere ; but the Prof. just had not the faintest clue to that.

There was an occasion when the Prof. was bidden to a luncheon given by the Vice-Chancellor for some royal personage, who had come for an unveiling, an opening or something of the sort. I asked the Prof. afterwards how the lunch had gone. 'It was perfectly frightful,' he said, 'everyone was so stiff and awkward ; one had not realized how terribly bourgeois our academic colleagues are.'

Included in the idea of an English gentleman, if we may use that old-fashioned term, is his ability to engage in easy conversation about any tittle-tattle that may be to hand ; in that respect the Prof. was well equipped. But also included in the idea is the possibility that, without any embarrassment, without any awkwardness, he may move away from the tittle-tattle and engage you, with equal naturalness, on some deep concern, something relating to the serious affairs of his life, or of yours, something touching the delicate fibres in our composition. In the case of the Prof. no such divagation was possible. He might leave the tittle-tattle, and embark readily enough on the serious affairs of politics or science. But on serious personal questions, there would be much awkwardness, jolts and jars, and a final halt. When one perceived this, one wondered whether his ease on the lighter plane was not itself something rather artificial, something acquired by a cerebral process to serve the social purpose ; it was not that really natural ease that comes from unpremeditated confidence in oneself, as being deeply rooted in the order of things, and thereby able to speak unaffectedly about them, whether they be light or grave. But it may be that this limitation in the Prof.'s powers was simply due to the fact of his extreme reticence and shut-offness.

*

This may be the place where I should try to probe further for the causes of his rather widespread unpopularity in the

inter-war period. First and foremost was, no doubt, the fact
that he was by birth an alien. This would not have mattered
in the least if he had shown some slight concession to that
fact in his deportment. The English are hospitable and cherish
those who come and settle among them. The Prof., who
undoubtedly loved this country and sought to identify himself fully with it — that was all to the good — rapidly took
up the position of teaching us all how to manage our affairs
and making it evident that he regarded most of our ideas
as very stupid ; and this was resented. Among the British,
and no doubt also among the members of any other nation,
there are certain subtle touches in their association with one
another, a kind of freemasonry, by which a natural fellow
feeling is engendered ; on the sure basis of this fellow feeling,
we can tell each other where we get off and how stupid we
are ; but the Prof. lacked the freemasonry and did not
establish the fellow feeling. And so, when he meddled and
even sought to dictate, he aroused suspicion.

Then there was his general attitude of superiority. By
small touches in his demeanour, he indicated that he regarded
himself as a great man ; and so indeed he was. But unfortunately between the wars he was not showing greatness in
the job that he was supposed to be doing ; the capital gained
by the *réclame* of his spinning nose-dive could not last for
ever ; perfectly good scientists, who were getting on with
their prescribed tasks more successfully than he, did not see
why they should be addressed *de haut en bas*. Then he had
a highly irritating habit, which caused deep resentment, of
informing scientists how they ought to conduct their research
in fields right outside the sphere of physics. He managed to
keep up with developments in many branches of science, and
had his own ideas. He had hunches, and the uncomfortable
thing about this was that they were often very good. But a
faithful scientist, who had devoted his life to a particular line

of research, say in the field of physiology, strongly objected to being informed by the Prof. that this line would lead nowhere and that his problems ought to be tackled by quite a different approach. More serious reasons for suspicion among scientists, which arose in the 'thirties, and gave rise to very strong feelings indeed, I reserve for their proper place.

I recall a remark by the Prof. which illustrates both his philistinism and his infuriating (even if well-meant) tendency to give instruction outside his own range. Even in my earliest days I should never have gone to the Prof. for lessons in deportment or in how to make myself socially acceptable. I happened to refer to someone as a 'great poet'. 'It doesn't do to talk like that,' he replied ; 'you shouldn't refer in an awe-inspired tone to "a great poet". What you should say is, "you know, the feller writes quite decent verses".'

The Prof. had another very bad habit, which, however, was by no means confined to him — that of speaking in contemptuous terms about someone who was his interlocutor's great friend. This bad habit appears to be more prevalent, I was about to say among academic people, but I should substitute among 'clever' people, than it is among ordinary decent people. A certain kind of clever person tends to think his judgement of character so important that its enunciation should have priority over a proper respect for the feelings of friendship entertained by his interlocutor for the person in question. The Prof. was by far the worst sinner in this regard whom I have ever met.

In his case, I judge, the motive was slightly different from a desire to display his own 'cleverness'. He had many highly unpopular opinions about things in general, and it was a part of his attribute of courage that he enunciated these views freely in all kinds of company, however unpopular they might make him, and even if he knew that he was losing the good-will of those who might be useful to him. He never swerved from his convictions. And he thought it his duty to affirm these convictions, as his contribution to the general well-being — that was an essential part of his moral code — at all times and seasons. And of course he was perfectly right not to mind incurring unpopularity, not to hesitate to upset people of the opposite way of thinking, whenever he thought it important for society that their way of thinking should be changed. Whether it was equally his duty to speak contemptuously of, say, Stanley Baldwin or Neville Chamberlain in the presence of a great friend of theirs, is an arguable point. Such men had elected to expose themselves and were in a position to affect our affairs for good or ill ; accordingly it could be held that it was just as important for the public weal to disseminate contempt for these men, if they really were contemptible, as to disseminate correct views about Germany or nuclear energy. Thus in that case too the Prof. could plead that he did well to have the courage of his convictions, and that his audience must take their chance if they chose to be friends of such significant figures. But then he extended his habit to trouncing perfectly harmless people, whose good or ill repute could make no difference to the public weal, in the presence of their friends. It was a case of extending a deeply ingrained habit which had grown out of his having the courage of his convictions, and applying it where no courage was needed and his conviction was of no importance.

I had much trouble with the Prof. on this score all through our period of friendship. I will give only one example, which almost led to a final breach.

Of those who came of age in the 'twenties, Robert Byron was one very much beloved by his friends and judged by many of his gifted contemporaries to have the greatest promise of them all. He published many volumes on a large variety of subjects within a brief space of time. They were of unequal merit, but all were written in a vital and original style, and packed with thought. He wrote voluminously because he felt passionately about many things, but also sometimes to earn money, since he was hard up. He was a most fascinating and brilliant talker ; his ideas were subtle and complex ; and what many of his friends felt was that, despite his numerous publications, he had scarcely yet begun to give expression to what was in him ; he had not yet achieved complete lucidity. We believed that he had the power to go forward and write works that might be great classics. Mr. Christopher Sykes has made an excellent study of Robert Byron,[1] which contains much that is good and true, but yet does not exhaust its subject.

Robert Byron's main fields of interest were aesthetic, and thereby of a kind about which the Prof. was abysmally ignorant. But he had political ideas also ; he was, incidentally, a fervent anti-Munichite. He was a man of great sensitivity and refinement. One should regard him as a fine flower of a high civilization. Compared with Byron, the Prof., for all his social graces, was basically, like some other men of great genius, a rough diamond.

It was with a sad and heavy heart that we heard the news in the early period of the war that Robert Byron had been drowned on his way to Greece. The Prof. was sitting at the head of the table at our wartime establishment at Marlow and I at the opposite end ; it happened to be a full evening, and both sides of the table between us were lined with members of our staff. It was not perhaps an appropriate moment for me to refer to the news, but my thoughts were full of it. I uttered some bromide : 'What tragic news it is about the loss of Robert Byron'.

'Oh, I thought him a very second-rate person,' said the Prof. I was not going to have this, and piped up in loud and distinct tones, 'Robert Byron was one of my greatest

[1] *Four Studies in Loyalty.* (Publ. : Collins, 1946).

friends, and one of the most brilliant men of his generation'.

'Oh, no,' repeated the Prof. in sneering tones, 'he was a very second-rate person.'

My instinct was to leave the room, to leave the house and to leave the Prof.'s employment. I had to cling hard to my chair and repeat a catechism that had become familiar : 'Would Hitler's victory in this war be a grave setback for our civilization ? Is Churchill playing a key part in preventing that victory ? Many people seemed to judge that he was. Was the Prof. helping Churchill in his task in an important way ? It was the firm conviction of our branch that he was doing so. Was I, in my tiny little way, helping the Prof. to help Churchill ?' I must stay where I was. Robert would understand.

But I could never quite feel the same about the Prof. after that. I could not think of any sufficient excuse. I have often wondered how this type of behaviour by the Prof. was tolerated in polite society. Perhaps he kept a closer guard upon his tongue there than he did among us intellectual ragamuffins — but that would not be to his credit either.

*

Many people thought that the Prof. was a Jew, or at least of partly Jewish extraction. Whether this was true should be a matter for research. There appears to be no doubt that his mother was wholly Gentile. His father was a German or a French Alsatian, and, at the time of his marriage, it was not usually supposed among his wife's family that he had Jewish blood. This does seem to suggest that the Prof. had no Jewish blood or that the admixture was quite small. I met his father once. He had a fine square beard and a guttural accent ; his appearance did not suggest the Jew.

The reason why this view about the Prof. was so widely

held was simply that he struck most Gentiles, including some of his French friends, as like a Jew. There were his rather heavy features. It should be added here that his brother, Charles, although quite like the Prof. in features, has no look of the Jew at all. But it was not only a question of features. There were many touches in his deportment, in his manner of conversation, in his modes of thought, and, notably, in his social attitudes, that suggested the Jew to the Gentile mind. It would be invidious, as well as probably beyond my powers, to make a list of these qualities. Such questions of resemblance are subtle, and hard to put into words. I would by no means be thought to imply that the traits in question were detrimental; they were good, bad and indifferent.

The question of whether the Prof. was in fact a Jew was a subject of frequent discussion. It has been suggested that, in England at least, where many German Jews have settled, characteristics that are basically German have become associated in the English mind with the Jewish race, so that it might have been the Prof.'s German characteristics — if he was indeed a German — that made English people think him Jewish. I have asked Jews if he was a Jew, and got at least one strongly affirmative answer as well as some negative ones.

This matter might, in itself, be deemed to be of no great importance; the supposition, whether right or wrong, that the Prof. was a Jew would not have prejudiced his career or subjected him to suspicion in this country. But there was another fact that put quite a different complexion on the matter. He was somewhat prone, especially in his younger days, to make anti-Semitic remarks. Now if his interlocutor was firmly convinced, whether by hearsay or by personal impression, that the Prof. was a Jew, and then heard him give vent to an openly anti-Semitic sentiment, that would create a very unfavourable impression and certainly be a ground for suspicion and distrust. Later he spoke in this vein less frequently, or qualified his anti-Semitic remarks by describing them in an amused way as the sort of things said in anti-Semitic circles. But even that was not quite satisfactory. If one was convinced that he was a Jew, it seemed odd that he should retail, even in a detached and sarcastic vein, stories or *mots* current in such circles.

He had many close friends, who were Jews, in the scientific world. Jews have shown themselves rather proficient physicists. In the early days of the Nazis he conducted a marauding expedition into Germany in one of his large cars, and made contact with a number of eminent Jewish scientists, in order to establish them at work in Britain. He seemed to have no fear of the Nazis ; but then he was, in any case, a brave man. He took great pains to forward the interests of these Jewish scientists. He found a permanent home for one in Christ Church. This would naturally put a curb on his tendency to anti-Semitic remarks ; but right up to the end he occasionally gave vent to something derogatory.[1]

He was up to all sorts of tricks, some of which I shall describe, to create desired impressions in his conversation, but I cannot believe — and my knowledge of his character is rather extensive — that he would have made the remarks he did, had he believed that he was himself of partly Jewish extraction. But of course he may have had Jewish blood without knowing it ; there may have been just one Jew among the multitude of ancestors, whose characteristics, while avoiding his near relations, came out, by an ordinary Mendelian process, markedly in him. To be oneself, without knowing it, something to which one is instinctively antipathetic, would surely set up strong psychological stresses, and might indeed be an important reason for his repressions

---

[1] I draw attention to his speech, however, condemning anti-Semitism, delivered in the House of Lords on April 10th, 1957.

and failures of adjustment, above all, for his deep sense of being unacceptable.

It seems curious that he never cleared the matter up. The belief that he was a Jew was so widespread that he could hardly have failed to be aware of it. Mr. Ivor Thomas wrote a short biography of Lord Birkenhead, in which he coupled the Prof. with Lord Melchett as examples of Lord Birkenhead's fondness for Jews (p. 201). Would not this have given him a chance of coming into the open? 'This fellow says I am a Jew; of course there is no truth in it.' It may be asked why we did not, on our side, take the opportunity of putting the question to him in some tactful way. But his early anti-Semitic attitude made that impossible.

I believe that it will always remain something of a mystery. It is possible that the reader who knows the Prof. only through these pages will find, if he perseveres to the end of the book, that he has formed his own opinion on whether the Prof. had Jewish blood.

I recall a clash that he had in the early days with Harold Laski, whose status as a Jew was not in dispute. It was at a crowded meeting of one of the College or University under-graduate societies, in some rooms in Christ Church. The Prof. was not very well known to the members and he made an excellent impression on them on his first run. The subject of the paper, to the best of my recollection, was Babeuf, the only Socialist of the French Revolution. Laski, however, interpreted his theme broadly, and gave himself plenty of space to dwell on the benefits that Socialism could bring to contemporary Britain. In particular he took the trouble to go into some rather elaborate statistics of coal production, in order to prove the advantages of the nationalization of coal-mining, and finally gave a figure for the annual output of coal that could be achieved in those favourable circumstances. The Prof. interrupted him. 'Would you repeat that figure for annual output under nationalization ?' I looked up ; the Prof. had taken his little slide-rule out of his waistcoat pocket, and I knew that something good was in store. Laski repeated the figure. The Prof. asked for further confirmation : was he sure ? Oh, yes, Laski was confident.

'Then,' said the Prof., 'they would be producing enough coal each year to cover the whole of England four feet deep in coal.' Laski eyed this strange person with his slide-rule, and recognized defeat. Some five minutes' worth of his speech evidently had to be written off as sheer waste of time.

So far so good. But later the Prof. made a riposte that might have been thought superb among some right-wing students in Germany or France, but was not suitable to the temper of any audience in Oxford, whether of the right or the left. It was during the general discussion, and the Prof. was making some observation to the effect that the conditions of life in Czarist Russia were not as bad as they were often painted. This time it was Laski who interrupted : 'You cannot expect me to agree with that, as forty of my relations were murdered under that régime'. (Was that indeed true ?) The Prof., with lightning speed and in a tone of supreme scorn : 'I was not discussing their attitude towards religious dissent'.

*

I have mentioned my frequent visits to his rooms without describing them. He had been assigned a spacious set in Meadow Buildings, overlooking the Christ Church meadow, with a distant view of the trees that bordered the river, whose name he later took for his title. He had done them up lavishly, with all regard to comfort, and installed a bathroom. White paint was used throughout, and the undergraduates used to refer to them as 'The White City'. The contents were hideous. Among all the objects there was not one that paid the remotest tribute to the human desire for something pleasing to look at. Later he framed some good photographs, which he had taken on his travels ; but even these he hung at the wrong height, so that the effect was displeasing. I do not think he realized how ugly everything was ; he just had no visual feeling at all. He had, I believe, some real love of music ; he had an upright piano in his study and, when I took him by surprise, I occasionally found him strumming.

In his dining-room he had two large oil paintings of Edwardian or late Victorian date. One represented two nude figures reposing in lush grass, the other two large-sized kittens playing round a box. I sometimes chaffed him about them.

'Prof.,' I said, 'you are an important person in this ancient university, and you just cannot have these daubs hanging in your dining-room ; they bring discredit on the whole of Christ Church.' To which he invariably replied somewhat acidly, 'I suppose that you want Picasso'. That was not in fact the case ; although I have endeavoured to keep myself reasonably well educated, my own personal taste is not for modernist work. But nothing that I could say would convince the Prof. of this. If I did not care for his pictures in the traditional style, it must be because I wanted something modernist. Over and over again I tried to persuade him that there were differences between pictures in the traditional style, that some were good and some were bad ; his, unfortunately, happened to belong to the class of very bad. I really think that in his heart of hearts he did not believe in these differences — provided that the picture had some rough resemblance in line and colour to the objects that they were supposed to represent ; he thought that the supposed differences in artistic quality were just a lot of mumbo-jumbo, devised by the alleged experts, to make themselves important and give themselves something to do. As he gave me credit for being an intelligent man, he assumed that I must see through all that rubbish, and he inferred that, if I did not like his pictures, it must be because, despite all my protests to the contrary, I wanted him to conform to modern tastes and have Picasso. Either one liked the traditional pictures or one liked the modernist pictures. To waste much time distinguishing between one kind of traditional picture and another was to mark yourself a fool, incapable of occupying your mind with anything more sensible.

That was a limitation in the Prof., which applied in other ways also. What was outside the range of his own powers of thought could not be of any great importance. He did not refrain, however, from passing judgements on paintings ; if others liked to indulge in these judgements, he was entitled to do so, as he really believed that his own view was as good as anyone else's. His judgements were governed, so far as I was able to make out, by his own private motives. We have a portrait in Hall of a deceased colleague, with whom the Prof. had had a good deal of friction — rather a displeasing painting in a highly finished style, not really a fine work, but far superior to the pictures in the Prof.'s dining-room. This portrait he roundly condemned as an extremely bad painting. We have one or two other rather poor contemporary paintings also in the traditional style in Hall, which the Prof. declared excellent. These judgements were determined by his attitude to the sitters.

As he was prepared to be dogmatic about paintings, I dare say he may have given offence to scholars and experts in this field also, if they had not previously been primed on the extremity of his philistinism. I simply closed my ears when he began talking on such subjects. Only in the last year or two of his life was this a source of any embarrassment. In 1956 the Christ Church authorities paid me the compliment of making me Curator of Pictures. This official is mainly concerned with our great collections of Old Masters, but he is naturally also involved in projects for acquiring new portraits. I made it a rigid rule never to speak to the Prof. on this topic, as I knew that he would make use of any knowledge that I gave him to start a campaign of intrigue and personal pressure. He sometimes made an approach. 'I hear that you are thinking of . . .'; but I snubbed him off at once. It was a little distressing. But I had had my full complement of difficulties with the Prof. over many years, and I was determined not to engage in fresh battles, or to allow him one iota of interference with me in my duty as Curator of Pictures.

It was in the very early days of my donship at Christ Church that I had a very dear friend to stay with me for a few days, Stephen Tomlin ('Tommy'), the sculptor. He remains in my mind as the most interesting talker that I have ever known and one of the most intelligent men. I have endeavoured to make a comparison of the intellectual powers and conversational aptitudes of the Prof. and Keynes. One is tempted into a sort of parlour game. Who was the greatest intellect you ever met? Who was the best talker you ever met? Winston Churchill comes up for consideration in any such class, but we must rule him out, as my personal acquaintance with him was less extensive than in the other cases. There are figures of the past like Alfred Whitehead and Frank Ramsey; I recall J. B. S. Haldane in his youth as very splendid. But let them be forgotten at the moment. Stephen Tomlin had not the mathematical training of the Prof. or Keynes; indeed he had little academic training, although he was a classical scholar of New College, and an exceptionally fine Latin composer; but he left Oxford after a short time. I would put him above, yes, far above, anyone else whom I have known as an entrancing talker. He had the great gift, rare among adepts in the loquacious art, of making *your* remark or thought the basic theme for his imagination to play upon. He never for a moment forgot the interests and personality of his conversational partner. He had a beautiful, mellow and soothing voice. Where he most excelled, I suppose, was in analysing the characters of people — and human nature, after all, is a subject that must bulk large in range of matters of rational discussion. The poor Prof. was not in the running here at all ; but Keynes' comments on men would seem very crude if brought into juxtaposition with those of Stephen Tomlin. He was a sculptor and could talk about the world of art. There again the Prof. not in the running, and Keynes limping along very far behind. He had a very wide knowledge of English letters. He was not merely an aesthetic type ; his brain had strong muscle, and he was a match for anyone in argument, where the issue depended on logical power. His imagination, his power of understanding many sides, his mental pliancy were very great ; he would not let you escape with loose reasoning ; he detected your fallacy very quickly.

I told him all about the Prof. — how much I was seeing of him and what an interesting man he was. I said that we must pay him a visit, as we had not happened to meet him in Hall, warning him of the frightful rooms. He did quail somewhat when I gave him my character sketch, but I insisted.

There could hardly be two more different people in the world. The Prof. was a tremendous philistine, Tommy an aesthete. The Prof. was shut up in himself, Tommy expansive. The Prof. was tart and caustic in argument, Tommy confounded you in the most gentle and winning way. The Prof. was a rigid Conservative, Tommy a Liberal. The Prof. was a great believer in the established order, Tommy very sceptical of it. The Prof. was highly prudish and conventional in his outlook on sex matters — except for his smutty stories which were themselves cast in a conventional mould — Tommy very outspoken and to some even shocking. For the Prof. the idea of homosexuality was utterly abhorrent, Tommy was inclined to regard it as a valuable element in society. For almost any human attribute, it would probably be safe to put them on opposite sides.

Nevertheless I wanted them to meet. I was giving much thought to the Prof. and I liked to talk things over with Tommy. I was not in the least afraid about the meeting. For among all their diversities, they had one thing in common : they were both of a very high level of intelligence such as one rarely finds, and that fact, I believed, would transcend all their differences. I take Sir Geoffrey Faber to task for finding it difficult to understand what Swinburne and Benjamin Jowett had in common. Is not the explanation simple ? Swinburne was probably one of the cleverest men that Jowett had ever met, and Jowett was probably one of the cleverest men that Swinburne had ever met.

The one danger in introducing the Prof. to a clever man was his utter hatred of any kind of showmanship ; it is to be admitted that many brilliant talkers have a touch of that. But there was no trace of it in Tommy ; that was one of his charms.

And so I took him up to the Prof.'s rooms, uninvited and unheralded, in the middle of a workday afternoon. I felt that if things were sticky we could go out as abruptly as we had come in. We should just have called to pay our respects. The Prof. was delighted, as he always was, to see a visitor. He put Tommy on the sofa and sat down beside him ; and there they remained chatting away for more than an hour, apparently with the greatest mutual satisfaction.

I asked the Prof. afterwards what he thought of my friend. His reply was characteristic : 'How does so intelligent a man come to be a sculptor ?'

I have set down the Prof.'s lack of discrimination in artistic matters in rather stark terms. But his broad preference for the traditional and his intense dislike of the modernist did represent something genuine, and perhaps important, in him. It was far deeper than a mere distaste for something because it was a new fashion. On minor points he was quite intrigued and amused by new fashions ; but not all the duchesses or the debs in the world would, I judge, have altered his aversion to modernist art, which was, in its own crude way, a deeply rooted conviction.

It was rumoured in Oxford that when the statue of Lazarus in the New College Ante-Chapel was pointed out to Mr. Khrushchev, he merely said, 'decadent rubbish'. The Prof. was thoroughly delighted by this and commented with an irritating gesture of taking you into his confidence, 'I am afraid that when it comes to artistic matters, there is something to be said for the Totalitarians'.

A few weeks ago I visited the Russian Pavilion at the International Exhibition in Brussels, in which contemporary Russian painting was displayed. All the western world was laughing. The point was, not simply that no modernist styles had been adopted, but that the mannerisms of the work were so intensely dated. They reminded me of the pictures in the Prof.'s dining-room, although naturally the Russian exhibits were of a much higher quality than those. The inspiration of the work came, not from all past ages, but precisely and particularly from the period shortly before 1917. It seemed that Totalitarian rule had managed to fix and sterilize the style of painting at just exactly what it was before the Bolsheviks gained power ; it had totally inhibited all new inspiration.

Then I went on to the splendid exhibition of modern art from all countries. As I went round its far-ranging galleries, containing so many styles of modernistic work, with the old-fashioned Russian painting still in my mind, I could not help observing that, whenever the human form was portrayed, whether elaborately or by a mere hint, it was invariably distorted, degraded, rendered hideous, or mocked at. Far indeed were we from the days in which it could be said of the naked form of a beautiful young woman : πρέπουσά θ' ὡς ἐν γραφαῖς.[1]

Now suppose that in dictatorial spirit, on the basis of disliking this kind of thing, you issue a ukase imposing one restriction, and one only : thou shalt not degrade the human form. That would, no doubt, be a grave infringement on the right of free expression ; but let us suppose it done. What would you get ? To judge from the Russian exhibition, you would merely achieve complete sterilization and inhibit all new inspiration.

But what does that in turn mean ? Does it mean that twentieth-century men must either be allowed to do portrayals that degrade and vilify, or be incapable of anything new and creative ?

I was brought up to believe that achievement in the high arts gave the best criterion for judging the spirit of an age. If one looks at the Welfare State, the diffusion of television, the gradual raising of the material, moral and mental condition of the great mass of people, then it seems that one ought to have optimism about our prospects, subject only to the avoidance of war. But if one argues that all these things just run along, and that, to find the underlying spirit of the time and to seek omens for future development, you must look at the creations of high art, then you are confronted with the degradation of the free world on the one side or the total sterility of Russia on the other. That does not look promising.

There is the ancient story of Noah's Ark. Does not the condition of art, if we concentrate upon that only, suggest

[1] Shining forth as in a painting. (*Agamemnon*, 242.)

that we deserve a second visitation ? Or since 'deserve' is a word drawn from that most subtle of all regions of human discourse, moral philosophy, which baffles the finest brains — how intellectually imperceptive are those who hold that moral judgements are merely emotive noises — we could substitute this question by another. Has the human spirit now reached a degree of masochism, at which it will not have the internal resources to save itself from self-destruction ? Only a hundred years ago there would have been violent protest at these mocking representations, or anyhow at their complete dominance in the exhibition — no one would mind a few caricatures amid other works portraying all that was most elevated in human nature. After all, each separate man is himself a member of the human species, and in the past would just not have tolerated its being insulted in so many ways by all the diverse devices of the artists. Some of the artists would, no doubt, claim they have merely been representing on canvas a civilization that has become degraded through other causes. But that would mean an abrogation of their old historic rôle, which was to inspire and to shape the character of an age. If there is no high inspiration at all, whether in the free world or Russia, then, to take the place of the swirling waters around Noah, we might have hydrogen explosions.

In this excursion I have gone much farther than the Prof. would have thought fit to do. He did not take artistic manifestations at all seriously. But just to the tiny extent to which he gave them his attention, I believe that he felt modernist work to be the sign of the breakdown of human morale and of evil portent.

*

As the 'twenties wore on, the Prof. involved me in certain escapades. The first that I recall concerned the

Chancellorship of Oxford University. This was in 1925. Curzon, who had held that office for many years, had recently died, and Milner, who succeeded him, occupied the office only posthumously. Who should follow now ? Among the voters, namely the M.A.s who had retained their names on the books of their Colleges, there was still, at that time, a substantial Conservative majority. But there did not appear to be any Conservative statesmen of sufficiently high distinction in public life to deserve this great honour. And so thoughts moved to possible Liberal statesmen, and of these Asquith (who had recently become Lord Oxford and Asquith) and Sir Edward Grey were thought of. On the face of it, it would seem that Asquith was much the more distinguished of the two. He had been Prime Minister ; in peacetime his government had carried through legislation, which, even more than the work that was to be done by the Labour Government of 1945–51, laid the foundations of our 'Welfare State'. He had carried a united nation into the war of 1914 and, for a time at least, conducted it with efficiency. Furthermore, he was a man of academic distinction and considerable learning, and some of his speeches were notable contributions to the treasury of English prose. All his life he had maintained links with Oxford, which he loved dearly, and he had recently been Chairman of the Royal Commission on Oxford and Cambridge. From an academic point of view, by contrast, Sir Edward Grey had no claim. It was not certain if he had any particular love for, or interest in, his old University. He was a man of great personal distinction, and he had been foreign secretary ; but in that rôle it was not agreed that he had acquitted himself well.

Despite these inferior claims, some of the more staid and senior Liberals in the University, like the Warden of All Souls (Dr. Pember), felt that Sir Edward Grey was the better man to put forward, since he was a less controversial figure than Asquith. Furthermore, he was a patrician which might be pleasing to some, while Asquith was a parvenu.

A gathering of the donnish clans was held in a College hall. The President of Trinity (Dr. Blakiston) rose and suggested that the Archbishop of Canterbury should be our man. H. A. L. Fisher, recently returned to Oxford as Warden of New College, and trailing the clouds of glory of his Cabinet office, then arose and proposed Asquith, making a grandiloquent speech of such interminable length, that in the end he had to resume his seat abruptly owing to the widespread shuffling of feet. That great man, massive and distinguished scholar though he was, had not yet succeeded in shedding his Parliamentary manner, which was highly uncongenial to Oxford dons. Sir Edward Grey was then proposed, and also Lord Crawford. This meeting was apparently held to ventilate opinion only, and was inconclusive. No one knew what would happen ; it was generally believed that Sir Edward Grey would be put forward, as the Liberal elder statesmen inside the university seemed to favour him.

The Prof. bade me come round to his rooms one evening, in a state of some excitement. F. E. Smith was very keen that Asquith should be Chancellor.[1] Despite their political differences F. E. had a great regard for Asquith ; furthermore, his high sense of the dignity of learning made him wish that the man who was, in his own person, a truer embodiment of learning and culture, should be the titular head of his beloved Oxford.

I was in delighted agreement. I was a friend of the Asquith family ; I was an ardent Liberal and, in particular, had been for some years what was called an Asquithian Liberal as distinct from a Lloyd George Liberal. I concurred with the

[1] In what follows I shall refer to Asquith, Sir Edward Grey and F. E. Smith, as that was how we always spoke of them in those days and how they were commonly thought of in the country.

argument that Asquith, being a man of far higher distinction in himself, would be a worthier Head of a learned institution. It seemed a shame for the Liberals not to put up their great leader on the ground that they hoped that a lesser man would get more Conservative votes.

But then the Prof. developed the point further. It seemed that I myself was to play an important rôle in this matter. There was to be something that might be described as an 'intrigue'. Well, I had always heard that the Prof. was an intriguer, and now I was to be personally involved. As I thoroughly espoused the cause, I was all in favour. I bade him tell me what I was expected to do.

F. E. Smith had acted quickly. He had obtained the consent of a number of prominent Conservatives in both Houses of Parliament (including the Marquis of Salisbury) to write their names down as supporters of Asquith, on the assumption, of course, that he was also supported by prominent Liberals. But it was on this latter point, oddly enough, that there was doubt. It seemed that Dr. Pember and his friends would continue to argue that Sir Edward Grey was a better choice. It was important to get the candidate widely supported with a view to there not being a contested election. In the latter event, there was every danger that the Conservative would get in. The electorate was more Conservative than the whole body of Oxford graduates, by no means all of whom kept their names on their College books ; it was rather heavily weighted by clergy, probably apt to be Conservative, who did so with a view to College livings. It would certainly be most inappropriate for that strong Conservative, F. E. Smith, to go and talk the matter over with Dr. Pember and other Liberals in Oxford. His quick work in collecting Conservative promises had, however, clearly been an excellent move, and the problem was to exploit this advantage.

And now for the essential nature of the intrigue. I came into it, although so junior, as being a Liberal of undoubted authenticity. I had been Gilbert Murray's agent when he stood for Parliament as candidate for the University seats in the General Election, and I was (or had been) secretary of the dons' Liberal Association. I was thus in a good position to approach Liberal leaders both in Oxford and in London. About the London Liberals there proved to be no difficulty at all ; they were entirely in favour of Asquith and against Edward Grey. But they did not know much about the electorate and the likely disposition of the Conservative votes. It was the Oxford Liberals that were the difficulty.

The Oxford committee met. But I cannot now recall whether under the guidance of H. A. L. Fisher, who was its chairman, they passed a resolution in favour of Asquith, or, rightly judging that this important matter would be settled at a higher level, abstained from passing any resolution.

The essence of the intrigue was as follows. It seemed hopeless to engage in a series of arguments with a number of prominent Oxford Liberals. The line proposed by the Prof., no doubt after full consultation with F. E., was that, as quickly as possible, the nomination of Asquith should be treated as a *fait accompli*. That was where the Conservative promises were so valuable. It should be represented that these Conservatives were determined to have Asquith and that his name would probably go forward whatever anyone else thought. That would put the Oxford Liberals into a tight spot. Of course, if all the Oxford Liberals flatly refused to nominate, that would make it rather difficult to 'accomplish' this 'fact'. F. E.'s Conservatives had no doubt made due reservations to the effect that the Liberals must join in support.

My task was to rush around with the greatest possible speed and collect all the Liberal names, without there being any further discussion among the Liberals as a body, on the basis of a *fait accompli*.   Fisher happily was with us from the beginning, and that was most valuable, but, oddly enough, he did not completely fill the bill, because he was still rather suspect among the true Liberals through having been a 'Lloyd George Liberal'.   And so I got to work among the London Liberals, and among those Oxford Liberals who were most likely to be for Asquith anyway.   But in the early stages, since I was not acting, and could not act, officially on behalf of any recognized Liberal body, conditions tended to be attached to the promises : 'I will gladly nominate Asquith if Blank also does so'.   I had to work the *fait accompli* argument hard.

The most obvious person of all to refer to in this game of conditional support was Gilbert Murray.   Well, I was a great friend of his and his agent ; so that looked all right.   But it was not so in fact, since he happened to be a fervent supporter of Edward Grey.   The reason was, not that he had anything against Asquith, whom he greatly admired, but that Edward Grey was particularly associated with the foundation of the League of Nations, to the support of which Gilbert Murray was devoting much of his life.   He was in constant touch with Edward Grey about League of Nations Union matters.   He felt a strong tie of personal devotion to Edward Grey and, since he knew quite well that there was a good chance of Grey becoming Chancellor, he was exceedingly reluctant to rush in prematurely and nominate Asquith. Actually, the League of Nations apart, there was something in the character of Edward Grey that appealed to Murray more strongly than did Asquith ; and Asquith's present entourage at the Wharf (his country house near Oxford) was a little too worldly for Murray's taste.

So I had to have extensive *pourparlers* with Murray ; once again the *fait accompli* argument came in ; Asquith's nomination would probably go forward ; it would be terrible if it

went in without his name. At last I wrung a conditional
offer from him, a curious one : he said that he would sign
the paper if the Corpus Professor of Latin (a Conservative),
Professor A. C. Clark, did so also. I could never quite understand this ; I suppose the idea was that if the paper seemed
more academic, if his name as Professor of Greek appeared
alongside that of Clark's as Professor of Latin, he could feel
that he was acting on academic grounds, namely supporting
Asquith as a scholar, and thus put the matter all right in his
own mind for deserting Grey, whom on personal and political
grounds he preferred.

Thus this became the key point in the proceedings. We
had to get Clark. On his name Murray's depended, on
Murray's a number of other Liberals and then, in the background, if we did not get these, F. E.'s Conservative supporters
might desert us. The position was reported back to headquarters, which, paradoxically enough, were simply the Prof.'s
rooms. It would have seemed odd to most people in Oxford
that the real impetus for this move came from F. E. Smith ;
it is safe to say that, without his intervention, Asquith would
never have been nominated.

We mobilized Fisher, and a most incongruous deputation
went to the rooms of Professor Clark in Corpus, consisting
of the Prof., Fisher and myself. Clark could not have guessed
that the whole business now turned on what he said. There
we sat in a circle. The Prof. mumbled out a statesmanlike
but inaudible discourse, no doubt provided for him by
F. E. Smith, on the great virtues of Asquith. Fisher then
embarked upon another lengthy oration, full of rotund
phrases, on behalf of that great statesman, our candidate.
The *fait accompli* argument could not be used with Clark ;
it would have no relevance for him. I hope that I said
nothing. I think I came with them, only because on the
very moment that Clark had spoken it was my duty to dash

round and see all sorts of people and put through many telephone calls, in order to have our complete list for the next Gazette. Clark sat there in his chair looking absolutely impassive, but, as the speaking went on, a look of distaste gathered upon his face. I became terrified. I am sure that the mentality of the Prof. and the mentality of Fisher were both entirely uncongenial to that mellow and crusted scholar. Then, when all the speaking was over, he turned his face away from us and looked straight into the wall beside him. It seemed that it was with difficulty that he was bringing himself to speak at all. My heart sank. Then he said in his funny high-pitched voice : 'Ah, ah, I have always thought that Asquith was the most suitable candidate'.

I found that almost every minute during two or three weeks was filled with these intricate negotiations ; I must have managed to take my pupils somehow ! There seemed to be need for fairly frequent references back to F. E. I was instructed to tell the operator, after asking for his number on the telephone : 'I wish to speak to the Secretary of State for India ; this is a priority call'. In those days one still expected to wait for ten or fifteen minutes on a trunk call to London. All this was rather exciting for a young man.

There were various excursions. I took the Prof. over to see Sir John Simon, who was obviously important on the Liberal side, and the Prof. took us both over to Charlton (F. E.'s country house), so that we could concert plans together. Thus I had an opportunity of witnessing a meeting between those two famous political antagonists, undergraduates together at Wadham College long before. F. E. was serene and composed, sitting comfortably in his white flannels and quaffing something, courteous, and with just a touch of the great man ; Simon, by contrast, seemed nervous ; he got hold of a tennis ball and passed it ceaselessly from one hand to the other.

I had to make an expedition to the Wharf. It seemed that there should be the names of as many bishops as possible on our list, and it was thought, correctly to the best of my recollection, that those men whom Asquith had elevated to the episcopal bench when Prime Minister, would be likely to put their names down for him. So I went through the list of bishops with him. He was touchingly keen to become Chancellor. Although he was destined to go down to history as one of our greater Prime Ministers, responsible for carrying through social reforms in difficult times, he had had the rebuff of having to resign in the middle of the war. He remained greatly respected, but had had no further chance of eminent public service, except through his sage speeches in the House of Commons. He had high regard for learning and loved Oxford dearly, and his keenness that our campaign should succeed showed that he had the sap of life still in him. I have the image of him walking up and down the room and saying with a genial grin on his face : 'We seem to have the Church in our pocket'.

There were little contretemps in Oxford. One of the points we had to clear up was that none of the outsiders would run ; for instance, some Asquith support was conditional on the Archbishop of Canterbury not being nominated. So I was told to call upon the President of Trinity and find out how the land lay. I was ceremoniously ushered in, and put my question. 'I am willing to inform any friend of the Archbishop's, but not a member of Lord Oxford's committee,' he replied tartly, and walked brusquely out of the room, leaving me to find my way out of his house as best I could. When I reported these brief words to the others, they decided that they could be safely interpreted as indicating that the Archbishop would not be nominated.

It seemed desirable to supplement F. E.'s London Conservatives by some well-known Conservative names in

Oxford, and I was asked to visit D. G. Hogarth, distinguished scholar and the man who had brought T. E. Lawrence forward. When I had stated my case, he replied, 'But I have been a lifelong Liberal'. One day I found a note in my rooms from Lionel Curtis, heavily marked 'Highly Confidential', bidding me go and see him at once. I rushed round, thinking that he might have some news on the Asquith front. Instead he put me into a chair and, standing in front of the fireplace, made a speech of great length, explaining the origin and purposes of Chatham House, as he wished me to be the secretary of a research committee there. After a quarter of an hour, when he was evidently far from the end of his discourse, I interrupted him. I said quite frankly, 'Mr. Curtis, I am afraid that I have not been listening to anything that you have been saying to me'. He turned upon me with some amazement. 'My mind is entirely full of Lord Oxford's candidature, and I was hoping that you had summoned me to offer your support'. He replied that he was personally strongly in favour of Asquith, but always refused to sign any document that did not relate to his immediate concerns, on the view that his signature tended to do more harm than good. (I did eventually become secretary of the research group, a prelude to many other activities in Chatham House !)

Finally our list appeared. It seemed resplendent. Great names from both parties were there, representatives of public affairs, of Oxford University, of the Church. But, alas, the Pember view was to prove, despite all our efforts, correct. Asquith was more than the Conservatives could endure. Mr. Grundy, Fellow of Corpus Christi College, set to work burrowing among the diehards. Two or three weeks later the nomination of Lord Cave appeared. Once this had happened, owing to the nature of the electorate, we could no longer have high hopes for Asquith. Our activities were renewed with a view to adding still more names to our list. There could be no public campaign on such an occasion, all had to be managed very discreetly, but a certain amount of canvassing was possible.

The main objections to Asquith are of some interest, and I give them in their order of importance, as they struck us at the time. (1) First and foremost was the fact that he had never taken his M.A. degree; he was plain B.A. This would merely have been a matter of putting down so much money, but he had not taken the trouble to do so. Aspirants for the Chancellorship of Oxford University should take note. (2) His having taken the title of Oxford on his elevation to an earldom gave considerable offence. This question of titles is apt to be a sore subject. Oxford men argued that, as he had honoured himself by taking our name, there was no need for us to convey any further honour upon him. (3) His Chairmanship of the Royal Commission on Oxford and Cambridge weighed heavily against him. Although I have no doubt that he was most skilful in meeting demands for reform in a way that did not injure the valued traditional ways of doing things in these universities, yet there were inevitably many points among its extensive recommendations that gave offence to various interests or points of view ; these were held against him, while the value of his work as Chairman was not seen in perspective. (4) Politics, I reckoned, came fourth only on the list. There, much the most important point of grievance was his handling of the Welsh Church.

In due course he was defeated. By the time that Lord Cave died, a few years afterwards, Asquith too had passed away. Sir Edward Grey succeeded to the Chancellorship on an uncontested nomination.

It fell to me to have an interview with Grey in his capacity of Chancellor. I cannot now recall why that should have happened, except that the interview was concerned with the Bodleian Library. The Chancellor had to be invoked in relation to difficulties that the University was having in persuading the Rockefeller Foundation to make a donation ; Lionel Curtis was involved in these negotiations. Grey received me in Brooks's Club, courteous, gracious, handsome and certainly embodying all that one would wish of dignity in a Chancellor. I felt that I was in the presence of an august person ; but he was at pains to put me at my ease and to be charming. He heard me patiently, and I have no doubt that the advice he gave was wise and to the point. But there was one thing that struck me, and that was that, while he entered fully into the diplomatic aspects of the point I put to him, he did not show the remotest interest in the problems connected with the reconstruction of the Bodleian Library that I had touched on. It was obvious that this question of the Bodleian problems was right outside his ken, and I could not help thinking that Asquith's attitude would have been very different.

The Prof. had a great distaste for Grey, and was always at pains to make some vilifying remark if he came into the conversation. I do not know if this simply arose out of our campaign in favour of Asquith, or whether he had other reasons of his own, or supplied by F. E. Among his conversational tropes concerning Grey, I will cite one because it illustrates the tortuosity of the Prof.'s mind in making personal comments, which I have already illustrated from his remarks about Margot Asquith, Maynard Keynes and Stanley Baldwin. It was sometimes said in praise of Sir Edward Grey that he had a hobby of bird-watching. This mode of commending Grey, or indeed anyone else, irritated the Prof. excessively. He thought that a man gained some subtle credit for this activity, which it really deserved no more than any other hobby. I think that what specifically annoyed him may have been the idea that these bird-lovers were deemed people of

knowledge, even of a kind of 'scientific' knowledge in relation to these fauna, and were sometimes given the grandiose
name of ornithologist. He resented the idea that a mere
memorization or recognition of the various species through
field-glasses could give any knowledge worthy to be ranked
with the scientific knowledge in the strict sense of those who
understand about the evolution of species, natural selection or
the physiology of birds.

Incredible though it may seem, he expounded the following conversational trope to me with evident self-satisfaction.
If Grey was mentioned in conversation, he said : 'Oh, he is
a great authority on the species of fish, is he not ?' The
conversation could then go in one of two directions. If the
interlocutor made no protest, the Prof. felt that he must have
damaged Grey in his esteem, since there was something
absurd about a high-thinking statesman, supposed to be
keeping a watchful eye over our foreign policy, interesting
himself in the species of fish. If, on the other hand, the interlocutor observed that he had never heard that Grey had this
special interest and thought perhaps the Prof. was thinking
of his renown as a bird-lover, then the Prof. would reply in a
tone rendered as indifferent as possible, 'Oh, it's birds, not fishes,
is it ?' Thereby he thought that he had shown plainly enough
how little regard he had for the hobby of bird-watching.

I recall other examples of this absurd tortuosity. There
was a joint meeting of the Mind Association and the Aristo-
telian Society in Reading (1924) at which Whitehead, being
in the chair at one of the meetings, made some observations.
The Prof. then rose to criticize him, and he categorized one
of the concepts he had used as 'illegitimate', adding that
perhaps owing to Whitehead's political proclivities it found
favour with him precisely because it was illegitimate. Afterwards I asked the Prof. why he had said that a concept would
find favour with Whitehead precisely because it was illegiti-

mate. 'Well, Whitehead is a member of the Labour Party, isn't he ?' — I did not know that, but the Prof. seemed to — 'and his leader, Ramsay Macdonald, is generally supposed to be illegitimate.'

He had no great regard for Gilbert Murray, not only, I should suppose, because of his somewhat difficult attitude in the Asquith campaign, but also because his views on international affairs would be deemed dangerous by the Prof. It was also the case that he was suspicious of anyone — this may have applied to Grey also — who was widely spoken of in tones of veneration ; he had a feeling that these reputations were often without real desert, gained by people who have not really done any hard thinking or made genuine contributions but have some quality of showmanship. The greatness of Gilbert Murray, as a poet, scholar, lecturer and wit, lay outside the Prof.'s field. When the Labour Government was in power in 1924, Gilbert Murray went as its official delegate to Geneva — a point not mentioned in his obituary notices, which dwelt only on his work for the League of Nations *Union*. In that year he actually operated in the League of Nations itself, and gained reputation for 'piloting' through a clause, which materially touched vested interests and the sovereign rights of nations on a number of prickly points, restricting the white-slave traffic. When Gilbert Murray was mentioned, the Prof. put on a puzzled expression as though the name was vaguely familiar to him. 'Wasn't that the feller who piloted a cargo of white slaves to South America ?' All these habits were very childish ; one could hardly believe that one was listening to a great man. He persisted with these obscure taunts all his life, and they may have damaged his reputation, since, if a stranger heard this kind of nonsense, he must have thought the Prof. a perfect fool.

Our campaign for Asquith might certainly have been called an intrigue. But I hope that it was no more deep-dyed than the manœuvres that often occur on this kind of occasion. Had we been wrong to embark upon it? We had involved Asquith in the humiliation of defeat. Our action would certainly have been wrong, if the alternative had been the nomination of an unopposed Conservative candidate. But it seems quite clear that, had the Prof. and I not interfered, Grey would have been put forward as an unopposed candidate. I judge that it would have been a greater humiliation for Asquith to have been simply passed over, *nem. con.*, by his beloved University, for which he had recently worked hard on the Royal Commission, in favour of *another Liberal*, his junior in political office and relatively unlettered. As things were, he went down under the serried ranks of Conservative voters in an honourable political defeat of a normal kind. So, even in retrospect, I judge that we were right to do what we did. The Prof. and I worked very happily together. His willingness to take a vast amount of trouble and his utter imperturbability in the face of setbacks were shown in a striking light. There was no trace of discord between us.

This adventure had a little aftermath, which was not so pleasant. It was an incident of minute importance in itself, but significant as a pointer. I was furious about it at the time.

In the course of the General Strike of 1926 Asquith rebuked Lloyd George in severe terms, which suggested a disposition to expel him from the Liberal Party, with which he and his followers had been 'reunited' not long before. Shortly afterwards the 'Liberal Council' was formed, containing many prominent Liberals, but not Lloyd George. This pointed to an attempt to ostracize Lloyd George. I held strongly that, whatever one might think of Lloyd George's manœuvres during the General Strike, Asquith had been wrong to express such severe condemnation.[1]

[1] This episode is more fully described in my *Life of Keynes*, pp. 375-378.

I had had occasional contacts with Asquith in a Liberal connection from very early days ; but ever since Anthony Asquith and I had been up as undergraduates together, I had gone over from time to time to the Wharf for a week-end, or to dine, and could be said to be a fairly familiar figure in that house. But I would not have dared to mention my misgiving to the great elder statesman, with all his vast experience, to whom I must still have seemed scarcely more than an undergraduate — the years pass quickly for the elderly. I felt that it would have been absurd and presumptuous for me to take him to task. In this respect there was a wide difference between Asquith and such a prominent Liberal leader as Sir John Simon, to whom I did not hesitate to express my views freely at that time. Perhaps I was over shy ? Anyhow that was how I felt. The most that I might have ventured would have been to utter some doubts to his wife, Margot.

The Prof., on the other hand, was greatly pleased by Asquith's *démarche*, both because he agreed with it on its merits and also because, by tending to renew the split in the Liberal Party, it was of advantage to the Conservatives. The Prof. knew perfectly well that I took an entirely different view.

On a Saturday afternoon while these events were proceeding, just a year after the Chancellorship contest, he rang me up, proposing that we should go over together to have tea at the Wharf ; he would drive me. At first I was surprised, since he had never involved me in any of his social rounds. This seemed to be quite a new departure. But I soon perceived his drift.

Asquith was beholden to him for the immense trouble that he had taken over the Chancellorship, and it was perfectly proper for him to wish to pay a call and sustain his acquaintance with the great man. The Wharf was a lively social

centre, where one might meet distinguished luminaries of the
past, or brilliant young people of the present. The Asquiths
liked to keep up to date and were very hospitable to the
younger generation. Among the young they sought out
writers or brilliant talkers. I do not suppose that it occurred
to them that the Prof., with his acrid Conservatism, with his
style of address which was obscure until one got to know it
well, with his scientific achievements about which they would
not necessarily hear good reports, struck them as the kind
of person whom they particularly wished to cultivate. His
friendship for F. E., or even for Winston Churchill, who by
then had left the Liberal Party, would not, for the Asquiths,
be an impelling or sufficient recommendation. What the
Prof. clearly wanted of me, as an old friend of the family,
was to give him the *entrée*, or at least, by accompanying him,
to give colour to his call ; I, on my side, would have the
advantage of roaring over in his super-charged Mercedes or
purring over in his Rolls Royce. It was a perfectly natural
pact of mutual accommodation between two friends. Accordingly I rang up the Wharf and proposed to bring the Prof.
to tea.

I was a fool. I should have smelt a rat. I should have
told a lie, and informed the Prof. that I was otherwise engaged
that afternoon. But it ought not to be a part of the pleasant
path of friendship to be looking out for traps all the time.

As soon as we arrived, the Prof. by a few deft words —
he could move quickly when he chose — transformed our
friendly visit into a sort of delegation from Oxford University
to compliment Asquith on the splendid line that he had taken
about Lloyd George. I felt that it would be utterly unseemly
to protest to Asquith that the junior member of the Party,
on the contrary, took the view that his action — about which
I judged that he was a little sensitive — had been mistaken
and wrong. I just had not the heart. For the Prof. a good

cause was always supreme ; and no doubt he thought it in the national interest that a wedge between the sectors of the Liberal Party ought to be driven home as deep as possible. But what about me ? What about his code of the elephant ? What about the injury to the feelings of his friend on being put in a false position in this way ? This was, I think, my first personal experience of those characteristics that were responsible for the prevailing distrust of the Prof.

I do not recall if I succeeded in mumbling some misgiving to Margot ; probably not. I was covered with embarrassment. But I well remember her succinct summary of the situation on that occasion. 'People blame us', she said, 'for carrying on a vendetta against Lloyd George because of 1916 ; but we never think of 1916 ; it is 1918 that we find it hard to forgive.' 1916 was the year when Lloyd George replaced Asquith as Prime Minister during the First World War. 1918 was the year of the khaki election ; by giving 'coupons' to his own followers and having other Liberal candidates opposed, Lloyd George caused a shattering defeat for the Liberals in that election, which displaced them from being the principal progressive party in the State. The whole future of the Liberal Party might have been different, had Lloyd George himself led a united party to the polls, but in order to do this, he would have had to have broken up the Coalition and jeopardized his own chances of representing Britain at the Peace Conference. This was precisely what Churchill in fact did in 1945. The unfortunate experience of 1918 and the following years may well have influenced the minds of the leaders of all three political parties in deciding what they ought to do in 1945.

★

The next battle that I will mention concerned the Radcliffe Observatory. It was in 1929-30. I had recently had the unusual honour of being elected to the Hebdomadal Council, the small governing body that rules the University, at the immature age of twenty-nine. I was pleased with myself, having received more votes in the election than H. A. L. Fisher himself. Presumably my primary duty there would be to concern myself with the needs of economics, which was about to enter upon a period of expansion in the university. But I knew full well that the Prof. would wish to work me hard on behalf of his scientific causes. I was quite prepared for that, since I was of his way of thinking.

The Radcliffe Observatory, which adjoins the Radcliffe Infirmary, had recently completed a negotiation with the latter body, which was flush of funds through the generous munificence of Lord Nuffield, and acquired the sum of £100,000. This would suffice for the construction of a new telescope of important magnitude. The question was raised where the telescope should be built, and it was pointed out that the skies of Oxford are often cloudy. It was decided that the climate of South Africa rendered it the most suitable site. To this the Prof. took violent exception.

It was true that John Radcliffe had in the eighteenth century left this portion of his money for the advancement of astronomy. But the Prof. pointed out that there were two aspects to his action. He sought to promote the study of astronomy, yes ; but he also clearly sought, by this and other benefactions — the Radcliffe Camera, the Radcliffe Infirmary —, to further the interests of Oxford. If one considers one aspect only, the study of astronomy, one might indeed think that South Africa could furnish the best site. The Prof. contended that he had not simply been thinking of astronomy in the abstract, but of astronomy at Oxford. Consequently the trustees ought not now to be thinking of South Africa at all, but of building a fine new telescope in Oxford itself. Although this could not be so useful as one in

South Africa, it would none the less be useful, and it would serve in an important way to attract distinguished scientists to Oxford and thus build up the scientific status of Oxford.

The Radcliffe Observatory was entirely independent of the University, being managed by its own trustees. Of these Dr. Pember appeared to be the most influential. Since his name seems to recur in these pages as being on the devil's side, I ought to mention here that he was a very charming man ; courtly, gracious, handsome, cultivated, a man of liberal views, he discharged to perfection his hospitable duties as Warden of All Souls College ; it was impossible to hate Pember, and I do not recall that the Prof. himself ever said anything nasty about him. My relations with him remained excellent, and he was on my side and most helpful in a greater battle that I had about the Bodleian Library, in which the Prof. was not involved. But he got rather cross with me about the Observatory.

It was arguable that the University had no *locus standi* in the question where the new telescope should go. As against this the Prof. had two points. One was that centuries of history entitled Oxford University to hold a watching brief on behalf of any higher studies, such as astronomy, that were carried out in Oxford city. If the trustees were acting wrongfully in relation to John Radcliffe's will by alienating the telescope from Oxford city, then it was surely the duty of the Oxford University authorities, rather than of anyone else, to protect the public interest by seeing that this wrongful act was not committed.

Secondly, the Prof. claimed that over the years the Observatory had received important financial benefit from the University, or from St. John's College, which was part of the University in the wider sense, by occupying land at a peppercorn rent, and perhaps in other ways. Thus, although the £100,000 came in the last instance from the pocket of Lord

Nuffield, via the Radcliffe Infirmary, it could be argued that fundamentally it was University money, since the Observatory would never have been in a position to do this deal if it had not been for the financial support of the University in the past. Therefore, the Prof. argued, the University should act strongly to prevent the alienation of the telescope.

The University authorities were extremely reluctant to interfere in this matter ; they felt it to be a point of delicacy *vis-à-vis* the Observatory trustees. That angered the Prof. very much. He felt it was part and parcel of the indifference of the University authorities to the needs of science in Oxford. Here was a chance to do something really big to promote it. Pember argued that they were more truly advancing the interests of science by building the telescope in South Africa. But it was with science in Oxford that the Prof. was concerned. How absurd to feel delicacy in relation to the trustees, who were only people like Pember ; what a trivial point this was in relation to the great interests at stake for Oxford itself. The Prof. felt that it was worse than indifference, and that some of the older pundits in the University were afraid of seeing science grow and prosper. There he probably overstated his case.

The Prof. busied himself among his scientific colleagues in Oxford, while I had to state the case for him to the Hebdomadal Council. I soon got into hot water. It was considered unseemly for a new boy, and a very youthful one, to intervene so actively in a highly controversial matter ; words like 'factiousness' and 'a racket' were used. The history of the relations between the Observatory and the University was a tangled one, and all this case had to be deployed.

It was, however, so strong that we prevailed upon the University to go to law about it. The University lost its action and the telescope was built near Pretoria. The Prof.

went up to London to hear the proceedings in court and claimed that the University case was shockingly badly handled. Our Counsel at that time was the great lawyer, Sir Wilfrid Greene, a figure much beloved in the University. On the day of the trial he did not appear ; he had to plead in an important case on piracy. A case on contemporary piracy no doubt had features intriguing to the legal mind. The Prof. was convinced that Greene would have somehow found a way of appearing for the University, had he not sensed that the University authorities did not have their heart in this case. If it had been put to Greene that this was a matter of major importance to the University, he would have felt it his duty somehow to manage to appear. Greene was on familiar terms with all the important people in the University. It may have been hinted to him that we were going forward with this as a mere matter of form, but that it was all very embarrassing and that we certainly did not wish to fight a bitter battle. So the Prof. thought, and I judge that he may have been right. It can be imagined that it left a very bad impression of the University authorities on his mind.

*

Somewhat before this affair, a dispute had arisen in Christ Church itself about the Prof.'s precedence in the seating at High Table. This sounds very absurd, but it gave rise to considerable heat and was the prelude to a more important dispute.

Shortly before the Prof. arrived in Oxford, Christ Church provided the money for three professorships in science. According to the Oxford system, each professorship is permanently attached to a Fellowship at a particular College. Fellows were normally, but not necessarily, members of the Governing Body of their Colleges. As the Governing Body of Christ Church was rather a large one, owing to the presence of six Canons, as well as two Regius professors, Christ Church decided that these three new science professors should not be on the Governing Body. At about this time it began to be evident that the University was likely to wish professors to be on the Governing Bodies of their Colleges, so that the interests of higher research should be adequately looked after in College policy ; and in fact some years later this was made statutory in all Colleges in consequence of the recommendations of the Royal Commission. Foreseeing this, Christ Church asked the University to have the three science professors assigned to other Colleges. This was before the Prof. was appointed. The existing incumbents of the other two chairs, Arthur Thomson and Professor Soddy, were given the choice of continuing, during the remainder of their periods of tenure, as Students of Christ Church (a Student at Christ Church is equivalent to a Fellow at another College) without being on the Governing Body of Christ Church, or transferring to the College to which their professorships were to be permanently assigned and having their full Governing Body rights at that College. Thomson preferred to remain with us without membership of the Governing Body ; Soddy transferred to Exeter College. When the Prof. was appointed he went automatically to Wadham College, to which his particular Chair had been permanently assigned.

But then the Dean of Christ Church (Dr. Strong), and some other members of Christ Church, thought it was rather a pity that, after we had supplied all this money, we should have no benefit from the presence in Oxford of this highly distinguished figure, reputed to be a most interesting man, and one who promised to be a foremost physicist in the country and was still covered with glory from his wartime experiments in flying. Although he was irrevocably attached to Wadham College, it was still open to us to make him a Student of Christ Church without membership of the Governing Body, the statute requiring all Students to be members of the Governing Body not yet having come into operation. This was accordingly done, and the Prof. was given the large set of rooms that I have already described, in which he lived for the remainder of his life.

The dinner-table dispute arose in this way. Did he have precedence according to the day of his appointment as Student of Christ Church, along with all the other regular Students, or did he rank below the Students who were also members of the Governing Body, who at that time comprised all the Students except himself and one other?

The Prof. was beginning to lose caste as a scientist at this time and was proving obstreperous in various ways. There were a number of our Students, perhaps a majority, who did not wish to grant him the precedence that he desired. The point seemed rather academic at the time since the Prof. was fairly low on our list; but he was looking to the future. It might be humiliating to him, when he was one of our oldest members and brought a Cabinet Minister to dine, for some beardless novice to have precedence over him and take the chair in Common Room. In those days the Prof. foresaw a long future for himself at Christ Church; indeed he did stay on after that for about thirty years, but he was thinking of something still longer. He was appointed before the enactment of a retiring age, and he used regularly to tease us about that. He told us that he had not the faintest intention of ever retiring, that he was fully determined to rejuvenate himself by monkey glands, that he would outlast us all, and our successors too. Poor Prof.; it did not quite turn out like that.

The Prof. claimed that, apart from the mere question of seating, precedence might involve other advantages. The only one that I can recall as cited was in the allocation of the

College garages. But I suppose it was possible that similar points might arise.

There was much unpleasantness about all this. The College decided that the easiest way out of the difficulty was to take Counsel's opinion about what the Prof.'s rights really were. They approached Mr. Gavin Simonds, and he laid down that the Prof. ranked after members of the Governing Body. The Prof. acted quickly and sought Sir John Simon's opinion. He decided the opposite. His authority was greater in those days than that of Mr. Gavin Simonds. Then much argumentation arose. Some of my colleagues wanted to take a firm line on the ground that the Prof. would never dare incur the mockery of his hostesses by going to law about where he should sit at table. That may have been so, but I am not quite sure. The Prof. was very pugnacious in those days. The College too might be made to look ridiculous in having a law case about its seating. All depended upon which side was able to do the better propaganda and make the more fun of the other.

I need hardly say that throughout I strongly advocated the more generous treatment. In the end it was decided to give the Prof. what he wanted.

At about this time a great tragedy occurred, when the airship R.101 crashed and many lives were lost. Simon was chairman of the tribunal of inquiry, and the Prof. aided him as *amicus curiae*. His usual prejudice against those who disagreed with him in politics had hitherto always caused him to speak in slighting terms of Simon. Perhaps he took F. E.'s gibes against his famous adversary more seriously than F. E. intended. But his experience at the tribunal filled him with a boundless admiration for Simon. He spoke in the highest terms of praise of his intellectual powers ; difficult scientific problems were involved in determining the causes of the destruction of the airship ; the Prof. explained the issues to

Simon, and he told me that Simon showed the most marvellous power, in questioning the witnesses, of bringing out
the relevant points, remembering precisely what the Prof.
had told him and perceiving instantly how the evidence bore
on the issues, in spite of the fact that the scientific problems
involved were beyond his own knowledge. It delighted me
that the Prof. should have been so impressed. We Liberals
had always assumed, of course, that Simon was a great intellect ; but the Prof. had hitherto been sceptical. Now he was
thoroughly converted. It pleased me also, as evidence of the
Prof.'s integrity ; political differences might lead him to
make caustic remarks in conversation, but, when the matter
was put to the test, he was willing to allow due merit where
he found it. The Prof. was very parsimonious indeed in
giving praise ; this high praise of Simon was accordingly a
notable tribute.

But the good effect of his experience was shortly to be
spoilt entirely. I happened to see Simon about this time and
mentioned in a casual way that I had been interested to read
his opinion about the Prof.'s precedence at High Table. 'Oh,
well,' Simon replied, 'I was glad to be able to do that as the
Prof. had been so extremely helpful at the R.101 inquiry.'
By a piece of sloppy and muddle-headed thinking, of which
I am much ashamed, I thought that the Prof. would be pleased
to hear that Simon, on his side, had valued his contribution,
and repeated his remark. But the Prof. immediately seized
upon the other aspect of the matter. Here was Simon speaking to a member of the Governing Body of Christ Church
in words that might be interpreted as meaning that he had
an ulterior motive for his opinion. The Prof. was furious.
He had always suspected that Simon was thoroughly untrust-
worthy and now here was the evidence of it. He would
never again in his life have any truck with Simon. I immediately endeavoured to take the whole blame upon myself.

It was I who was at fault for having repeated this remark.
I was an old friend of Simon's ; I had helped him long ago
in the Spen Valley by-election of 1919 and had since been a
frequent guest at his house. What he said to me was doubtless
in the strictest confidence. His saying that to me must not
be taken as implying that he would have said it to any other
member of the Governing Body. But the Prof. refused to
view the matter in this way. He cherished his wrath, and
this may even have had its effect many years later ; for the
Prof.'s memory was long.

*

The most serious clash in Christ Church connected with
the Prof. was on a more important issue. Even this might
be thought to have been concerned with a minor point,
unless it is seen against a wider background as symbolic of
more far-reaching questions.

In 1923 or 1924 the Duke of Westminster made a benefaction under covenant to support for a certain term of years
a research worker in physics at a stipend that was appropriate
at that time to a junior research Fellowship at a College. It
was a part of the agreement that Christ Church should make
the beneficiary a Student with all due privileges. At that
time the Statutory Commission of Oxford, appointed to give
legal embodiment in Oxford to the recommendations of the
Royal Commission, had not yet completed its deliberations,
and it was not known if they would enforce the rule that all
Fellows of Colleges must be members of the Governing
Bodies. The Christ Church authorities pleaded that there
was overcrowding in our Governing Body for the reasons
already explained, and suggested that this new research
Student should not be a member of the Governing Body ;
and that was agreed to by all parties.

Mr. Bolton King, a lifelong friend of the Prof., was the

first holder of this appointment. After a certain term it was agreed that he should be succeeded, partly perhaps because it was the original idea that this appointment should rotate among research workers fairly rapidly, and also because Mr. Bolton King's interests had taken a turn towards the more applied branches of physics, which might not be considered quite suitable for this particular benefaction. The term of the original grant had not yet run out ; accordingly the new Student would be appointed under the conditions laid down in the original agreement. This came up for discussion in 1930–31.

But meanwhile an important thing had happened. The new statutes had come into operation in all the different Colleges requiring that all Fellows of Colleges be members of their Governing Bodies. The Prof. made it plain that he expected that the new Duke of Westminster Student would be a member of the Governing Body of Christ Church.

Many of my colleagues demurred. They brought up the old argument about the overcrowding of the Governing Body. They pointed out that, when they originally agreed to the terms of this benefaction, they did so on condition that the Student in question should not be a member of the Governing Body, and they objected to this being altered. The Prof. pointed out that the new statute was perfectly general in character, affecting all Colleges alike, and applying to professorial Fellowships, research Fellowships and any other kind of Fellowship that there might be. To make an exception against the Duke of Westminster Studentship would be invidious. Furthermore, this change was not a mere accidental misfortune, like a period of bad weather ; it reflected high-level policy purposely designed to give the interests of research better representation in the deliberations of College Governing Bodies, concerning the use of their endowments and other questions of policy. All Colleges

alike had to face a certain dilution of their Governing Bodies
in order that this principle should be implemented. Christ
Church had no business to squeal ; the matter had been
argued out, and a certain decision had been reached, which
must now be implemented.

How, he inquired, could Christ Church legally avoid
having this Student on the Governing Body ? To which
it was replied that he should not be regarded as a Student in
the ordinary sense of the word ; he was a 'Duke-of-West-
minster-Student' ; he was thereby a 'Student', not a Student
to which the ordinary statute would apply. This made the
Prof. angry ; it had been a consideration with the Duke of
Westminster that, as a *quid pro quo* for his generosity, the
College should make his beneficiary a Student in the ordinary
sense of the word ; he would not have been content to make
the benefaction if he had been told that the beneficiary was
to be only a 'Student' or some special phoney kind of Student,
to whom the ordinary privileges did not apply. It is true
that he had agreed that his Student should not be a member
of the Governing Body, but *at that time* membership of the
Governing Body was not a necessary prerogative of a Studentship ; for example, Arthur Thomson was a Student but not a
member of the Governing Body of Christ Church, or of that
of any other College ; thus not being a member of the Governing Body *then* did not imply any derogation from the full
privileges of Studentship in the ordinary sense of that word.

Christ Church claimed that the Duke of Westminster
Student could not be regarded as a Student in the ordinary
sense, because the method of his election was peculiar, the
Duke of Westminster and the Prof. having a say in the matter.
This argument was not decisive, as in the case of University
professorships it was possible for special interests to be represented on the electoral body ; but my colleagues may have
had something on their side in claiming that there was a

difference in our case in that the Prof. had what amounted to a veto.

It may be plain from what I have said earlier why the Prof. attached special importance to this point. He felt strongly that Fellowships of Colleges, with full privileges, alone gave power and prestige in the Oxford scene. He had long lamented the small number of College Fellowships in physics ; he feared that, as the number of appointments in the various scientific laboratories multiplied, with the growth of scientific research, these scientists would come to form a sort of inferior helot class. Therefore he regarded member- ship of our Governing Body as a key point, now that this was compulsory for all Fellowships in the proper sense, and he made it plain that he would not yield.

There was only one thing that my colleagues could do, if they felt equally strongly. They could point out to the Duke of Westminster that the statute about Fellows necessarily being members of the Governing Bodies did not exist at the time of the original agreement, that this requirement did not suit them and that they would be reluctant to receive the benefaction for the remainder of the covenanted term. In that case presumably the Duke of Westminster would have agreed to withdraw the benefaction, and perhaps have placed it with another College.[1] This would be unfortunate, as it was understood that the Duke of Westminster was likely to be willing to renew his benefaction after the term of the present one expired, as in fact happened. If the Christ Church authorities were so obdurate as to cause the withdrawal of the existing benefaction and lose the chance of its further continuance, the Prof. would undoubtedly use all his powers to hold the College up to ridicule and contempt, both in private and in public.

[1] I seem to recall that he had recently given a similar benefaction to Wad- ham College.

To me it seemed that the Prof. had a thoroughly good case, and I supported his position strongly. I was at that time the Senior Censor at Christ Church. This is a position of great power and importance in our College, where the administration is more centralized than in other Colleges. The Senior Censor has some of the duties that in other Colleges are performed by the Head of the College, and also duties that in other Colleges are assigned to other offices. He is indeed much the most important man in the College. I would add here that I regarded this position as a most delightful one, indeed much the pleasantest that I have ever held. The Senior Censor knows everything that is going on in the College ; the life of the College pulses in him ; he knows all the undergraduates personally and all about their affairs ; he mingles much more with them than do the other dons ; he plays an important part too in the higher affairs of the College, being on many committees and briefing and guiding them. If one loves the College, and especially the ordinary undergraduate life of the College, then one must love particularly the office of Senior Censor ; I certainly did. Those were happy days indeed.

The dispute about the Duke of Westminster Studentship took some time to gather momentum. It came before the Governing Body several times ; there were resolutions and counter-resolutions ; compromises, *e.g.* concerning the mode of election of the Duke of Westminster Student, were put forward ; there were negotiations with the Prof. ; there was correspondence with the Duke of Westminster's solicitors.

All through this period I was strenuous in my advocacy ; I felt that the Prof. was altogether in the right. Finally I began circulating memoranda to members of the Governing Body. These were ill received ; it was said that the Senior Censor had no business to issue circulars on a controversial matter. I took a rather different line. I made it a rigid rule not to canvass individuals. I believe that in fact private canvassing would have been more in line with tradition. But I thought it wrong for the Senior Censor, precisely because of his high and responsible position, to have private talks in which he might stress different points to different individuals. It seemed better to issue memoranda, in which the same points were made to all, to friends and enemies alike. But what I regarded as my conscientiousness in this matter was not appreciated by my colleagues. At the same time I warned the Prof. heavily that he must on no account do any canvassing himself; I would see the matter through to the best of my ability. He was not a member of the Governing Body; he was on the other side of the fence as sponsor of the benefaction; if it was known that he was canvassing our members, that would inflame the ill-will against him.

He did, however, canvass one member, the Dean himself.[1] I have already expressed my discontent about the word 'snob'. I have tried to explain in relation to the Prof.'s so-called snobbery, that his excursions into high life had much more subtle explanations, being part of the tangled web of his complexes, his lack of ease among professional people, his need for affection. But in the case of the Dean of Christ Church (Dr. White) the word 'snob' applied in a quite ordinary sense. But what a shame it would be — this is another example of what a wretched word it is — to apply it in any derogatory sense to our former Dean, so good and loyal in all his dealings, as straight as a die, not a very intelligent and cultured man, but an assiduous and painstaking scholar and utterly devoted to Christ Church. His voice trembled with pleasure at the mention of a duke. I recall how, when there was discussion on our Governing Body about a garden party for a visit of the King and Queen on

[1] The head of Christ Church is called the Dean, and in his case this name has also its ecclesiastical meaning (Cathedral of Oxford).

the occasion of a quater-centenary celebration, and there was some question of overcrowding, a member protested that there seemed to be too many rather stuffy colonels representing the county gentry on our list. A sob came into the Dean's voice as he observed : 'For me a garden party without the county is not a garden party at all'. The Dean was an old-fashioned Conservative. He would have been a lesser man, not a greater man, if his voice had not trembled with a genuine emotion of pleasure at the mention of a duke ; still worse would it have been had he had those emotions while feigning indifference ; that would have been snobbery in a bad sense. The Dean's feelings did not cause him to deviate from the path of rectitude, for by an unhappy coincidence two dukes, who presented themselves at the College entrance examination — the only two, to the best of my recollection, during his period as Dean — were deemed unworthy of admission owing to their bad work in the examination, and the Dean agreed that they should not be admitted. The Dean's admiration for dukes was naïve and genuine. For him dukes were an important and honoured part of the establishment of Church and State, for which he prayed sincerely.

I feel sure that the Prof. was not so reticent about his excursions into ducal society when talking to the Dean, as he was in Common Room. The Dean really thought that great weight should be assigned to the opinions of a man who knew so many dukes. Consequently the Prof. was able to secure his vote on a variety of questions. It only occurs to me now for the first time, when writing these words, that the fact that the *Duke* of Westminster was the benefactor may have been one cause of the Dean voting so solidly on our side in this affair. The fact that the Dean had been 'nobbled' by the Prof. roused my colleagues to a higher pitch of fury.

The atmosphere in College became quite unpleasant. The

day approached when we should have to come to a final vote, as a successor to Mr. Bolton King would have to be found to take up his position at a certain date. The matter could be delayed no longer. Through the commendable frankness of my Junior Censor, I learnt that a meeting was to take place in College on the Tuesday evening immediately before the crucial meeting of the Governing Body on Wednesday afternoon. This meeting was to consist of eight Students who comprised the best known, the senior and the most important members of the College. There was one other equally important man who could not come to the meeting, but who was known to be the strongest of all in his opposition to the Prof. ; so there were nine. These were the people who would be named first if one asked at that time who the dons of Christ Church were. They were the people who were most fully identified with the College, and were men of some account in the University and outside ; it would be hardly too much to say that they *were* the College. There were other members of the Governing Body (in addition to the Canons) ; these included men of no less distinction than the nine pundits, but they were mostly men of comparatively recent election, junior, as yet little known, and men who very properly often allowed their votes to be guided by the views of the nine, since these had had so much more experience of College policy and had indeed earned merit by having already devoted substantial parts of their lives to the service of the College. When these men met together they might naturally think that what they then decided would be put through.

I was appalled when I heard that this meeting was to take place. They had not invited me, the Senior Censor, for the time being the most important person of all in the College. They had in mind that the College was being pushed along by the machinations of the Prof. into doing what it really did not want to do. The Dean had been 'nobbled'; the Senior Censor had been 'nobbled'. It was high time for the good and just to get together in an informal meeting and decide what should be done to defeat the Prof., and get the College into motion again on its normal lines, despite the Dean and despite the Senior Censor. It was time to take a strong stand. What they decided would certainly go through the Governing Body.

In the course of that Tuesday I went to the man in whose rooms the meeting was to be held. I said, 'I hear that you are having a meeting this evening about this Duke of Westminster business'. He looked extremely nervous; he took up the poker and began poking his fire in an agitated manner, and then said: 'Yes, I am having this meeting; I am sorry that I haven't been able to ask everyone to it, but there are not enough chairs'.

This was too much for me; I was, after all, the Senior Censor; I left the room immediately without saying anything more.

And then I was weighed down by sad and gloomy reflections. One fact stood out with appalling clearness. I should have to resign from the Senior Censorship. No such meeting had ever taken place before in my time at Christ Church, a meeting of weighty people to decide important matters, to which the Senior Censor was not bidden; and, indeed, I believe that no such meeting has ever taken place since. The College was evidently discontented with my handling of affairs; they did not like my memoranda. They took the line that the Senior Censor, by virtue of his office, should be a little aloof and above the fray when matters of sharp controversy were dividing the College. Indeed in this case it seemed to be I alone who was making the division, since the College was united against me.

Why could not these people make their speeches in the

Governing Body in the ordinary way, trusting to their influence on votes to get their decision normally ? They were likely to get what they wanted. It was very difficult to see why the addition of one member to the Governing Body should be regarded as ruinous, even if they did not approve of it ; it was hard to see how the whole welfare of the College depended upon it ; and yet nothing less than that would seem to justify such an extraordinary procedure. But they were absolutely determined not to be bulldozed by the Prof. — to use one of his favourite terms. This meeting was the most signal mark of lack of confidence in the Senior Censor that could possibly be given. It was absolutely clear that I must resign.

I did not feel any guilty conscience in this matter. I judged that the case in favour of the Prof. was impregnable. There was indeed my friendship for the Prof. ; but the arguments were strong enough on their own merits. I judged that it was in the interests of the College that the Prof. should not be irretrievably alienated. Thus I too felt that the matter was of some importance, and not one to which the doctrine that the Senior Censor should suppress his own view and stand aloof applied. I had issued my memoranda and would thereafter have been fully content to abide by the final verdict of the Governing Body. I should certainly then have done my best to patch up the relations between the Prof. and the College. But now this plan for a meeting, to which I was not invited, showed complete distrust of my whole handling of the matter.

I had some talk with my Junior Censor. I deliberately did not probe him for his views, but judged that on the whole he agreed with the majority, although seeing the force of some of my arguments and reluctant to part company with his Senior Censor. He had been summoned to the meeting, and we agreed that he ought to go and report back to me, not indeed their general plan of campaign but in the event of anything really outrageous being decided. He also put it to me that his presence would tend to prevent the meeting developing into a sort of conspiracy against the Senior Censor. That was good of him, but I did not attach much importance to it for myself, as I was already fully determined to resign. The Junior Censor did in due course inform me of the resolutions that they proposed to put forward at the Governing Body the next day, but these were quite useless from my point of view.

I had not the heart to go to dinner in Hall that evening. I decided to dine in my own rooms and was lucky enough at the last moment to get Maurice Bowra, always a pillar of strength in times of trouble, to come along ; I also got the two cheeriest undergraduates whom I knew in College, Ran Antrim (then Dunluce) and Francis Lennox-Boyd. A plentiful supply of champagne was laid on, to drown my sorrows. I told them all my troubles, pledging them, of course, to secrecy ; I do not think, however, that I mentioned my intention of resigning. It was suggested that the two undergraduates might go and listen through the keyhole at the meeting to hear what was being said. I cannot remember if they actually went ; I believe that they did, but found the room empty, the venue having been changed at the last moment, presumably in order to get more chairs, but evidently not enough for the Senior Censor. This may seem rather a scurvy way for a Senior Censor to treat his colleagues ; but I was very furious. Furthermore, as I was fully determined to resign on the next day, my having my little fun this evening did not matter very much.

On the Wednesday morning I woke up with a heavy heart. As I looked about my room, containing all the documents and trappings of the Senior Censorship, I reflected that at the end of the day I should have no more interest in them. The time dragged heavily. There was one thing, however, which it still fell to me to do. I had issued my memoranda, but canvassed no one. I would go down with flags flying. I would make the finest speech in the Governing Body that afternoon that its members had ever heard there.

And then the incredible happened. The Dean voted the right way; he had been 'nobbled'. To the best of my recollection the Canons, always an unaccountable factor, were evenly divided. I suspect that the Prof. had done a little canvassing in that quarter, thinking it safe since the Canons were somewhat remote from our main body. Spokesmen of the nine delivered their weighty speeches. But then it happened that the riff-raff — but that is not the right way of speaking of them, as they were men of distinction, who have since made reputations in the world. They were mainly the juniors and one or two others whom it had not been thought necessary to summon to the important meeting. These peripheral members were convinced by my arguments. Almost all of them voted for me, and my motion was carried by a narrow majority.

Thus I did not, after all, have to resign from the Senior Censorship, and the Duke of Westminster Student became a member of the Governing Body, as he still is. But it was a considerable time before I resumed cordial relations with some of the nine.

It is incumbent upon me to state here that since those days Christ Church policy has been entirely transformed. It has gone further than most Colleges in Oxford in electing to Studentships with full membership of the Governing Body men who are doing no specific work for the College but hold research positions in the University. Perhaps the great Duke of Westminster controversy did have some effect in initiating a new trend of opinion. Cynics might attribute the change of policy to a more humdrum cause. It was at some time

during the 'thirties that we acquired a much larger table for
our Governing Body meetings. We also acquired a Dean
(Dr. Lowe) who gave a lead in these matters in the right
direction.[1]

I do not recall that the Prof. ever thanked me for my
efforts about the Duke of Westminster Studentship. I am
sure that I should remember it, had he ever done so. Nor
do I recall that I expected him to do so, or had even the least
flicker of a grievance for his not doing so. We had fought
together in a just cause ; it was no more for him to thank
me for my efforts than it would have been for me to thank
him for 'nobbling' the Dean. That was my firm view of
the nature of our joint enterprise ; I was full of young
enthusiasm.

However, an experience can have an effect and its moral
can have an effect, even if no recognition of that moral flits
ever so fleetingly across the conscious mind. I was bom-
barded with representations all through the inter-war period,
not least from my own colleagues, that the Prof. was a very
tricky person to work with. I repudiated those suggestions
indignantly, affirming that it had not been my experience.

The fact seems clear, however, as I look back from my
vantage point of 1958 upon the joint enterprise, that our
positions were not quite parallel. It was the Prof. who was
interested in physics ; it was the Prof.'s friend, the Duke,
who was putting up the money ; this money would sustain
an extra worker in the Prof.'s Laboratory. Furthermore, my
whole life and career were bound up with Christ Church in
a way in which the Prof.'s were not ; he was occupying
rooms in College by an act of special courtesy. He had no
stake in the College, nor was he in any way dependent on it.

[1] Dean White had been sound about the Duke of Westminster, but held
no decided views on the broader question of adding men not engaged on
college teaching to our Governing Body.

Those same nine people, who had conspired against me, were my colleagues in a much closer sense than that in which they were colleagues of the Prof., and they were my friends ; I did not wish to quarrel with them ; in due course I hope that after the passage of months or years our friendship was fully reconstituted. Then again, I had a natural ambition to give satisfaction in the Senior Censorship, an office that I so particularly valued. When I first became Senior Censor, I was due, in accordance with the College practice at that time, to hold the office for two years, but Mr. Dundas, who was the high authority on these matters, intimated that it was likely that I should be asked to stay on for a third year. I should have liked that, but now it was utterly out of the question. One of the nine had me to lunch shortly afterwards alone with him. He said that under my Senior Censorship the College had been raised to a pitch of domestic strife such as he could not recall during his long period of service there ; everyone was very angry at the way in which the Dean had been 'nobbled'. For all these disturbances he held me to blame. But as a matter of actual fact, during all my time as Senior Censor I had *no* points of friction whatever with my colleagues, so far as I can recall, except about matters touching the Prof. I did not grudge this, as it seemed to me that his cause was a just one. If one starts, as I did, with a capital of goodwill, what better than to treat it as expendable, for a fight in a just cause ?

It would, I now judge, have been appropriate for the Prof. to have thanked me. Or, if he was too shy to do that, he could have shown by some little sign or token in the years that followed that he felt indebted. His not doing so I do not attribute to lack of generous feelings towards me. I attribute it, not to callousness, but to his total lack of perception that I had had a rough time in my own person in consequence of our joint campaign. For him it was just a question of advancing to the next encounter. In certain circumstances there might be danger in co-operating closely with someone who was so very impercipient.

I am now sure that, although I never expected thanks at the time nor consciously felt the lack then, and although I never agreed to the view so often pressed upon me that the Prof. was 'tricky', those experiences had an effect on me at an unconscious level, and had an insensible influence on the little story of our wartime relations, which I shall presently have to tell.

★

In the 'thirties I found myself seeing the Prof. a great deal less. The cause was partly on my side. I suppose that the creed of conversation is one of youth, really. The *Weltschmerz*, the yearning to probe the secrets of the universe, even the confidence that one may succeed in doing so, wane, and give place to settled habits. I was then becoming, what I have since remained, one of the world's hardest workers. Gone were the days of morning sessions during term, chatting with David Cecil. Many years later the Prof. used to recall with pleasure what I said when I first arrived as a new don in the Christ Church Common Room — I have no recollection of it myself : 'I *cannot* work hard'. It was not only the sentiment that pleased him, but also the air of authority and finality with which I informed my senior colleagues of this interesting fact.

At the same time I should suppose that the Prof.'s social preoccupations outside Oxford were taking up still more of his time, and his political preoccupations also. At some date early in the 'thirties his ambition to have a parliamentary career took definite shape. F. E., who died in 1930, was no longer there to dissuade him ; and I have no doubt that Churchill continued to urge him on. The situation grew more anxious, as the Nazis advanced in strength and finally obtained power. The Prof. felt that he had valuable contributions to make as regards both foreign policy and defence.

But how get into Parliament ? A university seat, if one were obtainable, appeared to be the obvious solution. I do not think that the Prof., with his shyness, his complete lack of touch with the ordinary man, his fear, his contempt for sobstuff, which in his view included all forms of political oratory, would have found the rough and tumble of a fight in an ordinary constituency possible. There were two Oxford members at that time, Lord Hugh Cecil and Sir Charles Oman. The former was a parliamentarian of ripe experience and one of the finest speakers of the twentieth century in the House of Commons ; he sat very securely in his University seat. Sir Charles Oman was older and expected to resign shortly, as in the event he did at the General Election of 1935.

But how get the Conservative Committee to nominate such a person as the Prof. ? Churchill had no influence there. It was one of those bodies that might unkindly be described as a caucus ; no one was quite sure how it had come together. It contained Conservatives of distinction, both of London and of Oxford. The London members were no doubt men who liked to maintain their University connection and probably thought mainly in terms of the young men who had shown brilliant promise in pre-war days. They might like to think of Oxford in traditional terms. The Prof. was relatively a newcomer ; he was far indeed removed from the traditions of Oxford. He might have a 'great brain', but being a scientist was probably not in his favour, and old fogies are not in all cases readily able to recognize a 'great brain' for themselves. Furthermore, the Prof. was already a suspect character in many quarters ; he was not even an Englishman by race.

All the same his reputation was growing in certain circles,

especially in what we may call high society. It could not
be said that he had no chance at all, and so he got to work.
I was not involved in all this, and can only speak of what I
learnt casually from day to day. The first thing to do appeared
to be to reform the Committee. It seemed desirable to bring
in representatives of younger elements, who did not know
so much of pre-war Oxford and would be prepared to
back the Prof. as the great friend of Churchill, and formerly
of F. E. Little though the Prof. appreciated the virtues of
democracy in general, this seemed to be a case for some kind
of democratization. The Committee should be reconstituted,
with certain specified groups having their representatives on it.

All this involved much negotiation. I noticed signs of it
in his rooms. They began to get silted up with card indices
and other paraphernalia of democratic organization. Mr.
Bolton King, deviating for a time from his scientific interests,
did much to help the Prof. in this matter.

The Committee was reformed, and the great day came
when they had to choose a successor to Sir Charles Oman.
In the event, after all the work that the Prof. had done and
the trouble that he had taken, and I believe that this was quite
considerable, the reformed committee selected, not the Prof.,
but precisely the kind of man that the old committee might
have been expected to choose : Mr. Cruttwell, the Principal
of Hertford College.

Mr. Cruttwell had been a scholar of brilliant promise in
pre-war days and obtained a Fellowship at All Souls, which
was one of the channels by which Oxford maintained its
contacts with London life. After the war Cruttwell retained
his position in Oxford, as a distinguished and highly respected
historian. He was reputed a wit and had a sharp tongue,
although in my recollection he rather over-worked one
particular way of describing one or other of his academic
confrères — 'grinding his intellectual barrel organ'. He was

not a man of experience in public affairs, and it was not expected that he would be an effective orator ; he was distinguished and respectable, but not by any means of the same calibre as the Prof. in the view of those who regarded the Prof. as a man of real genius. The Prof. felt deeply humiliated.

At this moment Mr. A. P. Herbert, a brilliant wit and accomplished writer, soared over the political horizon. He decided to offer himself as an independent candidate for our University seat. He pursued quite unconventional methods. It was customary for a candidate to issue one short election address only, signed, not by himself, but by his supporters, who would normally be men of eminence in public life or Oxford luminaries. Mr. Herbert did not bother with all this, getting the statutory number of supporters from among less famous men, largely, to the best of my recollection, assistant masters at the Dragon School in Oxford. And then, greatly daring, he wrote his own election address at considerable length. He told the electors that he 'knew nothing about agriculture' ; but he discoursed with point and pungency about a large variety of other topics. In those days, when a spirit of weariness had been produced by the prolonged period of economic depression, and anxieties about the international situation were beginning to mount, the freshness and unconventionality of Mr. Herbert's approach caught the imagination of the voters, many of whom already knew his literary work. There were four candidates : Lord Hugh Cecil — quite safe — and Mr. Cruttwell, the two Conservative official nominees ; Mr. A. P. Herbert ; and, for the first time, an official Labour Party candidate, whose chances were not considered good. There were two seats.

I went round to the count. I had no *locus standi* there, but I had been to that count so often as Gilbert Murray's agent, that I think I was regarded as part of the permanent furniture of the place. Perhaps I could have been regarded as representing the Liberal Party, although it had no candidate. I may also have had it in mind to say a friendly word to A. P. Herbert ; although I had had no part whatever in his candidature, I had instructed him in the mysteries of Proportional Representation, about which he wrote some articles for Punch.

Two facts became evident to me before the count was finished ; I knew the procedure very well. One was that the Conservatives had lost a seat, A. P. Herbert getting in and not Cruttwell ; and the other was that Cruttwell had forfeited his deposit. I then ran as fast as I have ever done in my life ; the nearest telephone I could think of was in my rooms in Canterbury Quad. I got through to the Prof. and announced briefly, 'Cruttwell has forfeited his deposit'. The Prof. was not addicted to manifestations of joy and enthusiasm or to throwing his hat in the air. I have never heard from the Prof. such a whoop of triumph, such genuine joy in his voice, as came to me over that telephone. It was pleasing to be bearer of the news that would salve his wound after the deep humiliation of the Committee's choice.

Actually Cruttwell did not do so badly as this suggests. The matter of the deposit had not been adjusted to the peculiarities of Proportional Representation. It was natural for most Conservative voters to give Lord Hugh Cecil their first preference ; only a few gave Cruttwell a first preference ; but the question of the deposit was determined by the first preferences and not by the final count. Still the fact remained that Cruttwell had lost his money — or the Conservative Committee had lost theirs.

It was not long after this that a by-election occurred in Oxford, owing to the acceptance by Lord Hugh Cecil (later Lord Quickswood) of the Provostship of Eton. The Prof. made up his mind that he would put himself forward as a candidate, whatever the Conservative Committee might do.

A. P. Herbert had blazed the trail for independent action. But it is fair to add that the Prof. lacked the wide appeal of Herbert. The Conservative Committee put forward Sir Farquhar Buzzard, the Regius Professor of Medicine in Oxford. Sir Arthur Salter (later Lord Salter) stood as an independent, being deemed to be on the left of centre in politics. As there was only one vacancy, the procedure of Proportional Representation lapsed.

By that time I was extremely anxious, for reasons presently to be explained, on political as well as on personal grounds, that the Prof. should win. But the political gulf was still too great for me to do anything positive to aid him. I did one negative thing, however. Sir Arthur Salter wrote and asked me, somewhat apologetically it is fair to add, since I had become rather senior for such a run-about job, if I would act as his agent. He could not think of anyone with comparable experience to mine in this particular type of seat. In the ordinary way I would have gladly done so. But I wrote to him and explained that I could not take any part against my old and dear friend, the Prof.

Winston Churchill intervened in this election ; it was a characteristically generous action, since he must have known that it would give rise to much adverse comment. He had to address one of the Oxford University political clubs, which had booked the Union Debating Society's Hall for the purpose, and a large gathering was mustered. Churchill frankly admitted that what he had to say was unconventional, but pleaded that our situation was so stern and threatening that ordinary conventions should be waived. He made a strong plea in favour of the Prof. ; he stressed that the Prof., with his proved understanding of defence matters, and of other matters, would be able to make unique contributions in the House of Commons debates. The inevitable criticisms occurred. What business had Churchill to come and make this speech ? The audience that he addressed consisted mainly of undergraduates, who had no votes. It was absolutely *de rigueur* in this election that there should be no canvassing of any kind and no speeches. Just one short election address was the rule, although I seem to recall that Salter hotted up the election a little by sending out more than one envelope. Churchill was not even an Oxford man. But I guess that he thought that those who made these stuffy criticisms would not vote for the Prof. in any case, but that there were others who were deeply anxious about the nation's plight and the state of her defences, and yet were uncertain whether the Prof. really had the credentials claimed for him in his address. Churchill may well have been correct in thinking that his firm categorical statement that the Prof. could in fact render invaluable service may have swayed those wavering electors to vote for him.

In the event the Conservative vote was split, the Prof. and the official candidate got about the same number of votes each, and Salter was returned. Salter got more votes than those of the two Conservative candidates put together.

*

Although I had fewer contacts with the Prof. in the 'thirties, there was one thing which, surprisingly, drew us nearer together than we had ever been before. It was an agreement on politics. I may put the matter controversially by saying that we were both against Hitler, and, beside the Hitler question, all other political questions seemed trivial indeed in the late 'thirties.

'Being against Hitler' must be defined more precisely. Of course in a vague general way everyone was against Hitler; it was a question of the correct policy. The Prof. and I were at one in thinking that appeasement was not the right line. It is apt to be forgotten now that this was the view of a minority, even of a small minority, in the early days. As late as Munich, the nation seemed to be divided into two roughly equal parts. But at the time when Hitler occupied the Rhineland (1936), there were very few people who were extremely keen that the French should check him by invading the Rhineland immediately. I was used to being in a minority. Had I not been a faithful member of the Liberal Party ? But it was odd to be in a minority on a political question with the Prof. ; it would have been amazing to think of it only ten years earlier ; in the House of Commons almost the only person who represented our views appeared to be Winston Churchill, who soon became my hero.

Opposition to appeasement does not mean opposition to any concession, made in order to gain time or because one thinks one gets a greater countervailing advantage ; appeasement consists essentially in making a concession with the idea that, by removing a grievance, one would create a more friendly disposition on the part of one's adversary. Even appeasement may be the correct policy in appropriate circumstances. Opposition to appeasement in the late 'thirties was based on the view that the time had long since passed for concessions to produce any such effect on Germany. Vitally interconnected with this question of foreign policy was the question of defence. Once one reached the view that Germany could no longer be placated, it was urgently needful to build up armed strength as quickly as possible, so as not to be too frightened to resist acts of aggression, so as not to allow Hitler to extend his domain, so as not to discourage and lose allies, so as to deter Hitler from the final act of general war, and so as not to be defeated in war, should that occur. In those gloomy years there was present in our minds, quite as much as the thought that by failing to make our defences strong we might fail to deter Hitler, the still more forbidding thought that, should war come, we might be defeated.

I did not acquiesce in these new views without strong mental resistance. As a Liberal, I had assumed that our policy should be founded upon the League of Nations, that we should continually strive to get agreement on disarmament and even to give a lead in that direction by our own example, and that, in regard to Germany, we should take such action as might remove grievances. Whatever might have been the rights and wrongs of the First World War, for the sake of the future it was better to let bygones be bygones and not to hold the German nation down in an inferior status, whether by unilateral disarmament or by various forms of restriction upon her sovereignty within her own territories ; there was even the question of whether it would be wise and expedient to give her an outlet, such as the other principal powers in Europe had at the time, by restoring certain Colonial territories. I have already indicated that the Prof. did not take this view even in the early 'twenties. Whether rightly or wrongly, I did take that view. It was only by an arduous process of conversion that I came to recognize that, after a certain point in the career of Hitler, it had become obsolete.

I had many heated arguments with the Prof. on this subject. I remember one evening, although I cannot date it, when everyone else had withdrawn from Common Room, except only the Prof., A. J. Ayer and myself. Ayer and I joined together in deploying the usual Liberal arguments, and in Ayer I had an ally of no mean debating power. I remember saying gloomily to him as we walked back through the dark quad, 'I do not see the answer to all that'. He gave a little shudder, like a dog shaking off water, and replied in tones equally depressed, 'No, it is difficult to see the answer'.

I took the view that, if one cannot answer an argument, one must change one's own position. There may be times, no doubt, when one cannot answer an argument in dialectical debate, and yet has some inner hunch that it is wrong. But on this occasion, unfortunately, my inner hunch was in the opposite direction ; that too suggested that the Prof. was in the right. If that was so, one must make the utmost haste in getting very strong in arms and be resolved to yield nothing, merely for the sake of removing grievances or in the hopes of creating a friendly attitude on the part of the Germans. When one had made up one's mind on the point, it was obvious that it was one of supreme importance. One felt too that most of one's fellow countrymen had not yet grasped its full implications.

I recall an incident in the General Election of 1935. In 1931 I had been strongly opposed to the deflationist policy of the 'National' Government, and offered myself to Transport House to speak on any Labour platforms in divisions where no Liberal was standing ; I spoke on a number. In the years immediately after that I was admitted to the 'pink' Lunch Club in Oxford, which consisted mainly of professed Socialists, and I went to some of the Fabian Research Bureau conferences. And so even in 1935 I found myself on a Labour platform in the General Election. I dealt mainly with the question of Abyssinia, holding that we should take all steps to check Mussolini's aggression. This line was greeted with enthusiasm, and, when I mentioned Anthony Eden with approval, since he seemed to be taking a different line from his Conservative colleagues, his name, even in that Labour meeting, was greeted with applause. Then the candidate came in, and she made an impassioned speech in favour of disarmament. 'How could you,' I expostulated, 'when I had devoted my speech to the need for taking a strong line with Mussolini and everyone seemed to favour that?' 'But we ought to disarm,' she said, 'as an example to the others.' 'You think our example will cause Hitler and Mussolini to disarm?' I asked. 'Oh, Roy,' she said, 'have you lost all your idealism?' I am afraid that, confronted by the spectacle of Hitler, I had. In all these matters the Labour Party, so it seemed to me, was profoundly unsatisfactory. Churchill appeared to be the only hope.

There were some right-wing Conservatives in those days, who, lacking knowledge of, or turning a blind eye on, the atrocities that were proceeding in Germany, believed that co-operation with Hitler should be possible. Hitler was reported to have said, 'Give me Europe to manage, and I will let Britain have the world'. Extreme right-wingers might have a sneaking sympathy with Fascism, on the ground that it imposed discipline and was a safeguard against possible excesses of democratic socialism. From the very beginning the Prof. would have no truck whatever with such views and in conversation dismissed them summarily with a trenchant aphorism, 'You cannot hunt with the tiger'.

From this time onward the Prof. and I had this strong bond of sympathy and we watched events from our common point of view. In this period I saw the Churchills from time to time. Mrs. Churchill was always kind and I stayed at Chartwell occasionally.

★

A few days before Munich I returned to Oxford from the country. I went in to see the Prof. and found him in a state of considerable annoyance, as a plan had just gone wrong that afternoon. He told me about it. As this is a very weighty matter in the pattern of British foreign policy, I will say at once that my memory of what he told me may be at fault. He told me the story then, in those days of terrible excitement just before Munich, and I never happened to mention it to him again. Subject to these reservations, it seems that my memory, such as it is, of what he did tell me should go on record. It could, no doubt, be made a matter of research. We may call it 'The Prof.'s Tale'. He had some link with the Foreign Office, or with some top men concerned with these matters, perhaps one should call it an underground link. Someone had the bright idea, I do not recall if the Prof. claimed to have originated it himself, that the B.B.C. should ascertain the wavelength on which Hitler was to make one of those important pre-Munich pronouncements,[1] and come in *on that wavelength* half a minute or a quarter of a minute before Hitler was due to speak, announcing officially, on behalf of the French and British governments, that if Hitler committed an act of aggression against Czechoslovakia, the French and British would declare war upon him. There were fears here that it had been concealed from the German people that, if Hitler went too far, France and Britain would actually fight. The vast mass of the Germans would have turned on their sets to hear Hitler speak, and, according to the plan, just in those few seconds of waiting, they would hear a clear statement of the French and British intentions. This seemed to be a way of getting at the German public not to be missed.

But, according to the Prof., the B.B.C. had misunderstood the plan and made no preparations for executing it ; they thought that they merely had to give out an announcement on the ordinary wavelength for British broadcasts to Germany. When at the last moment the mistake was discovered, the B.B.C. took a double line. First they pointed out that this would be a contravention of international law in regard to broadcasting and that they could not possibly do anything of this sort without an explicit Cabinet order that they were to break the law in this way. Secondly, it was too late to carry out technical arrangements, which would be extremely diffi-cult, to make a broadcast on the desired wavelength. So the plan had flopped.

Then the question arose whether the statement should

[1] I believe the one in September 26.

none the less be made, although the consideration which alone, it was understood, had caused the Cabinet to agree to it, had gone ; they had decided that it was expedient on the understanding that the whole German people would hear it. The Prof. doubted, so I seem to recall, whether the Chamberlain government would ever have agreed to so bold a statement, but for the extraordinary advantage that would be gained by its wide diffusion among the whole German people. The relevant authorities — whoever they may have been — took the line that, since the statement had now been authorized by the Cabinet — albeit for a special purpose that had become obsolete — and since the French had also agreed, there was no harm in giving out the statement on the ordinary wavelength without reference back to the Cabinet. The Prof. was just waiting to see if they would give it out. It was given out,[1] and was one of the few firm warnings given in those anxious days. But, of course, its effect was all washed away by the Munich meeting. Such was 'The Prof.'s Tale'.

*

When the news of Munich came, the most shattering political event of my lifetime, I retired to bed for a day or two.

A few days later I recall our telephone bell ringing shortly after lunch. When I lifted the receiver, I heard a well-known voice : 'This is Winston Churchill speaking'. It was an excitement indeed to hear the great man's voice come over directly ; usually on such occasions one gets some premonitory inquiry from a private secretary. He was seeking about to discover whether it was possible to build up some united front, which would naturally include himself, in opposition to the Chamberlain policy ; this was prior to the debate in Parliament on Munich. He knew that I had some

[1] Referred to in *The Times* (Sept. 27) as an " authoritative statement."

contact with my old pupil, Mr. John Dugdale, who was then Mr. Attlee's private secretary. I had indeed sounded my friend, but I had nothing of value to report to Churchill. Regretting this, I made the suggestion that he should get in touch with eminent Trade Union leaders who were not in Parliament ; these might be willing to be more forthright than the parliamentarians, who were inhibited by the complicated claims and loyalties of day-to-day party strife. 'I have done that already,' he replied ; 'they are worse than Chamberlain.'

Shortly after Munich I took an initiative by writing an article for our local paper, proposing that the Labour and Liberal candidates in the forthcoming by-election in Oxford city should stand down in favour of an Independent anti-Munich candidate. This proposal received support, and I became the chairman of a committee that formed itself to negotiate this project, which, despite much goodwill, proved very complicated and vexatious, and met with obdurate resistance. Mr. Lindsay, then Master of Balliol College, was put forward as the Independent candidate. As he was normally a member of the Labour Party, it was thought fit that I, as a Liberal, should be chairman of his executive committee — but I have to admit that Lindsay took its business very much into his own hands. I devoted most of my time to continuous speaking on platforms and in the streets.

We had an enthusiastic campaign, drawing support from the whole spectrum of politics, and having well-known Conservatives, as well as Communists, on our platforms ; help poured in from all over Britain. My Canadian pupil, Mr. Graham, conducted a survey of opinion before polling day. To the best of my recollection his results, which were sent up to the *News Chronicle*, were correct within one per cent, showing the defeat of our candidate ; there was a modest majority of men in his favour, but this was outweighed by a larger majority of women against. The Prof. did not come out openly on our side, although he was wholly sympathetic. I induced him to compose a leaflet for general distribution on the state of the nation's defences. This was highly effective.

Although our candidate was defeated, Mr. Vernon Bartlett ran a campaign on similar lines at Bridgwater shortly afterwards and gained a victory.

In those days after Munich I did some writing outside my normal range on the need for a change of policy, and received encouragement from Churchill.

They were trying times. The Prof. sometimes brought me curious questions. For instance, one day he told me that he was in touch with a German who was prepared to take the risk of assassinating Hitler, on condition that our Foreign Office would guarantee him a safe asylum in advance, should he succeed in escaping. Was political assassination justifiable ? And if so, how should one approach the Foreign Office ? I found this a little difficult ! One did not like the idea of political assassination, but was not Hitler himself an exception to all rules ? As regards the approach to the Foreign Office, that was altogether outside my range.

He put another question in that period, which I found much easier to answer. I cannot date it precisely save by saying that it was in 1938 or early 1939. The Prof. explained to me that scientists in Berlin had succeeded in splitting the nucleus of a uranium atom and that a chain effect had been observed. That might mean that it would be possible to construct what we have since come to call 'an atomic bomb'. It was by no means certain that this could be done ; there were still certain fundamental problems to be solved. It surprises me in retrospect how accurately the Prof. was then able to describe the nature of what the bomb would be when the possibility of constructing one was still quite uncertain. He said that it would cause a total destruction of life and devastation over an area of some two square miles. Even if the fundamental problems were solved, it would take a long time — some five or ten years — to construct such a bomb.

Should he write to the *Daily Telegraph* about this matter ? Although I knew of his close friendship for Lord Camrose, which would predispose him to communicate with that newspaper in the first instance, I could not refrain from asking him whether he also thought of writing to *The Times*, as a complementary medium for publicity. He replied that *The Times* was not willing to publish any letters from him. I do not know whether this was in fact the case, or merely another example of his suspicion that the world was against him.

His reason for wishing to write was as follows. He thought that at some point Hitler might claim to have a 'Secret Weapon' which, by instilling alarm, might carry us farther along the road of appeasement. If he explained from his precise scientific knowledge what had been done, how it was still quite improbable that a bomb could be made, and how, even if it could be made, there was no chance whatever of constructing one for five or ten years, then people would know exactly where they were, and not be unduly frightened by Hitler, or pushed off their proper course of action by the fear that his secret weapon might be an atomic bomb.

I had no hesitation whatever in advising him against the letter. If Hitler talked of secret weapons, the British people would show their usual phlegm and treat him with indifference — as in fact happened. But if the Prof. had given this alarming information about the bomb, then, whatever he might say to reassure people that it could not happen for a considerable time, he would have sown the seed of uneasiness. If people knew, as a matter of hard scientific fact, that there was this fearful possibility, and that the site of the crucial experiment had been Berlin, then they might fear that what the Prof. said about the long postponement of fruition was merely his private opinion. The letter was never written.

I experienced in my own person how right my advice had been. I had no further information thereafter about the progress of research on the bomb. When in due course Hitler began to talk of a 'secret weapon', I did have, I believe, just a tiny fraction of greater uneasiness than the average man on account of what the Prof. had told me.

I never raised the subject with the Prof. again, although I was working in his office during the war and we discussed many secret matters. Having heard nothing for a couple of years and lazy-mindedly inferring that probably this business had petered out, I asked Mr. Tuck at dinner in our establishment one evening — it was among a few members of our staff, who were all accustomed to discussing top secret matters — how uranium was getting along. Tuck put on his most lachrymose of voices : 'Uranium is a dr-e-a-dful subject, and I cannot bear to think of it'. I could have bitten my tongue off. I never asked another question. But in due course I became dimly aware that there was a certain seepage of scientists across the Atlantic and guessed that things were proceeding.

I had one very bad day towards the end of the war. I was then working for the Fifth Sea Lord and, after we had concluded our business, he turned to me and said that he had been to a meeting of the Chiefs of Staff and learned that the enemy had a weapon to which we could have no answer. I left his room. Was this then IT ? I was a coward all that day. If the Germans really had it, that was, after all, the end of everything. It was not a question only of one's own life, but of everyone in the world who was dear to one. I slept badly that night.

Next day I could bear it no longer. Deeply ashamed of myself, I found some trumpery excuse for an interview with the Fifth Sea Lord. After dealing with that, I turned to him

and, reminding him of what he had told me the day before,
I asked him : 'Would you mind telling me if this weapon to
which we have no answer would be something very serious ?'
'It would be something very serious indeed', he said, and
looked exceedingly glum. I must have eyed him in an
appealing way, for then he came out with it. 'The enemy
could drop a warhead of 12 tons of high explosive without
our being able to intercept it.' This was the first exaggerated
account of what was to be known as V2. I breathed again.[1]

★

It was in these pre-war years that the Prof. became involved
in certain activities that earned him deep distrust and ill-will
from his fellow scientists. He did not speak to me of these
matters except in a casual way ; I heard something about
them from others also. I did not think that it was my business
to inquire more particularly. I have no knowledge of these
affairs, and I am not a person who could be called as a witness
about them. Nevertheless it seems proper for me to record
here what I believed at the time, adding that my belief may
have been inaccurate.[2]

He was on a committee, or possibly several committees,
concerned with scientific aspects of our defences. He was
particularly interested in a balloon barrage. When the war
came, he said that something much better could have been
done, had there been more research on his own ideas at an
earlier date. He had had some interest in this in the First
World War. Towards the end of it he was exceedingly

---

[1] Sir George Thomson (op. cit. page 64) tells us that from the beginning
the Prof. derided the idea that a V2 could have a charge of 12 tons, and that in
fact it was one ton.

[2] Sir George Thomson gives an authoritative, but brief, account of some
of these matters (op. cit. page 58). More detailed research into these episodes
might reveal matters of much historic interest.

keen to carry out another hazardous experiment in his own person, by flying an aeroplane, to which a cow-catching device had been affixed, into the cable of a barrage balloon. He was not allowed to do this.

There were other defence questions in which he was also interested. The gravamen of the charge against him was that he utilized information acquired at these committees in order to brief Churchill for his criticisms of the Government. According to the Prof. there was a committee which was dissolved on this account, and then shortly afterwards re-formed again with more or less the same personnel but without him.

In my own person I was delighted to believe that the Prof. was doing this sort of thing. Of course as a general rule it would be deeply wrong to divulge secret information obtained on a committee in order to brief someone who was criticizing the Government, or indeed for any other purpose. To do so was, in the strictest sense, immoral, since knowledge that committee members might behave in that way would entirely obviate the usefulness of such committees. To most moral rules, however, there are exceptions. One would have to go a long way back into history to find anyone of so black a character as Hitler in a position of such enormous power and so menacing to all that was best in the world. Again the question arises whether the threat of Hitler was not such as to justify irregular behaviour that in normal circumstances would be unforgivable. It would have been unlike the Prof. to do anything that actually contravened the law ; but it would not be difficult for him to give some hints about the general directions in which things were moving on his committees that would be helpful to Churchill. Was it wrong to do so ? After all, Churchill was at that time a man of enormous political experience, discreet, and a patriot.

In the dire conditions prevailing before the war broke

out, Churchill seemed the only hope. Even at the price of some irregular behaviour in relation to a committee, it seemed that all strength should be given to Churchill's arm in prodding a Government which seemingly lacked the capacity or will-power to increase our defensive strength with all possible speed.

I do not judge that it is making light of the moral obliga-tions of a committee member to hold that, in the peculiar circumstances of those times, the more that the Prof. told Churchill the better. But his scientific colleagues did not see the matter in quite that light.

CHAPTER 2

THE WAR AND AFTERWARDS

WHEN the war broke out, the Prof. disappeared at once ; he had gone off to help Churchill. It occurred to me that I ought to pay a call upon him. The porter at the Admiralty had some difficulty in directing me to his room. 'I do not know where he is, although I know exactly what he is doing.' 'I wish I did', said the Prof., when I eventually found him. He was sitting quietly in his room in the Admiralty, not far from that of the First Lord, passing his paper cutter up and down his trousers. Harvey was in the next room, acting as his private secretary. It was not until after many months that the Admiralty assigned to the Prof. a professional civil servant as secretary, and, as the Prof.'s business was extremely multifarious, Harvey had a heavy task — as indeed he had throughout the war.

The Prof. told me something of what he was doing. Churchill wanted to have him on hand to give him independent advice on a wide variety of topics. The Prof. has often been referred to as Churchill's 'scientific adviser' during the war. He certainly did give scientific advice, and followed all the secret scientific developments. But he also gave advice on many other questions, and particularly on economic questions. Although I was eventually to be adjacent to him, it was not easy to measure the distribution of his day among his various interests. He had many scientific callers and went to many committees dealing with scientific matters. None the less from my own observation I would say that he devoted

more time to economic questions than to those of science.
If we judge the matter by his own staff, in 1940 he had eight
economists of university training assisting him, but only one
scientist.

In this first phase he explained to me that, while Churchill's
primary responsibility was as First Lord of the Admiralty,
he was also a member of the Cabinet, and, as such, regarded
it as his positive duty to keep himself well informed on all
matters on which the Cabinet, as a whole, had to decide. Of
course he had the benefit of perusing the various papers that
were circulated in abundance — even too great abundance —
to Cabinet Ministers. Some no doubt were content to accept
the views of their colleagues on matters touching their several
departments. Churchill felt that he wanted an independent
mind to digest and criticize these papers. It was not enough,
amid the heavy pressure of his duties at the Admiralty, to
have a cursory knowledge of matters outside his province ;
he wanted to have a deeply critical knowledge, and what
better person to aid him towards getting that than the Prof. ?
That was how I understood the position when I left him
after my call.

It was not long after this visit that the Prof. rang me up
with a request for help. Churchill's inquiries about economic
matters were multiplying ; for instance, there was the question
of the amounts of the various kinds of foods to be allowed
on the rations ; Churchill was by no means satisfied that
these were being correctly assessed. Could I suggest an
economist ? He trusted my judgement not to send him a
stupid man ; the one qualification mentioned was that he
must not be too squeamish about figures, but willing to
make a rough assessment on inadequate data ; the Prof.
implied that he attributed a very high standard of meticulous-
ness to professional economists. I immediately promised to
find him someone.

There was no lack of economists on the market at that time. The various Departments had hardly yet begun in October 1939 to absorb economists for the war effort; it was only when Churchill became Prime Minister in May 1940, that Mr. Francis Hemming obtained the authority of Mr. Arthur Greenwood to sweep the board almost clean, by taking under his wing a large cadre of economists, who in due course provided the personnel of the Central Statistical Office and the Economic Section of the War Cabinet Office, or went off into other Departments.

None the less the matter required very careful thought. I knew so well the Prof.'s habit of laying down the law to ripe scholars on matters on which he himself had no special qualifications. An economist might easily take offence if he found that his own *expertise* was totally scorned, and, if offence was given too often, the partnership would not be a happy one. This seemed to point to the need for a young man. When the Prof. said 'not stupid', this meant that the victim must be one of quite first-rate intellectual calibre. What I had in mind more than anything else, however, was the Prof.'s insistence on putting everything into quantitative terms; a merely abstract argument meant nothing to him; the beautiful refinements and subtleties of economic theory would be wasted on him; the terms of the equations must be quantified. I must accordingly find someone with this habit of mind. Furthermore, he must have no inclination to 'show off'; that would be fatal. On the other hand, he must be tough and not quail before the Prof.'s overbearing manner in the first round of an argument. For the Prof. was essentially a reasoning man, and ready to learn if he perceived that his adversary had a good case.

I regard my choice of man on that occasion as a stroke of genius, and my best contribution to the defeat of Hitler. One single act may presumably do more to frustrate the enemy than six years of honest plodding. At that time Mr. MacDougall (now Sir Donald) was only beginning to be known among economists. I had examined him when he took Modern Greats at Oxford, and supervised him when he was working for an advanced degree there, and his intellectual calibre, as well as his toughness, then became evident to me. He proceeded to a Lectureship in Leeds University, where, under the guidance of my old friend, Professor T. H. Jones, he directed his attention to applied economics, and made a study for a committee of the British Association on the Advancement of Science on economic trends in Britain in the 'thirties. It was this work that suggested to me that he had a very special aptitude for quantitative economics.

I told him that I had a war job for him, the nature of which could not be divulged in advance, and bade him take the train from Leeds to Oxford without delay. He arrived late one evening, and I presented him to the Prof. in the Christ Church Common Room. His appointment was quickly fixed up. It was an unqualified success. My idea that he had a feeling for quantities was proved correct ; he rapidly learnt to understand the Prof.'s modes of thought, which were peculiar, and worked in beautiful harmony with him, as he on his side worked in beautiful harmony with Churchill. Indeed, in relation to certain economic aspects of our war effort, one should think in terms of a Churchill-Prof.-MacDougall triangle, with the Prof. as the go-between. Their joint thinking, the initiating spark for which might, according to the occasion, come from any one of the three, caused decisions of no little consequence to be taken. If history could be written at a really fundamental level, not in terms of events, but in terms of the thoughts of which the events are the remote effects, or, deeper still, in terms of the tendency of certain types of mind to generate certain kinds of thought, then the existence of this triangle would have to figure quite prominently in the history books.

Soon afterwards the Prof. came to me, asking for more. I looked around busily. The next batch that I sent him consisted of G. L. S. Shackle, Miss Helen Makower and H. W. Robinson. More followed.

And then a new note began to come into the Prof.'s inquiries. Why did I not come along myself? At first it was tentative — 'why not?' Later it became more insistent, 'you must'.

I was very hesitant, indeed very reluctant. I had the idea that the Prof. might be making this proposal only from a feeling of friendship — to give me something to do. I had expressed restiveness to him. For me, as for others, those months of inactivity during the phoney war dragged heavily ; I had expected an immediate mobilization of the whole nation when the war broke out, but that could not be. Many years later, when winnowing through Keynes's papers, I came across a little note written by him to the Treasury at the outset of the war, saying that the only two people that he had in mind as suitable for immediate incorporation in the Treasury were Mr. Richard Kahn and myself. I never got that summons from the Treasury, which would have been so welcome then, nor, to the best of my knowledge, did Richard Kahn ; later he went into the Board of Trade.

What weighed most heavily with me was the idea that I should be a fifth wheel on the Prof.'s coach. Indeed I had a strong sense that, by going there, I should spoil my own artistic handiwork. By supplying MacDougall, and then the others, I had built a nicely balanced edifice. I had given the Prof. what he really needed. I began to see, still from the outside, how his department would work. I knew well that the Prof. was not an empire builder. When Churchill became Prime Minister he encouraged the Prof. to create a large department, so that there could be an ample staff mapping out all aspects of the war effort. This did not appeal to the Prof. He liked to be selective, not comprehensive, in his range. He sought to pick on some point of real importance, to get the high-powered thought of a few chosen spirits, with all of whom he was in daily contact, to bear upon it, and to reach his conclusion with high speed. He did not wish to be surrounded by the cumbersome paraphernalia of a large research organization. The point to be studied might be suggested by Churchill, or by his own thinking, or indeed, as events proved, by MacDougall himself. MacDougall then got busy with the statistical aspects, with the aid, if need be, of the others. It did not seem that I should have a useful part to play ; I should be an excrescence on my own carefully constructed edifice.

Other thoughts came into my mind. Would I be happy, subjecting my judgement, as I knew well that I needs must, to the Prof. ? War was a time when subjection is accepted, even welcomed. My friend, John Sparrow, joined the ranks of the Army, because he felt that, war not being his *métier*, he wished to have his efforts directed by others ; I understood that point of view. I felt that I would gladly have been a subaltern in the Army, or in the vast organization of the Civil Service, with defined, albeit narrowly restricted, responsibilities. But this was a different kind of subordination. Could one happily be an adviser to an adviser ? That was all right for MacDougall, because he was still very youthful ; but I was in what might be supposed to be the prime of life.

And then there was that tendency of the Prof., which I knew so well, to lead one along a little farther than one intended to go. It was all right when I was fighting the battle of the Duke of Westminster Studentship. I had gone farther in my quarrel with my Christ Church colleagues than I had originally intended. But I had never at any point lost my freedom to say to the Prof. : 'Now I have done all that I can for you ; I will go no further'.

There were counter considerations. Since we had indisputably one common aim, the defeat of Hitler, it did not seem that there could be differences on fundamental issues. I did not deem myself to have any special *expertise* on the economics of war and would be glad to sink my own immature judgement. The Prof. would presumably be working in close accord with Churchill and, if these two great men were in agreement on how to conduct the war, it did not seem likely that I should wish to be adamant in a contrary sense. Of course I had to envisage the possibility that the Prof. would advise Churchill in a sense that *both* Churchill and I believed to be wrong. How should I then be placed ? In the event I do not recall that such a situation ever arose. But what I thought about that possibility in anticipation was wrong. I imagined that my prior contacts with Churchill, which were slight indeed compared with those of the Prof. but had existed, would be of service, and that Churchill would occasionally seek my independent judgement. In fact this did not happen, and the official hierarchy was rigidly maintained. Although I was composing minutes for Churchill's perusal almost daily, I felt farther removed from the possibility of direct access to him than I had been before I went into his office. Presumably that was natural. To this day I cannot judge how far my relation to the Chief was exactly analogous to that of the Number Two in any ordinary departmental set-up, or whether the Prof.'s dictatorial tendency, on which J. J. had commented long ago, served to create an abnormally wide gulf between me and Churchill.

There were naturally strong forces impelling me to accept the proposal. There was the exciting interest in being so near the centre of things ; there was my impatience to be doing something ; there was my friendship for the Prof. ;

and there was my intense veneration for Churchill, which all came to share in due course, but which I had entertained already in the years before the war.

There was one further consideration which weighed much with me, but which proved to be erroneous. The little department that the Prof. was building up was unconventional and outside the normal machinery of government. I supposed at the time that this was due to the fact that, although it was quite proper for the First Lord of the Admiralty to wish to be thoroughly well informed on all matters, including those of a broadly economic character, for which, as a member of the Cabinet, he was responsible, it was unusual. It seemed quite clear that before very long Churchill would become Prime Minister. Indeed that was an inducement held out by the Prof. to me. He assured me — although such assurance was hardly necessary — that Churchill would not throw his little staff overboard, but that, on the contrary, he would need their services still more.

Where I was wrong was in supposing that, when that change took place, we should cease to be what might be called a 'band of irregulars' and would somehow be incorporated in the normal machinery of government. It is unusual for a First Lord of the Admiralty to wish to be primed about economic matters, but not for a Prime Minister. Accordingly I supposed that, when the change came, Churchill would desire us to be integrated into some kind of General Economic Staff, which was largely lacking under Chamberlain — of the kind indeed that Mr. Hemming actually tried to build up under the inadequate leadership of Greenwood.

Until I went in, I had not fully grasped the situation. It was not only because Churchill was First Lord, and not Prime Minister, that we had to be 'irregulars'. It was also because Churchill wished, and continued, when he became Prime Minister, to wish, to have around him a band of critics, who, precisely because they were not fully merged into the general machinery of government, would give him an independent judgement on how things were going forward. And then there was another factor — the special character and aims of the Prof. It would not at all have suited him to be a part of any general organization whatever ; and he would have been most difficult to fit in. Even had Churchill, on becoming Prime Minister, judged that on general grounds there was no need for him to have a private economic staff, yet, if he was to get full value out of the Prof., it was needful to retain him in an anomalous position, and that meant retaining his staff along with him. I am sure that Churchill acted wisely. But I did not foresee this. Whether, had I done so, I should none the less have accepted the Prof.'s offer, about which I had the gravest doubts at the time, it is naturally impossible in retrospect to say.

I began work on January 1st, 1940, and was immediately plunged into activities of an exciting kind. On about the third day I was taken by Churchill and the Prof. to a Ministerial meeting, which discussed a variety of problems. Among these there was an item on the agenda relating to the alleged under-loading of the ships bringing in our imports. Churchill spoke on this from a brief by the Prof. ; neither the Prof. nor I said anything. Sir Cyril Hurcomb (now Lord Hurcomb) was there, as the departmental head of the Ministry of Shipping. He rebutted the criticisms, and went further ; with his eye on the Prof. he said that it was wasting the time of all the Ministers present to bring up all these ill-informed allegations, implying that they were mere rubbish. It seemed to me that this was rather a strong rebuke to administer to the great Churchill ; but Churchill sat quietly there, blandly puffing away at his cigar, and did not seem to mind.

When I got back to our office, I expected to find the Prof. somewhat crestfallen. His figures had been confuted, and Churchill had been humiliated in the presence of a committee of Ministers ; the whole affair struck me as deeply shaming. But I found the Prof. entirely unperturbed, and cocksure as usual ; he got us all to work away again on the figures, in preparation for further attacks upon the Ministry of Shipping on similar lines.

A couple of days later, I was bidden by the Prof. to go round to the Ministry of Shipping to see Sir Cyril Hurcomb, with whom I had had a slight acquaintance before the war. Why was *I* to go ? From the beginning the Prof. was somewhere betwixt and between a Civil Servant and a Minister ; about halfway through the war he was given Ministerial status as Postmaster-General. The Prof. never stood on his dignity. He interviewed persons of the most lowly status, if he thought that there was a brain to be picked. But this was a different kind of occasion. I suppose that in our tiny little irregular department, being senior under the Prof., I was to be regarded as on a diplomatic level with a 'permanent secretary'.

Hurcomb gave me a thorough 'dressing down'. He had a good command of rough and strong rebuke, available for his service, when he required it. Members of Professor Lindemann's staff kept ringing up the Ministry of Shipping, asking to be supplied with irrelevant figures ; then the First Lord was briefed to make ridiculous criticisms. His, Hurcomb's, people were busy, trying to contribute to the war effort, and their work was interrupted and their time wasted by these idiotic questions. Unless a stop was put to this, he would feel it his duty to report the matter to the Prime Minister. I did not mind his rebukes, not yet knowing whether they were well justified or not ; there was something endearing in his rugged features and forthright manners. The Prof. always stigmatized his expression as 'gloomy', and I believe that Churchill shared this impression ; but I did not find them so. I did, however, regard it as rather ironic that I, who had been in public service for five days only and had during my life no executive responsibility, save those accruing in university or college administration, should be threatened with a report to the Prime Minister himself for my misdeeds. I reported this interview to the Prof., who was greatly amused.

This may be the place to mention another interview of a rather different tone, which I had some months later with Sir Edward Bridges (now Lord Bridges). On this occasion, to the best of my recollection, I was not bidden to go by the Prof., but had a direct personal approach from Bridges. Churchill was by then Prime Minister. Bridges began by observing in his quiet way that 'although it sounded rather pompous to say so, he regarded himself as responsible for the efficient working of the machinery of government'. 'Not at all pompous, my dear sir,' I thought, 'but very modest, and very impressive.' What a frightful load of responsibility — to feel oneself responsible for all the vast, and in wartime rapidly shifting, complications and ramifications of the government of Britain, not to say of the British Commonwealth and Empire. In fact, Bridges was one of our foremost war-winners.[1]

What worried him was the time absorbed in Cabinet, or Ministerial meetings, by the fact that figures put forward by the Prime Minister, under the briefing of the Prof., were challenged by the Ministers concerned ; this led to acrimonious disputes about figures, recriminations and much waste of effort. Surely we could arrange that any figures put forward by the Prime Minister had been previously agreed to by the Ministries concerned.

I explained that we always used the basic figures that were officially supplied to us, but that sometimes it occurred

[1] Cp. my *Life of J. M. Keynes*, p. 613.

to us to 'process' the figures, by adding certain items together, by taking percentages, by working out a moving average. The consequence of these operations might be to bring to light matter for criticism. Of course it would be possible to ring up the Ministries, to find out their explanations, their reasons or excuses. But we had instructions from the Prime Minister not to proceed too far on those lines. He did not wish the native hue of our resolution to be sullied over with the pale cast of Ministerial explanations ; if these were indeed but excuses, he would prefer to hear them for himself in open Cabinet discussion. Some of our criticisms might be wrong ; but, if they were right, then it might be useful for the Prime Minister to have cognizance of them, so that he could apply prodding. In all cases the additional prestige given to our findings by the Prime Minister having mentioned them, might make the Ministries concerned look at certain aspects with a fresh eye. But I was impressed with what Bridges said, and inwardly resolved to do my best.

*

The Admiralty, having no doubt exhausted most of the alphabet for its various branches, gave us the name of S Branch (S for Statistics). And that was how we long continued to speak of ourselves after we had moved across to the Prime Minister's office. What did we do ?

Our bread and butter work was the construction of graphs in pen and ink or colour, to keep Churchill informed of the progress of events ; these were bound into albums which he inspected every few days and sometimes showed to his visitors in order to acquaint them with certain aspects. I referred to this as bread and butter work since it was our continuing task ; but the construction of each new graph — the volumes continued to grow in bulk — was a highly skilled task. It was needful to select what was important, to present it in a readily intelligible way, and, above all, to bring home the essential truth. The choice when to use quantities, when percentages, when averages, etc., was all-important. The Prof. himself had great skill in devising the right mode of presentation ; if one of us tried our hand, we seldom got it past his critical eye without numerous modifications. MacDougall too was very skilful, as indeed were all our members. The best was good enough for Churchill, and I believe that in this respect he had the best that the art of man could devise. I recall one matter which I believe we never succeeded, despite great efforts, in getting into good graphical form ; we wanted to show the relation between the flow of a given type of aircraft from the factory and the size of a Battle Array of that type that could be sustained, having regard to wastage, training needs, etc. It sounds very simple !

Our graphs related both to economics and to defence matters. When still in the Admiralty we naturally provided a large amount of naval information. After Dunkirk, when most of our equipment was lost, we constructed charts showing for each division separately the gradual and slow build-up of its required complement of each of the main weapons. The Navy, the Air Force and the Army were assigned, as their special responsibility, to different members of the staff. We provided information about such economic matters as the distribution of manpower, the degree of utilization of machine tools, imports, etc. etc.

After the fall of France the Prof.'s brother, Brigadier Lindemann, was attached to the British Embassy in Washington as adviser on scientific questions. His duties in regard to the despatch of olive oil for the Prof.'s nutriment have already been mentioned. Churchill asked us to have duplicate copies of his albums made, and these were sent out to Washington

in the Foreign Office bag ; it was the duty of Charles Lindemann to pay a personal call on President Roosevelt from time
to time and to place these volumes, as also the supplements
which followed, in his hands. The United States was still
neutral. The idea was that it would be a good thing for the
President to know exactly how Britain was faring, for good
or ill, and have the same information that Churchill himself
used. It was desired to by-pass the State Department and
any other 'departments concerned'. It would be for the
President himself to use his discretion in deciding to whom
else, if anyone, he showed his precious information.

Then there were our advisory duties. These might arise
out of a direct query by Churchill — I recall that within a
few days of my arrival he asked me to discover whether the
canals of Britain could be a useful supplement to our transport
facilities — or out of the annotations, which he made in red
ink, on the various Cabinet papers that he had to read. Those
annotations were sure evidence of Churchill's wonderful grasp
of detail over the whole vast range of our war effort, economic as well as military. Or the advice might arise out of
some bright idea of the Prof.'s or of any of us.

I have already referred to the dispute with the Ministry
of Shipping, which was proceeding when I first arrived, on
the under-utilization of our shipping capacity. There appeared
to be a wide discrepancy between the tonnage capacity of the
ships coming into port and the tonnage of the imports delivered. Of course we had to find our way through the
intricate maze of gross tons, net tons, deadweight tons, etc. ;
some cargoes (*e.g.* timber) were too light in relation to their
bulk to use the full tonnage capacity of the ship ; allowance
had to be made for wrappings and awkward parcels.

In order to develop our criticisms we had to supplement
the information contained in official papers by further inquiries
from the departments that had put them forth. Up to a point

we were anxious to learn the reasons for certain discrepancies, but we were specifically instructed not to go too far on these lines. The distinction between those facts, like the space occupied by wrappings, which are proper reasons for other facts, and those facts that are in the nature of excuses, is no doubt a fine one ; but it was our duty to make it. The excuses Churchill wanted to hear, not from us, but directly from the departments concerned. He did not want his S Branch to be drawn into the position of feeling that it had to plead the case of the departments. And so the departments were doubly burdened. They had to spend time furnishing us with much information, the relevance of which they could not see, only to be rewarded by a flaying criticism by Churchill at a Ministerial meeting, which they deemed unfair. We owed much to the extraordinary tact and persuasiveness of MacDougall in pressing his queries. I can see him calmly sitting at his desk with his telephone receiver glued to his ear, day after day.

After a time, largely owing to the efforts of MacDougall himself, our position changed somewhat. As we became more trusted, we extracted the information more easily, and not only that specifically requested, but other relevant information that in the earlier days might have been held back from us. Much was also due to the position of the Prof., which changed greatly after the time when he first arrived in Whitehall in 1939, trailing clouds of suspicion. When those concerned began to realize that, like it or not, the Prof. was the man whom Churchill trusted most, and that not all their refutations, aspersions, innuendoes or attempts at exposure would shift Churchill from his undeviating loyalty to the Prof. by one hair's-breadth, they began to deem it expedient to take a different line. I recall the account given me by a private secretary, which was doubtless over-dramatized. It was understood in the office that any memoranda known to emanate from Professor Lindemann were to be given short shrift ; he knew nothing about the subject ; he had no business to butt in and must be effectively refuted. Then one day the Chief came in and, instead of mouthing the words 'Professor Lindemann' with considerable asperity, as was his habit, he referred in a seemingly almost affectionate voice to 'the Prof.'. That gave them all the cue for a change of tone.

Furthermore, our staff itself, which was green at first, began to feel that Churchill's original instruction not to enter too deeply into departmental excuses was no longer applicable. As their own knowledge and experience increased and the respect in which they were held increased, they felt that they could talk more freely to those in other departments, while sustaining their own independent critical judgement. They were no longer in danger of being contaminated. Thus, as the war proceeded, excellent relations came to be established with opposite numbers in all the various departments.

In regard to the under-loading of ships, my impression is that, after many months of guerrilla warfare, S Branch, including the Prof. himself, became convinced that, although there was something in our criticisms, there was not as much as we originally believed, and that it was not a big war-winning point of the kind for which the Prof. was in search.

There were other matters concerning the efficient use of shipping. We discovered that the time taken for the turn-round in our ports was abnormally great and not to be accounted for by the difficulties of the 'black-out' alone. We exerted pressure accordingly. I recall an interview with a senior official in the Ministry of Shipping. He explained to me that the different shipping companies had their own quays and that ships sometimes had to wait about accordingly. 'But must not all the quays be pooled,' I said, 'so that, if there is any quay capable of accommodating the ship, it should go straight in, whatever the Company ?' He explained that the different companies had different routines and that labour difficulties might arise. 'But surely all these difficulties can and must be adjusted.' I added a bromide. 'You know we have got this war on.' He turned to me with a very sad and wistful expression. 'When I hear you talking with indifference about scrapping all the old practices of the shipping companies for the sake of the war, I begin to wonder whether, when the war is over, we shall find anything left that has been worth fighting for.'

I recall receiving a personal instruction from Churchill to explore the possibility that troop-carriers returning from Egypt via the Cape should touch in at the Plate to pick up some meat on their way back. This would not greatly lengthen the round trip. I entered into negotiations, and it seemed that the plan was feasible.

In the end our recurrent preoccupation with the loading of ships yielded a large dividend, and may be deemed easily to have justified all the trouble that we had given the Ministry of Shipping by less relevant probings. A growing quantity of shipping had to be earmarked for the transport of troops and their equipment, and of the latter the most bulky part consisted of the enormous number of vehicles on wheels. (We made some attempt in the early days to criticize the amount of army transport 'required' — much to the indignation of General Jacob, I recall.)

MacDougall raised the point that, if these hordes of vehicles, instead of being run aboard, were dismantled and boxed and reassembled at the point of disembarkation, that would save a vast amount of shipping space. This was a point after the Prof.'s own heart. The case against this procedure was evident — the enormous administrative headache that would be caused by the need to have reassembly plants and skilled personnel at the ports of disembarkation. Anyone would shy at having to make all the arrangements. But the case in favour was overwhelming. It rested essentially on the quantity of shipping involved. It must be remembered that much of this army transport had to be shipped on the long haul round the Cape of Good Hope to Egypt. I do not recall the figures. The main battle, which was a long and arduous one, was fought after I had already left S Branch. If the extra shipping made available by the resulting economy in the use of space was equivalent to sinking, say, half the enemy's fleet of submarines, then you clearly had a large war-winning point, and the administrative inconveniences, great though these might be, were of relatively trivial significance. The resistance to the project was tremendous, and it is doubtful if this great gain would ever have been garnered in, but for the influence of the Prof., his passionate interest in the quantitative aspect of things and the drive that he was prepared to put to the service of a cause of the merits of which he was convinced. In later years the Prof. liked to take the boxing of army vehicles — when his reticence allowed him to speak of such things at all — as an example of a contribution that he had been able to make to our victory.

Alongside the controversy with the Ministry of Shipping about the loading of ships in the early days, there ran another about the presentation of periodic figures for our current gains and losses of shipping. The Ministry thought it expedient to present these in the most pessimistic light, in order to brace the people with the idea that the situation was grim. Churchill took the opposite view ; he wanted to keep the people in good heart. Neither side, it need hardly be said, wished to depart from the truth ; but there were many day-to-day events about which it was legitimate to argue whether they constituted a true gain (or loss) or not.

An example may be cited from the launching of the *Queen Elizabeth*. New launchings were counted as 'gains' ;

but the Ministry of Shipping, arguing that this was a wholly exceptional event and that the *Queen* would be of no use whatever for our war effort, omitted her from the reckoning, thus converting a substantial net gain into a moderate net loss. Churchill was furious. Even from the Ministry of Shipping point of view, he was proved right in the end, since the *Queen Elizabeth* did valiant service later in the war, transporting thousands of troops across the oceans. Churchill wrote a terrible minute to Sir John Gilmour, who died shortly afterwards, suggesting that, instead of trying to depress the public with gloomy and inaccurate figures, he would be employing himself more usefully if he took steps to see that the ships at his disposal were fully loaded.

Drawing on his vast vocabulary, Churchill sent us a little note one day, asking why it was necessary to ingeminate the doleful news of shipping losses on the air and in the newspapers. This made us wonder ; could it be — but this never happened — that he had overlooked a mis-typing for 'inseminate' ? No. To ingeminate (gemini) is to say the same thing twice over.

Our inquiries and comments covered a very wide field. One of our main interests came to be the balanced use of our resources, notably of manpower and of the shipping available to import our food and materials. I have heard it alleged that Churchill was not so strong on the economic side of things as on the broad issues of foreign policy or on military matters. It is true that he did not concern himself much, to the best of my knowledge, with such matters as foreign exchange arrangements, Payments Agreements or Treasury Deposit Receipts. But the central theme of economics is the right distribution of scarce resources among alternative uses, in order to get the optimum result. About this Churchill took a passionate interest, extending not only to the broad lines of policy, but to meticulous detail. Over and over again the red ink markings on the Cabinet papers that passed through his hand showed that he had a firm grasp of minutiae and a retentive memory for previous decisions about them.

I recall a little note that he wrote for us in the summer of 1940. He had been much concerned because after the outbreak of war it had been necessary to fix the meat ration so low. The decision was the result of careful calculations of the amount made available from the slaughter of British cattle and the amount that could be imported in our refrigerated tonnage, which was unhappily especially suitable for conversion into troop carriers ; some of the allied tonnage had to be earmaked for providing the French with a balancing supply of meat. Then amid all his distractions after the fall of France, the Battle of Britain not yet fought, sea-borne invasion a real possibility, our equipment largely lost at Dunkirk, fresh divisions having to be formed and supplied, coastal defences to be looked at, new weapons to be promoted, the Home Guard to be organized, the smooth running of the Government, of which he had but recently become Prime Minister, to be attended to, President Roosevelt to be kept in play, and — we may recall — speeches to be made to sustain morale at home, he sent us a minute as follows. Now that France had fallen and it was no longer our duty to ensure that the French people had a balancing supply of meat, why was it that there had been no proposal to increase the British meat ration ?

At fairly frequent intervals there were reviews of the best distribution of our diminishing supply of shipping among the principal items of imports. And whenever the Services asked for more, the distribution of manpower had to be reconsidered. On both these questions S Branch played a crucial part. The normal machinery of government churned up certain proposals, which finally came to the Prime Minister ; it was our duty to counter-brief him on what we knew to be the lines of his own thinking. When MacDougall had completed his calculations, the Prof. sketched out a re-allocation ; after the Cabinet we usually learnt that Churchill had carried the Prof.'s proposals through.

I believe that S Branch was the governing influence in the disposal of our available shipping during the war ; anyhow in my time it seemed to be so. On manpower too it did important briefing ; but in the later part of the war Sir John Anderson (Lord Waverley) organized a committee on manpower, which I attended once, and I believe that Churchill was willing to devolve upon him some measure of final responsibility.

That was all at the level of directives. There remained the question how faithfully these were implemented in detail. Sometimes the subsequent returns showed discrepancies, and then the Prof. became very cross. We were especially anxious to decrease the importation of timber. But timber imports seemed to have an especially obdurate tendency to remain above the level of the previous directives. Nothing raised the ire of the Prof. so much. There were excuses, of course. They had expedited imports because the St. Lawrence would soon be frozen, or they had used timber as a balancing cargo, etc. But the Prof. was not one whit appeased. I think that he suspected that there were some bearers of a degree in the Arts — 'classics', he always called them — who had too sentimental an eye for the preservation of the British woodlands and were working away to frustrate him. 'Timber' became almost like the name of a personal enemy ; the very word stank in our department.

In regard to all these matters, I had a great surprise when I arrived in S Branch. I had supposed, along with the majority of people, I fancy, that Churchill, who had for so many years inveighed against our neglect of the Services and was now calling upon the people for the utmost sacrifices, would be striving to pare down civilian consumption to the greatest possible extent, in order to make the utmost possible quantity of productive capacity and manpower available for the fighting forces. When I arrived, I found that the whole tendency of our briefing was quite the other way round. More often than not we were asked to make the case against the Services being allowed more resources and against having civilian amenities further pared down. The paramount danger was conceived to be that the Services would get too much and the civilians too little.

There were two aspects of this. On the one hand, it was thought that it would be bad for civilian morale if the common way of life was made too harsh. This argument would not necessarily have availed by itself. On the other side, it was held that the requirements of the Services were normally exorbitant and that the resources released on their behalf, to the detriment of civilian life, would merely be wasted.

Of course no effort was to be spared in getting the maximum production of really key weapons — aircraft, tanks, small arms ammunition, scientific devices of all kinds, secret weapons. It was our daily duty to keep our eyes on the output of all these things and to warn the Prime Minister of any short-fall below the target. Sometimes we had to work out a plan for the projected production of some item, such as bomber aircraft, with which the Prime Minister could prod the authorities to greater efforts.

But Service requirements stretched over a much vaster area than the weapons designed to destroy or deflect the enemy. There were all the stores and reserves, the uniforms and camp equipment. On the side of manpower Churchill was convinced that there was a vast accumulation of redundant personnel in the tail of the Army. A so-called 'requirement' of the Services was just any figure that a junior staff officer chose to write on a piece of paper. There was a classic occasion on which the Prof. got the requirement for anti-aircraft shells defeated at some staff committee by calculating how many thousands of shells would, according to this requirement, be needed to bring down each separate enemy bomber and showing that the resources required for their production would be many times as great as the damage that the enemy bomber could, on the most pessimistic assumption, inflict. It was our duty to winnow through the various figures in order to find instances where the 'requirements' could be reduced to absurdity.

Waste of effort involved in the production of redundant stores and of shipping required to import the materials for them might have a cumulative adverse effect. If it meant that the civilian population had to be worse fed, clad and warmed, and that transport facilities were reduced and queues made even longer, then the productivity of the country would in due course decline.

I have no doubt that in 1940 the civilian population would have been willing, with unimpaired morale, to undergo any sacrifices, however onerous, that it was called upon to make. There was no lack of will to endure the utmost at that time. But it may not always be wise to accept the full measure of sacrifice offered. Many weary years lay ahead in 1940. It may be noted that the great words with which Churchill called upon the nation, 'blood and toil and tears and sweat' did not include the word 'austerity'. He was against it. If people were under-nourished, if they lacked sufficient fuel, if transportation became ever more difficult, then there was the danger that their productivity, yes, and their morale too, would decline by imperceptible stages. Before Pearl Harbour, when it remained exceedingly difficult to see how a decisive victory over Germany could be achieved, it was the dictum in our office that victory would go to the nation in which civilian morale was the better sustained over a seemingly interminable term of years. Churchill was determined that the standard of living of the people should be kept up to the greatest possible extent. I do not believe that it is to this day widely appreciated that the British owe to Churchill not only victory, but also the maintenance of a much better way of life during the dragging war years than they would have had, but for his unremitting attention and repeated interventions on behalf of the comfort of the civilian population. That is a point that the official war histories tend not to stress, but it is one most relevant to the final assessment of Churchill's qualities as a war leader.

These doctrines were promulgated to S Branch by the Prof. They clearly represented his own views. I at once became uneasy. Was it right to assist in composing briefs against asking for greater sacrifices by civilians, against what in common parlance was called an all-out war effort ? Was I being led along by the Prof. ? Was this precisely what I had feared, when accepting service ? Was there some quirk in the Prof.'s mind that wanted to make him kind to the civilians, or, better, I should say, to do down the Services ? With this in mind I scrutinized Churchill's red ink markings on the Cabinet papers with exceptional acuity. It soon became evident to me that this was Churchill's own genuine personal view. Churchill and the Prof. evidently thought alike on this topic. In due course I was eventually to have abundant evidence of what Churchill thought.

It was remarkable how completely the minds of Churchill and the Prof. worked in harmony, not only on this matter, but on many others connected with the war. It occurred to me to wonder, having regard especially to the Prof.'s views about France and Germany in the 'twenties, whether the Prof. was nothing more than a sort of emanation of Churchill. One could entertain such a view only to dismiss it. I already knew the Prof.'s mind intimately as early as 1923. I do not believe that in that year he was as yet closely in Churchill's confidence. The Prof.'s methods of thought were very characteristic. There was a complete continuity from 1923 onwards. Furthermore, the Prof. conveyed his thoughts to me about many subjects with which Churchill had no concern. There was a certain characteristic mark upon all those which rendered them unmistakably his own. The ˙ fact appeared to be inexpugnable, that these two minds moved alike — independently. Perhaps that was why they had, in the first instance, come together and formed a lifelong friendship.

Confronted with the fact that these two great men thought together on this question of sustaining civilian morale, I felt that it was not for me to interpose an opposite view. I had sufficient modesty to think that Churchill knew better how to run a war than I did. In the end I became entirely convinced that their common point of view on this matter was right.

The consequence of these background assumptions was that we tended to argue against fresh demands for manpower by the Services ; in the allocation of shipping we favoured giving a higher quota to food and a smaller one to materials. Within the domain of food we had our special ideas. We favoured the continued maintenance in this country of live cattle, a 'reserve on the hoof', and of chickens also. If there was one thing that seemed obvious to the official planners on the outbreak of war, it was that the importation of animal feeding stuffs must be cut right down ; of course they were in fact greatly reduced ; but we were against carrying this policy to the final extreme, if it meant a premature slaughter of cattle here. And we argued that chickens were highly economical converters of imported grain.

Medical experts and dieticians were called upon to furnish their views through official channels, and these eventually came up to the top level. They met with the Prof.'s extreme scorn. He assured the Prime Minister that he need pay no attention to all this rubbish. We were told by the experts that vegetable protein could to a great extent serve as a substitute for animal protein ; at one point it looked as if, should the worst come to the worst, we would be reduced to a diet largely consisting of oatmeal. The views of the dieticians seemed to chime in with those who wished to reduce the livestock in Britain and eliminate the import of animal feeding stuffs. All this aroused the utmost wrath of the Prof. Although a vegetarian in his own person, in relation to public policy for the war effort he was an extreme anti-vegetarian.

The Prof. implied in his verbal comments that he knew just as much about the processes of human nutrition as the experts ; he could tell them exactly where they got off. This may sound very improper. But the fact of the matter was that he did have an extraordinarily wide range of scientific knowledge ; he was something of a pantomath within the field of science ; and he had most excellent hunches. I had had so long an experience of his refuting and confounding scientists in the Christ Church Common Room on matters within their own special fields and right outside his own, that in my heart of hearts I thought that the Prof. might quite well be right on these dietetic questions.

Not only did he want the people to get the full amount of calories and animal protein required to sustain their efficiency, and to this end he was prepared to reduce imports of materials, which would merely go to swell the stores of army quartermasters, but he was also extremely keen that our diet should be as palatable and varied as possible. Alas, I do not recall that our diet in the later years of war was very delectable or varied. But of this I am sure, that it was a great deal better than it would have been, but for the persistent advocacy of the Prof. with Churchill, who was, of course, entirely of like mind. The quiet, but supreme, self-assurance with which the Prof. expressed his withering contempt for the views of the dietetical experts must have been a comfort to Churchill in his resolution to pursue this policy. The encased and reserved Prof. may not have felt a warm glow of sympathy for the 'common man'; but, when it came down to brass tacks, I guess that he did more than any other person concerned with the planning of our war economy, except only for Churchill himself, to make the lot of the common man less dreary.

*

While the others in S Branch were busy with their telephones, their masses of documentation and their slide-rules, I had the more cushy duty of going out to attend committees, Ministerial and official. I used to go regularly to such bodies as the Production Council and the Food Council. It was not my duty to intervene at these high-level gatherings, but only to report proceedings back; I had many opportunities of forming impressions of our wartime Ministers, but this is not the place to describe them.

There were many other inter-departmental meetings. I recall an occasion at a meeting of the committee on drop forgings, which were in very short supply in one phase; the chair was taken by an able and determined civil servant; I happened to sit next to an economist from the Economic Section of the War Cabinet Office. The chairman on arrival cast a stern look in our direction, and said in distinctly audible tones: 'The usual time-wasters here, I see'. I felt this a little unfair, as I made it a rule to say nothing, unless there was some special point on which I was briefed; my main duty was to report back, with a view to our having a comprehensive view of what was going forward in the different sectors of the war effort.

Soon after Churchill became Prime Minister, the Treasury invited the Prof. to come for a talk, and I went with him, with a view to our taking cognizance of the work of the Exchange Requirements Committee. I attended its meetings regularly ; the chair was taken by Sir David Waley, who was very kind and hospitable to my views. But there was only one line on which I ventured to make comments. In the early days of the war, before Lend-Lease, and before even the Jesse-Jones loan was arranged, there was an appalling conflict between the need to save dollars and the need to buy our imports where the shipping haul would be the shortest. It made a great difference to shipping whether one bought wheat in the United States or Australia. In the later part of the war we tended to buy as much as we possibly could on the short North Atlantic haul ; but in the early days, when the American Administration was not allowed to give us credit and we did not see where the dollars to pay for orders for aircraft and other vital weapons already placed were coming from, the dollar shortage just could not be ignored. The tendency of my advice was to encourage the Treasury to go for the longer haul, on the ground that, in the opinion of our Branch, the estimates by the Ministry of Shipping of future availabilities tended to be biased on the pessimistic side.

There was one inter-departmental committee where I was by no means inactive. Early in 1941 we discovered that twenty million pairs of trousers had been produced for an army consisting at that time of only about two million men, i.e. ten pairs per man ; furthermore, the plan was that production should run at a still higher rate. We found similar figures for other items of Army uniform and for Air Force uniforms also.

I had already been regularly attending the inter-departmental committee on the allocation of materials. The chair was taken by Colonel Llewellin (later Lord Llewellin), and I was immensely impressed by his tactful handling, to which I have never seen an adequate tribute. It was a case of a 'dual rôle'. He was Under-Secretary to the Ministry of Aircraft Production, whose Minister, Lord Beaverbrook, was known to be — very rightly — grabbing all available materials on behalf of the Air Force. At the same time Colonel Llewellin had the quasi-judicial task of confronting the serried ranks of officials from all the different departments and apportioning the precious materials among them. Despite the fact that on most occasions he openly assigned a hundred per cent of requirements to the Ministry of Aircraft Production, he never seemed to lose the confidence of the meeting for his fairness. The other departments also could make claims that their needs were vital for our war effort. I remember one occasion when an assignment to himself, personifying the Ministry of Aircraft Production, of the lion's share seemed particularly blatant, Llewellin directed our attention upwards by a gentle motion of his arm, and we heard the drone of enemy bombers engaged on a daylight raid on London.

This seemed the correct place to raise the question of Army trousers, etc. But I also burrowed down into the various offices where the requirements were computed, and entered into all the detailed figures with the officers concerned. My researches took me to the Admiralty establishment at Bath. According to our calculations the Navy record was much the most satisfactory of the three. The reason seemed to be a simple one, namely, that the ratings were given an allowance for their clothing which they bought at shops ; thus they were able to economize as much as they could, provided only that they kept themselves sufficiently smart.

Curbing the requirements for clothing was a long-drawn-out campaign. I recall a dreadful evening. At a sub-committee we reached agreement on certain principles. Colonel Llewellin wished to catch a train to Scotland at dinner-time and would not be back in London until the following Monday, when we should have to face the large meeting. As we had agreed on the principle, he thought it would be all right for him to depart for Scotland. I eyed him firmly ; I did not think it was enough to have agreed on the principle ; if we had not seen how it worked out under the detailed heads, things might go wrong at the big meeting. He was upset at the idea of not catching his train, but I remained ruthless. I reminded myself that I was in effect speaking for the Prime Minister. He put off his departure. Afterwards I felt a little rueful about my stern treatment.

For that evening there occurred what proved to be one of the worst night raids on London. We sat in an upper room of the I.C.I. building overlooking the Thames. The man on duty put his head round the door and said, 'We are going to have a rough night'. We looked out of the window ; the enemy had dropped lights, which hung low in the air and outlined very clearly the whole curve of the Thames. The bombs crashed down and the table shook repeatedly ; it was the night on which the Admiralty had a hit. Colonel Llewellin was a soldier, and assured us, quietly and confidently, 'they won't hit us', and we proceeded with our figures until a very late hour.

When I reported to the Prof. that I had secured a cut in the requirements of, say, fifty per cent of what we had sought, expecting compliments, I got none. A hundred per cent was good enough for him. I should have to go back to the Committee. Sir Arnold Plant was the head of Colonel Llewellin's set-up, and sometimes took the chair at the big meeting. I recall that, when I came back for the third time, asking for still more, he got quite cross ; I could hardly blame him. On the whole, Colonel Llewellin and Plant were fully co-operative, and between us we secured large economies.

It was not long afterwards that the official proposal for

a clothing ration came to us. The Prof. reacted in the usual way. The proposed ration seemed very small. It was intolerable that the people should be oppressed by these wretched officials. They would be sufficiently patriotic to be economical in their clothing on their own account ; different people had different requirements ; some might already have a large wardrobe in hand. He was determined to oppose a clothing ration with all his wonted skill in argument.

But here was a point on which I felt that I could no longer go with him. We had made a tremendous cut in Service requirements ; it was true that their allotment exceeded many times over what was proposed for civilians in the rationing scheme, and the Prof. made much of this point. However, the civilian population was larger. Imports of cotton and wool occupied a substantial shipping tonnage — of course we knew these figures very well. The textile industry was also engaging very considerable quantities of manpower, of which by 1941 a shortage was becoming acute. My friend, Richard Kahn, was busy in the Board of Trade, working on schemes for releasing manpower and materials from inessential civilian output ; I had some talks with him at that time. I told the Prof. that I could not see that there was a case against the economy in men and materials that would result from a clothing rationing scheme. We had cut down the forces ; now it was the turn of the civilians. I did not think that it would damage morale to have people curbed on their purchases of clothing ; they would not mind being shabby, if everyone else had to be shabby too.

But the Prof. was adamant. He wrote out a skilful minute for the Prime Minister, packed with arguments and figures, and I believed that, armed with this excellent brief, Churchill would block the project in the Cabinet for the time being. I argued strenuously on the other side.

I returned to him shortly afterwards. He showed me a

new version of his brief. It seemed very much the same as the previous one, except that he had added these words. 'Roy Harrod, favouring austerity as usual, does not agree with these arguments.' This made me very furious. I asked the Prof. how he could possibly say such a thing, considering all the work that I had done extracting figures, composing minutes, engaging in negotiations, all designed to help him in his campaign against austerity. How could he say that I 'usually favoured' austerity? This was the first time that I had flatly opposed his view on any major point. I lost my temper. I stormed up and down his room. I summoned up all the fire and fury of which I was capable. This was the fiercest 'row' that I ever recall having with the Prof. I told him that I would not only resign, but that I would tell Churchill that I was resigning because he misrepresented me in his minutes. (I believe that I had one other instance in which I thought that he had misrepresented me concerning the great controversy of the 'reserve on the hoof'.)

The Prof. jettisoned his minute. He composed another one in much milder terms, still expressing opposition to the rationing scheme, but furnishing no figures and arguments, so that it did not give Churchill a brief for opposing it in the Cabinet. The measure went through according to the official plan. I have no doubt that a clothing rationing would in any case have come in two or three months; but I like to think that my stormy interview succeeded in preventing a postponement at that time.

My regard for the Official Secrets Act naturally prevented my giving a warning in the home that a ration of clothing was coming along. But, after it was announced, my vanity impelled me to boast that I believed that it was entirely due to my personal effort that it had been expedited by a few months. This was not at all well received.

It was a little later that on another point connected with

rations we were all able to work together in the happiest accord. The Ministry of Food suddenly confronted us with a proposition that they intended to introduce six new coupons for the rationing of six new types of food. I forget now how the list was made up. There were such items as biscuits, rice, sultanas and currants, etc. In each case the proposed ration appeared to be meagre in the extreme. Churchill and the Prof. were both entirely opposed to this further dose of austerity.

The economists of S Branch had the idea that the hardship would be greatly mitigated if these various foods could be put on to a single 'points rationing' scheme. The consumption of the six foods in the aggregate could be cut by as much as the Minister of Food desired, but each individual would be free to use his points on those particular items that he valued most. This idea appealed to the Prof., since it preserved the individual freedom of choice. Of the foods that each individual preferred he would be able to get, not merely the derisory amount proposed under the rigid rationing scheme, but probably as much as he wanted. If under the general allotment of points one commodity went into short supply while the other became redundant, this could be adjusted by a change in the points value of the various foods in terms of one another ; if biscuits ran short one could increase the quantity of rice that had to be sacrificed to obtain a pound of biscuits ; or conversely.

To the best of my recollection this scheme was initially sponsored, not by us, but by the Economic Section of the War Cabinet Office. Unhappily the Ministry of Food pronounced it administratively unworkable. There was a precedent for it in the clothing rationing scheme, where the available ration could be implemented alternatively in the purchase of a pair of trousers, or of so many shirts, etc. I do not know why it was deemed workable in one case and not in the other ; it may have been that the different types of food had more diversified channels of trade. Thus we were in happy accord with the Economic Section, as I recall, and both offices were annoyed by the negative attitude of the Ministry of Food. At that time S Branch had somewhat greater power than the Economic Section in a situation of this sort. It was difficult for the Economic Section to carry the matter further, if a Ministry said a scheme was unworkable. But we could bring into action our great big gun — Churchill himself.

Churchill told the Minister of Food that he would not agree to his proposal for rationing six new items of food. He, Churchill, was responsible for sustaining the morale of the whole people. He could not allow them to be curtailed in the few remaining items of food that might diversify their diet. It was the duty of the Minister to maintain a supply of these foods. Churchill was in a strong position, as he could point out how he had consistently striven to help the Minister of Food, by getting for food imports a larger allocation of the available shipping. Thus, so far as the Prime Minister was concerned, there just would not be any rationing of these extra foods. But Churchill had been well briefed by the Prof. on the possibility of a points rationing scheme. Of course if the Minister proposed a points rationing scheme his attitude might be different. After that the Ministry of Food discovered that the points rationing scheme would be administratively workable after all. Thus I believe that S Branch may claim the credit for that modest amelioration of the rigours of rationing.

*

I have referred already to the large group of economists who were gathered together by Mr. Francis Hemming in the summer of 1940, with a view to building up some kind of general economic staff under the auspices of Mr. Greenwood. This party was subsequently split into two separate organizations, the Central Statistical Office and the Economic Section of the War Cabinet Office. This splitting was due to the strong insistence of the Prof. The Central Statistical Office was to have the duty of supplying figures for the information of the Cabinet and others concerned, but would not be allowed to make any comments on the figures, other than comments of a purely statistical character, nor to tender any economic advice. It was the duty of the Economic Section to make comments and tender advice in relation to those figures, or generally. The Prof. held that it was wrong in principle that identical people should be responsible both for establishing the correct figures and also expressing opinions, which might be controversial, about the lessons to be drawn from the figures. The figures themselves must be above suspicion ; however honourable the statisticians, there might arise an embarrassment, if these statisticians were using their own figures in support of some policy, with which others disagreed. It was one of those cases where it was expedient not only that justice should be done, but also that justice should be clearly seen to be done.

The Prof. may have had it in mind that an embarrassing situation could arise in the event of a disagreement between S Branch and what came to be the Economic Section. Happily, I believe that, as mutual consultations between members of S Branch and members of the Economic Section became closer, for the reasons which I have stated earlier, there was less and less chance of any such embarrassment arising. But this could not be foreseen. I believe that the division of Hemming's happy party of workers into two separate parts caused some ruefulness at the time. But I am confident that the Prof.'s basic principle was correct, and that he did well to insist upon it at an early stage. I was put on a small committee, including Sir Edward Bridges, to supervise the setting up of the two separate bodies, but I do not recall that the committee had to meet more than once or twice; all went forward smoothly.[1]

I have already referred to the view, shared by Churchill and the Prof., that it was undesirable to err on the side of pessimism in presenting the facts of the war situation to the public. The official mind seemed inclined to think that it was good to represent the facts as a little worse than they really were, in order to brace the public for further sacrifices. Churchill was entirely opposed to this policy. Let the truth be told, but not a pessimistically biased version of the truth. In all this S Branch had its part to play.

There was another quite distinct aspect of our battle against 'gloominess', which surprised me very much when I first apprehended it. Just as Churchill wished to safeguard the public from an unduly gloomy version of the progress of events, so did the Prof. want to safeguard Churchill himself. Thus, when reports or forecasts came in that, in our view, presented matters in too gloomy a light, the Prof. was anxious that we should get busy quickly in contesting these views and putting a more favourable forecast before the Prime Minister. I made the Prof. aware of my surprise that he should have anxiety lest Churchill be unduly depressed. Churchill's own morale was surely in no danger of collapsing!

[1] Sir George Thomson (*op. cit.* p. 60) refers to this episode, but in a manner that might cause confusion. His account seems to suggest that there were only two bodies involved, viz. the Central Statistical Office and what he calls 'The Section', presumably referring to the Prime Minister's Statistical Section (p. 58). In fact there were three quite separate bodies, viz. the Central Statistical Office, the Economic Section of the War Cabinet Office, and the Prime Minister's Statistical Section. The genesis of the first two of these is described in the text above; the third was simply S Branch, which had existed from almost the beginning of the war in the Admiralty and moved with Churchill to the Prime Minister's office.

Of course it was our duty to see that he had the best possible estimate ; but I did not understand why the Prof. was so deeply concerned that any estimate tending towards the pessimistic should be quickly corrected.

In one of the most serious talks that I ever had with the Prof. about the utility of S Branch, the Prof. put this forward as almost its most important task. 'If S Branch were broken up, then Churchill would be left to the tender mercies of the officials with their gloomy forecasts.'

I found it hard to see the force of this argument at the time. I could not see Churchill as a person who had to be put in cotton wool. He would not quail before a gloomy forecast. I have often thought over this matter since, and, the more I have thought of it, the more I have tended to think that the Prof. was right.

Churchill was carrying a tremendous load of responsibility at that time. Of course the Prof. never hesitated to put forward any item of bad information that was real and important. Indeed it was our primary task to be on a keen look-out for any shortfall in key supplies, and from time to time we had to give Churchill some terrifying piece of information. Why should the cares of this man, waging such a formidable battle against odds as he was, be increased by a piece of woeful information that we ourselves believed to be phoney ? And there is this point to be borne in mind. Although in so many ways Churchill was an Englishman to the core, the proud emblem of our race, he had one characteristic that was not perhaps typically English. If an Englishman is given a piece of bad news, his reaction is too apt to be that we carry on just as before and hope for the best. But Churchill's reaction to a piece of bad news was that something must immediately be *done* about it. That was where he differentiated himself in his attitude to Hitler during the 'thirties. If these doleful prognostications really represented the facts of the case, then he would immediately worry himself about the need to devise some measures for correcting the situation. But suppose that the whole thing was a false alarm. Suppose that the situation was not as bad as it was painted. Churchill would have been worried needlessly. He had quite enough real problems to contend with. Why set him thinking about a problem that was not a real one and merely represented the pessimistic outlook of a compiler of figures ?

I have tried to state what I believe to have been at the bottom of the Prof.'s extreme concern that gloomy forecasts which came up to the Prime Minister should not be allowed to stand uncorrected. But there was a touch of humanity in it too. If Churchill wanted to keep the people in good heart, the Prof. wanted to keep Churchill in good heart. Churchill should not be depressed in any way, except in so far as was needful for the efficient discharge of his duties as Prime Minister and war leader.

Experiences since the war have tended to make me still more sympathetic with the Prof.'s perennial annoyance at gloomy official forecasts. Over and over again since the war gloomy official views about the position of Britain have been falsified by the subsequent events. It may be that gloominess is an occupational malady, caused by the way of life of officials or their expert advisers. They seem to have a tendency to view matters in a more pessimistic way than those who are out in the field, getting on with the job. These gloomy interpretations have had many adverse practical consequences, because they have tended to undermine world confidence in Britain at a time when world confidence has been much needed. It is a paradox ; but I believe that the Prof., despite his innate tendency to pessimism, and despite the tortuosities of mind that he sometimes manifested, took a more sane and balanced view of our position throughout the war than the average denizen of Whitehall. He saw things in better proportion. And he was determined that Churchill should see things as he saw them and not be the victim of the pessimism of any chance official.

*

In the Admiralty we had rooms conveniently adjacent to those of the First Lord. The Prof. had to wait up to a late hour ; Churchill often chose to have appointments with important visitors, such as the First Sea Lord, in the early hours of the morning, and he liked to see the Prof. at the end of the day's work. This was not out of accord with the Prof.'s settled habits, except that now he had to keep reasonably early hours in the morning. We did not all usually sit up so late unless there was some 'Action This Day' paper to work upon or the Prof. was seeing Churchill on some matter about which he might wish to refer back to one of us. We did often sit up very late. I once asked the First Lord's first private secretary how he was enjoying his work. He replied that under Churchill's predecessors he had in effect been First Lord of the Admiralty, but that now he found himself simply Churchill's secretary ; on the whole he found the *latter* job the more interesting. What about the late hours ? He could take them in his stride ; but he confessed that he had found it rather irksome when at, say, 3 A.M. he put his head round the First Lord's door, to discover if things were drawing to a close, to see Churchill and the Prof. sitting on each side of the fireplace quietly reading the next morning's newspapers.

When Churchill became Prime Minister we migrated to Richmond Terrace (and at the end of 1940 moved over to Great George Street, where we were immediately above the Prime Minister's suite). When the night blitz came on Mr.

Francis Hemming offered me a bed in some space that he had acquired for his group of economists in a basement of Scotland Yard. There I found myself among old friends; it was a pleasure to be with them. Our night quarters were not as secure as I, at least, imagined them to be at the time. We went down to a low level under the large Scotland Yard building and had to walk a considerable distance between beds, on which members of the police force were lying, ready for action, with their boots sticking out at the end of their blankets. Some of us slept in a little room where there was a vast boiler, which made strange noises during the night. One had gone so far that one fancied oneself secure. But actually one had gone too far, and almost gone out at the other end. On subsequent investigation I found that there was little dividing us from the paving stones of the Thames embankment. It was not surprising that we were severely shaken when a land mine dropped on the London County Hall.

During this period of the blitz the Prof. had an awkward interval during the evenings. Naturally members of the Branch wished to get to their respective homes in reasonable time, unless there was some special business requiring their presence. But the Prof. had to wait on for his early morning session with Churchill. He began to get a little worn; I suspect that his heart was already giving him some trouble, although he never complained of ill-health; his routine was certainly more strenuous than anything he had been used to for many years. What he principally complained of was that in the final stage of the evening he had to wait about in a cellar and there he was in the company of other members of Churchill's entourage; he found their conversation uninteresting, and this got on his nerves.

I was given a mandate to find a house not too far from London, for S Branch to use in the evenings. I had a splendid bit of paper, giving the Prime Minister's authority to commandeer suitable premises. After visiting a number of houses, I came to one that the Prof.'s own family had previously lived in at Marlow. I have an uncomfortable memory that, flushed with self-importance, I spoke brusquely to the old gentleman living there, with a menace of dispossession. By a coincidence a larger and more suitable house next door was vacant ; one night shortly before that, our success in deflecting the enemy's beams had caused them to unload a vast quantity of bombs into the meadows outside Marlow, presumably supposing that they were over Coventry or some such place. The lady who lived in the larger house decided that Marlow must be the prime target for the enemy, and moved herself to the Lake District ; we went in.

At about five-thirty or six in the evening, we transferred ourselves, along with piles of cabinet boxes, into three or four cars, provided by the good offices of the W.V.S. — Lady Reading was a friend of the Prof.'s — and proceeded to Marlow. Mrs. Montagu Johnson proved a very efficient organizer of transport. She proved efficient in another way also. We had two man-servants at Marlow, who were called up in due course. The Prof. was extremely indignant at these two men going into the 'tail' of the Army, instead of doing valuable work for him, and was appeased only when the higher authorities informed him that the male staff of Buckingham Palace had also been called up. I appealed to Mrs. Montagu Johnson, who promptly found us two women. But she got into grave trouble with the W.V.S. for doing that, since she was responsible for transport, not domestic service. When pleading on her behalf — in vain — with Lady Reading, on the ground that it was clever of her to have found us servants so quickly, I remarked that my friends told me — this was in 1941 — that it was becoming quite difficult to get servants. 'You must have a very gloomy set of friends', Lady Reading replied.

When we arrived at Marlow we settled down to further labours, working from the papers that we had brought or discussing problems with the Prof. We probably got through more work in this way, since there was no longer any question of getting home in reasonable time, and we often worked very late.

I do not recall that the Prof. had any recreations during all that time. He was content to study his documents until a late hour. His only distraction that I can remember was his attempt to develop a theory for relating the distribution of prime numbers to general probability principles. He worked out something and sought the advice of Professor David Champernowne, who was in S Branch for a time. The Prof. continued to pursue this line of thought for some years.

Hospitality was greatly curtailed during the war. The Prof. told me that he tended to refuse such invitations as still came to him, because he found it trying to be cut off from all subjects of serious conversation. His close proximity to Churchill meant that special significance would be attached to whatever he said or indeed to his refusal to express an opinion. That brought home with startling vividness to my mind the fundamental limitations to his range of discourse. How one welcomed in those war days an occasion when all reference, direct or indirect, to matters relating to the war was taboo, and one could engage in cosy, comfortable, human talk. For the Prof. the taboo entailed a void, which he shunned.

He had very conscientious, perhaps even exaggerated, views on the security question. They fitted in well with his natural inclination to secretiveness. In the early days of the blitz we had dining with us in Christ Church a distinguished banker, who was a member of the Common Room and a familiar figure there. The Prof. was asked how London was faring, and replied that the bomb damage had so far been trivial. The banker did not quite agree, affirming that out of so many hundreds of their branches in London over 90 per cent had sustained some damage. On analysis this probably meant only that their windows had been broken ; London had lost most of its glass by that time. The Prof. turned on him furiously, to the embarrassment of our colleagues, and said that he would report him to MI5 for spreading false information, calculated to undermine the morale of the people.

One evening at Marlow Mr. Bensusan-Butt, then the Prof.'s private secretary, went over to dine at a neighbouring Air Force unit at Medmenham. There they had a complete collection of the photographs taken by bombers over Germany, which they thought that they might show to Mr. Bensusan-Butt, since he was a member of the Prime Minister's private branch. What the photographs revealed was appalling. The vast majority of our bombs appeared to have fallen on the open countryside. This was a case when we had to carry very bad news to the Prime Minister. I believe that this little incident caused him to heighten the pressure for the production of scientific equipment designed to improve the target finding of our Air Force.[1]

In defining his duties to me, the Prof. explained that Churchill wished him to range over the whole field of our war effort. There were only two topics with which, by mutual agreement, he was not to concern himself. One was actual military operations. The other was everything to do with personal appointments and promotions. The latter was probably a very wise restriction. But it seems that all human rules have exceptions, for one evening the Prof. asked that we should drive in our car together without anyone else.

[1] Sir George Thomson gives an account of this (*op. cit.* p. 62).

They were much worried, he said, by the difficulty of thinking whom they could send to Washington in succession to Lord Lothian, who had just died. The post was very important, and they could not think of anyone suitable. I reflected a few minutes. 'Why not Lord Halifax?' I said. The idea seemed quite new to him, and he reacted badly to it at first. 'We cannot send a man of Munich.' I argued back. That was all past history now; anyhow Lord Halifax had not been the prime architect of our foreign policy in the late 'thirties; if he was good enough to be our Foreign Secretary (as he was at the moment), he was good enough to be our Ambassador in Washington; he was basically a man of first-class intelligence, and we should need that sorely in our relations with the United States during the coming years; as soon as the Americans got to know him well, they would like and respect him. Although the idea seemed to be novel and was at first rejected, he appeared to be convinced by my argument. But whether he passed it on to the Prime Minister I never inquired.

Our daily migrations to Marlow continued for more than a year.

*

In the course of 1941 a new interest arose for me. During that year the Atlantic Charter was signed, and it was evident that the Mutual Aid Agreement would eventually be signed also in one form or another. Article 7 of the latter provided for mutual discussions about post-war economic policy. In the autumn of that year Keynes was already getting busy on his draft for a 'Clearing Union'.[1] It was thought that Britain would have to decide upon her attitude to, and possibly frame, proposals under other heads also, such as commercial policy,

[1] For an account of these matters see my *Life of J. M. Keynes*, pp. 509-517 and 525-585.

international investment and commodity plans.

I became much involved in these questions. I had correspondence with Keynes on his various drafts of the Clearing Union. I attended meetings of small groups and of the official committees dealing with these matters. I recall that I spent much time upon, and attended all the meetings of the committee dealing with, Keynes's plan for post-war buffer stocks. I wrote some memoranda of my own on these problems.

The Prof. was entirely satisfied at my engaging in these activities. I showed him my memoranda and explained to him what was going forward. There was a difference of opinion in official circles. Keynes, in due course, came to advocate a bold policy of active co-operation with the Americans in making far-reaching plans for a more satisfactory international economic order than we had had before the war. Others were inclined to be more reticent, urging that Britain's post-war difficulties might make it unwise for her to commit herself to American ideology too far, and that we should allow ourselves to be drawn into these discussions only to the extent that our hand was forced. The Prof. was entirely in favour of the more active response to the American initiative. Thus we thought alike on these matters, and no difference arose. The cautious party was very reluctant in regard to our signing Article 7 of the Mutual Aid Agreement ; there were arguments over the form of words ; there were genuine difficulties in regard to Imperial Preference. It was hoped that, when Churchill went over to the United States shortly after Pearl Harbour, he and Roosevelt would come to a final settlement on this disputed point. Churchill told the Prof. that he found it very difficult to get Roosevelt to discuss these matters, and we heard from American sources that Roosevelt had found it very difficult to get Churchill to discuss them ! The Prof. used his influence in favour of an early signature.

There was complete sympathy between myself and the Prof. on all these matters. I did not bother him with my detailed comments on Keynes's plans. They did not interest the Prof. and he was willing to leave the matter to me.

*

It is now necessary for me to go back in this narrative to May 1940, when Churchill became Prime Minister. It will be remembered that this was a great crisis in our affairs. Hitler had started his major invasion of Western Europe, and no one knew how things would turn out. Bad news began to come in rather quickly. We still did not know what damage he would be able to inflict on Britain herself by air attack.

As I have explained already, my original idea about the project of joining the Prof. in the Admiralty was that Churchill needed a special band of helpers and servers there, outside the ordinary Civil Service establishment, because it was desirable that he should take a more active part in Cabinet decisions than is normal for a First Lord of the Admiralty. The whole point of the business was that, although Churchill was actually First Lord, we felt that he ought to be Prime Minister. Everything should be done to help him to get a grip on the whole situation, and not merely on naval affairs. For this he needed a special staff; so far as that was concerned I was most glad to join it. My only mental reservation had been as to whether I could play a really useful part or would be a fifth wheel on the coach.

When Churchill became Prime Minister he could organize everything as he liked; the whole nation was at his disposal. As stated before, I had not fully grasped, when I joined, that he would still feel the need to have a special branch outside the regular machinery of government. For a First Lord to have a special branch, when he is *en route* for the Prime

Ministership and perhaps already doing some work that might have pertained to the Prime Minister, and for the Prime Minister to have a special branch, are two quite separate ideas. I was aware, of course, that during the First World War Lloyd George had decided that it was useful to have his own set of private advisers, his 'garden suburb', as a make-weight to the official machinery.

So far as I was concerned, this idea did not appeal to me. I had no special knowledge of the advantages and disadvantages of a Prime Minister having a 'garden suburb'. This was entirely outside my range of knowledge. All I did know was that such a plan was uncongenial to my own temperament. I was quite sure that I did not wish to become involved in it.

Accordingly I asked the Prof. what was to happen to us now that Churchill was becoming Prime Minister. At first it was not quite clear what the answer was, because grave events were moving so rapidly in France, that one had to continue living, so to speak, from day to day, and we carried on as usual. But gradually it appeared that this was not a mere makeshift, pending an opportunity for giving the matter full consideration and making new arrangements, but that we were to continue to carry on just as before *sine die*.

And so, after a lapse of a certain time (two or three weeks?), I told the Prof. that I did not care for this arrangement, that I did not wish to continue to serve on this basis. I had joined him owing to the special circumstances in the Admiralty, and now expected some regularization of the position; otherwise I would prefer, for my own part, to drop out. I pleaded with him in favour of a new kind of set-up, such as the merging of our office into some kind of Economic General Staff.

He unburdened himself to me at this juncture in a sincere and natural way. We were walking together in St. James's

Park. We sat down on a rough bench to continue the talk more easily. St. James's Park was beginning to suffer from the general untidiness of wartime ; there seemed to be a lot of poor people milling around ; I thought that I had never known the Prof. place himself in such close proximity to the proletariate. But he wanted to talk without more ado. 'This is not the time for false modesty', he began. It certainly was not ; France was falling ; the situation was grave. 'I happen to believe that I have more brains than all these other people', and he made a gesture with his arm. I took 'all these other people' to include the Cabinet Ministers, except Churchill, the chief officials in the Civil Service, and I do not doubt that he also had in mind such Admirals and Generals as were available to command our forces. Because he had more brains than all the others, he could render unique service to the country. For this purpose what he required was *power* ; that was to be gained by acquiring more and more knowledge of all that was going on. If he had ample leisure to study certain aspects of the war effort deeply while others were engaged on routine duties, this would give him the knowledge, both wide and deep, that others lacked ; this in turn would give him power, and that power he would deploy in the service of his country and of Churchill. Such was the gist of his confession, mumbled rather, in sentences that were sometimes obscure. But his general plan of campaign was perfectly plain. He told me, as we sat on that bench, that Churchill, as soon as he became Prime Minister, had offered him a position as a Minister of the Crown in charge of one of the great departments. He had refused that. He did not think that it was the way to get the power that he wished.

I could not but admit that I understood what he meant, and that from his own point of view his decision was probably right. But I still added that I did not think it was the right thing for me. This was becoming slightly unfriendly. Could

I not help him in his scheme for power? But I persisted. It was not what I had originally supposed that he meant when he told me that Churchill would still need us when he became Prime Minister. I went on worrying him, despite his disarming confession of faith, like a dog that will not release an article of clothing. As I did so, I began to feel very petty and ridiculous. There were these people milling around, looking dejected; the country could easily be defeated within a few months. Where should we all be then? So much depended on Churchill. In the light of this, what really did it matter whether my war work precisely suited my taste or not?

And yet I persisted. I felt that this was a crucial point and that I ought to persist, although it seemed so paltry and egoistic to do so. Finally the Prof. became cross. 'Things are too serious. I really have not time now to enter into all your personal difficulties.' And there the matter rested.

I dimly recall that he said that he would look at the problem again after things had settled down a little more, and that I did have a second discussion with him at the end of some months, leading to the same result.

I believe that I am right in saying that I mentioned my own personal problem only to one other person, namely Mr. Brendan Bracken. He was an acquaintance of mine of old standing; and, as he had been so stalwart a supporter of Churchill over many years and was now so close to him, I felt that I could mention the matter to him without being disloyal to Churchill. He was sympathetic, and promised to think if anything could be done about my case. But really there was nothing to be done.

I judge that the Prof. was open to criticism at this juncture, although the extenuating circumstances — the greatest crisis in the country's history and his intense preoccupation in helping Churchill in every way he could during those frightful times — were very great. On a strict view, he should have reopened the matter for unprejudiced consideration, if not at once, then after the lapse of a few months. Churchill had now become Prime Minister, and the situation had entirely changed. Did we, in the new circumstances, wish to continue as 'irregulars' or would we prefer some alternative? Churchill and he would understand, whichever way we decided.

I have no reason to suppose that Churchill himself had any knowledge of the way in which the Prof. handled this little problem. It would have been perfectly correct for the Prof. to ensure that the Prime Minister was not bothered with it. And I should suppose that he did so.

*

In the spring of 1942 I decided to resign. I think it is proper that I should set out my reasons for doing so to the best of my ability. And I will state at the outset that, after the events of 1940 that I have narrated, I had no further grievance against the Prof. He treated me with the greatest consideration and we worked in perfect accord. If we had an occasional rumpus, as over the question of the clothing ration, that did not serve to impair our relations and we remained on excellent terms.

Early in 1942 the idea returned strongly to my mind that I was a fifth wheel on the coach. For a time that had not been so. I had been very active for a considerable period and done much work that I felt to be useful. But the position was altering both inside S Branch and outside it.

Within the Branch the members had tended to settle down into an established routine and to have their own pigeon-holes. One was responsible for naval matters, one for the Army, etc. MacDougall's work remained more diversified.

He had established a perfect liaison with the Prof. and had demonstrated his wonderful talent for extracting from the official statistics the kind of point that appealed strongly to the Prof.'s mind. By his special character and talents he had become unquestionably the Prof.'s right-hand man.

Outside the Branch the position was altering. Sir John Anderson (Lord Waverley) was making his mark in his handling of questions of general economic policy. It seemed that in Anderson Churchill had found a man whom he could really trust for this purpose, and deservedly, and that therefore he would not think it necessary to give so large a part of his own mind to economic problems. For doing the kind of work that S Branch did for Churchill, Sir John Anderson had the advantage of the services of the Economic Section. Meanwhile a Ministry of Production had been formed, and it was the task of this organization to concern itself with production programmes, requirements, and the availability of supplies. It was evident that the staff of this Ministry would deal in a systematic way, as part of their regular duties, with many of the problems with which we had dealt in a free-lance way, precisely because there had so far been insufficient co-ordination within the normal machinery of government. In the early years of the war there was a flurry of inter-departmental committees. The central economic problems of the war were discussed in these committees, but the handling was not always adequate. I used to go from one to another as the representative of the Prime Minister's office, and the knowledge that I gleaned of how things were proceeding, or failing to proceed, was useful when I reported it back. As the war wore on, policy became less subject to change, the responsibilities of the different Ministers became better defined and they were able to settle down to their assigned tasks. There was less scope and need for the unattached watchdog.

There were periods in our office when work was slack, at least as far as I was concerned. There were always times when Churchill became so deeply immersed in critical operations, that it was felt that we could not usefully put a new point to him. The Prof., on his side, was interested only in a certain type of point. It must have a statistical background. I often raised questions with him about problems that I judged were being wrongly handled ; we might have a long discussion about them in which he seemed quite interested ; but if the matter was not closely related to a statistical question, he would just rise from the discussion, arguing that the point was not one for us. So I realized that I had been wasting my time.

During the earlier period of my active attendance at the inter-departmental committees I had not had much time to devote to research on statistical raw material. In 1942 I should have had to start up some new lines of investigation ; but really MacDougall had the whole statistical side thoroughly well mapped out. And so I came back to my old original analogy of the fifth wheel.

I have referred above to my contacts with Keynes and my attendance at inter-departmental committees concerned with putting forward proposals to the Americans for implementing Article 7 of the Mutual Aid Agreement and for post-war economic planning generally. During my last six months in S Branch these matters occupied the greater part of my active time. It might be supposed that this was a congenial occupation — it was — and well suited to my interests and capacities. Could I not find a suitable niche for myself in this work, now that the kind of work that I had previously been doing in S Branch seemed to be coming to a natural end ? It was in reflecting upon this matter that a thought occurred to me that, I believe that I am right in saying, was the most weighty reason for my decision to resign. I saw, as they say, a cloud no bigger than a man's hand.

So far the Prof. and I had been in cordial agreement on this range of questions, but he had not gone into the matters very deeply. He held that we should show ourselves thoroughly willing to co-operate with the Americans ; he was favourable to the idea of greater freedom of trade ; and he was not opposed to discussions at an early date. But as and when these discussions developed, there were bound to be controversies at home on a wide variety of points about what our right line should be. The Prof. was likely to have strong opinions on all these points, and I could not be sure in advance that they would coincide with mine.

On questions relating to the war effort, such as the proportions of resources that one should devote to the Services or to maintaining the civilians' standard of life, I was perfectly willing to believe that Churchill and the Prof. had a much better judgement than I had. But when it came to the economic planning of the post-war world, that would not necessarily be the case. These problems were very near the centre of those studies to which I had devoted my life and about which I held well-defined views. I was by no means sure that the judgement of Churchill, or even the joint judgement of Churchill and the Prof., would be better than mine. I was already reaching some maturity of years and not prepared to subordinate my opinions. If there was anyone at that time in deference to whom I might be prepared to waive my own opinions, it was Keynes, not the Prof.

It was precisely at this point that both the 'irregular' character of our establishment and the peculiar characteristics of the Prof. counted for much. If one was in a regular department of government in an advisory capacity, one stated one's views to the best of one's ability, but would not necessarily expect them to be accepted. One's station and its duties were fairly well-defined. One might hope that one's own views would prevail, but, if they did not, there was no personal implication or involvement.

But our little branch was different. It was too small for differences of opinion to be convenient. Its informality and intimacy, which from one point of view constituted its charm and attraction, carried danger. We all worked closely together, constituting, so to speak, a single spearhead. We had one view. That was the Prof.'s view. I am not suggesting that he was not open to persuasion. I believe that we persuaded him to change his views on a number of points ; but the most effective method of persuading him, almost the only method, was by bringing forward a *quantitative* argument. If we could show that the statistics were on our side, and presented him with the relevant figures, then he might well yield to us. But in the matters relating to post-war planning there might be alternative views that could not be determined by statistics alone.

And then there was the Prof.'s tendency to lead one along farther than one had originally intended to go, of which I had had twenty years of intimate experience. On the first engagement one might have a slight qualm, yet not think the difference material enough not to be willing to join forces with him. Then before one knew where one was, one had become involved in a further engagement, about which one's doubts were much more grave ; and then in another engagement, and so on. He might argue that the logic behind the third engagement was precisely the same as that behind the second, and that, having engaged in the second, one could not, if one was reasonable, hold back from the third.

I might have decided to hold my hand for the time being, and not leave the Branch unless and until my fears materialized. I had an uncomfortable feeling that, precisely because of the Prof.'s 'leading along' tactics, I might be put in a false position. There might be great embarrassment, and even ill will, connected with resignation on a particular point. It might be very difficult to explain to Churchill why, if I had agreed to B, I was unable to agree to C.

I still believe that my thinking on this subject was correct in principle. It seemed likely that the Prof. would function as Economic Adviser to Churchill on important points of post-war economic policy. I was not prepared to accept the Prof. as an authority on these economic problems superior to myself.

Such was the most weighty argument in my mind in favour of resignation. In the event my scruples were un-necessary. I kept in touch with the Prof. on these matters, and I do not think that any serious disagreement arose. The only point at which I can conceive that there might have been trouble was in regard to his attitude at Octagon (Quebec, 1944), had he consulted me about that. This was an episode about which I have little knowledge, but something might be learnt about it from the voluminous tape recordings or Mr. Morgenthau. In 1945 we had a General Election before the conclusion of the war against Japan, and Churchill was thrown out and S Branch dissolved. Thus the whole set-up came to an end before the period in which acute differences about international economic policy could have come to a head. But I do not think that the pattern of events in 1945 could reasonably have been foreseen in 1942. It was more natural to suppose that Churchill would be heavily involved in such matters as were thrashed out at the time of Keynes's mission to request a loan from the United States (autumn of 1945) and afterwards, and that the Prof. and S Branch would be called upon to play an active part in all these matters. Had I been able in 1942 to foresee the actual course of events, I might have continued to have an interesting time in S Branch right up until the fatal General Election.

I must not attribute my resignation exclusively to cool reason. That it was temperamental also I will not deny. I just could not bear it any longer. There were many days when I had literally no work, and that I found it hard to endure. I could have borne them, had I had the sense that on the other days I was making a useful contribution to the war effort. I would not have minded the sense that I was making no useful contribution to the war effort, had I been working hard all the time. The combination of partial idleness with a general sense of futility got on my nerves.

There was a feeling of rebellion also. Despite the boundless admiration that I had always had, and continued to have, for the Prof.'s great qualities, I was unwilling to be his 'stooge', and to sit about day after day hearing him talk a lot of nonsense, just because there was a personal difficulty about changing my position. This very personal difficulty increased one's rebellious feeling. There ought not to be any personal difficulty. If the Prof. was a reasonable man, he would have noticed that I was no longer fully occupied and said, 'Look here, we must find you a more active job somewhere else'. If he was not like that, it was an additional reason for resigning.

Of course I knew that he was not like that. The question of personal loyalty and allegiance meant everything to him. There was the old familiar doctrine of the elephant. I had had recent experience of his extreme possessiveness. So long as I was in S Branch I was its Establishment Officer. One or two of our people became restive after a time and wanted to change their occupation. As I had been responsible for getting them into S Branch, I felt it my duty to carry as much as I could of the burden of getting them removed somewhere else, and to shield them as much as possible. Negotiating these matters with the Prof. proved embarrassing, and indeed unpleasant.

Accordingly I felt in relation to my own resignation that,

if anywhere in my disposition there were any resources of tact, I must deploy them now. To leave him without quarrelling with him still strikes me as the most difficult task that I have ever had to undertake.

My main argument was naturally the perfectly correct one, that I was not fully employed. I pointed out to him how smoothly S Branch was running and suggested to him that my departure would make no difference.

Further to this, I worked on two lines. There was a period at the beginning of 1942 when he himself became disgruntled and talked of closing S Branch down. I never got a full view of the causes of this. Lord Beaverbrook's name was mentioned. Lord Beaverbrook had done most splendid war-winning work at the Ministry of Aircraft Production. When he felt that his work there was truly done and his dynamism no longer needed to promote the output of aircraft, there was a period of uncertainty about what he would do, and he became Minister of State. I think that the Prof. had the idea — whether it was correct or not I do not know — that Churchill wanted to make Beaverbrook mainly responsible for the economic planning of the war. The Prof. felt that this would make his own position difficult.

When he was in this mood, I suggested that I too would find it convenient in many ways to return to Christ Church. There were many threads there that I wanted to pick up. I talked in a vague and mysterious manner. Thus it seemed that it would suit us both to return to Oxford.

In fact I never for a moment believed that the Prof. would leave Churchill ; I knew full well that this was but a passing mood of discontent. But, while the discontent was on him, I sought to get it accepted by him as an established fact that I was shortly to return to Oxford, so that, when the mood passed, the established fact would remain. Thus instead of having to give him reasons for going, it would be he who would have to put up reasons for my not going.

The second line that I worked on was this. I was not really leaving him at all. All I wanted to do was to go off his pay roll and have the free disposal of my time. I should come into the office frequently. I should remain subject to the Official Secrets Act, on the basis of still being a member of his staff. As I had had so much idle time in recent months, I should probably be able to do for him almost as much as I was doing before.

And so we parted without mutual compliments or re-criminations. I doubt if he ever formally accepted my resignation. To the best of my recollection all that happened was that I asked the Establishment Officer to cease sending me cheques.

I kept my word about maintaining contact. I made it a rule to look in at the office at least once a week. But after a time it became apparent that one could not truly be of S Branch without being in it. I felt that the Prof. and the other members were merely interrupting their work in order to maintain polite conversation with me, and after a passage of months my visits became less frequent. I did, however, carry on with some of my work in relation to the Anglo-American discussions on post-war economics. I continued to attend some of the meetings of the inter-departmental committees as a member of the Prime Minister's private branch. I reported on all these to the Prof., and wrote him certain memoranda from time to time.

That my connection with S Branch continued to be real, an incident that occurred as late as September 1943, more than a year after I had given up whole time employment, is evidence. I was advising the Prof. on the negotiations which Keynes was then carrying through with Harry White in Washington. A telegram had been sent which seemed to me mischievous and likely to sabotage Keynes's negotiation.

Drafted under the influence of a temporary shift of emphasis in Whitehall, it required Keynes to insist on more liberty for each nation to change the value of its currency than he had himself proposed in his original plan for a 'Clearing Union'. For this telegram the Prof.'s assent was required but had been mistakenly taken for granted, since he was at a meeting. I pressed that it was urgently needful to send a counteracting telegram, but, by the time that all had been unravelled, it was found that the coding staff at the Foreign Office had packed up for the night. Thus there was much telephoning and going to and fro, and I had to hang about in the office until after midnight. It was quite like olden times. I believe that the matter was put right in the end.

★

After I left S Branch, I resumed my teaching and committee work at Christ Church. But by this time there were not many undergraduates remaining in Oxford and my employment was by no means full. I told Sir Richard Hopkins, who was always kind to me, exactly what had happened, and he said that he ought to be able to find me a place under the 'Treasury umbrella'; but some weeks later I got a letter from him saying that he had looked into the matter and found his project not to be feasible. There was also a proposal from Dr. Dalton, then President of the Board of Trade, to whom I had paid occasional visits on these post-war questions. I learnt from my friend, Mr. J. E. Meade, who was working on post-war commercial policy at his desk in the Economic Section, that the Board of Trade was being quite co-operative. Dalton's idea was that I should act for the Board of Trade as its representative on the committees concerned. This seemed attractive, and I waited for some months to hear about it. But in the end it was found necessary to put this on a stronger basis and Sir Percival

Liesching, a civil servant of high standing, was brought into the Board of Trade for this purpose.

In my own mind I had not built much hope on these suggestions. On the contrary, I was convinced that the pattern of events had rendered me unemployable for any task that would fully engage my economic *expertise* for the remainder of the war. I had no illusions about this before I left the Prof. I did not for a moment believe that I should find suitable alternative employment. S Branch had been engaged in highly controversial activities, which ramified widely ; although the Prof.'s position had immensely improved since the outbreak of war, he was still suspect in many quarters, and I had identified myself with him ; above all, no one knew anything about the circumstances of my departure, nor what Churchill's attitude about it was. They would not wish to employ someone who was a *persona ingrata* in those high quarters. My continued attendance at certain committees did not clarify this matter ; it only served to deepen the obscurity and ambiguity of my position. I knew from the very beginning that I should have to be content to devote the rest of the war to relatively minor activities.

Had I been wrong to join the Prof. in the first instance ? From a worldly point of view it was certainly a fatal error. But from the point of view of real service to the country, I still cannot see that it was wrong. For two and a half years, the very period in which the country was in most mortal peril, I was fairly actively engaged in what I truly believe to have been useful work. I had the impression at the time that my economic colleagues in the Economic Section had not yet found anything so useful to do ; their chances were to come later, especially after Sir John Anderson began to get a grip on economic policy questions. Once I felt that I was no longer doing useful work, I resigned. If I was unable, in consequence of the pattern of events, to do anything very useful in the later years of the war, that did not matter so much. The most critical phase was already over. To have been able to do really useful work in the most perilous period was satisfactory. Of course the position in which I found myself in 1942 was exceedingly irksome and frustrating ; but the war was a period of irksomeness and frustration for many ; and there were many thousands who had met with a far worse fate. It would be paltry indeed to be sorry for oneself ; and I hope and believe that I was not.

There was one point about my resignation which saddened me very much. I have already indicated that I had certain links with Churchill before the war, and it had naturally been pleasing to think that, after a number of years of faithful service, those links would be strengthened. I consulted Sir Edward Bridges about what Churchill's attitude would be if I left S Branch. He was not encouraging ; he even went so far as to characterize the Prime Minister as 'temperamental' about personal questions. Should I accordingly have put my loyalty to Churchill as a decisive reason against resignation ? One clearly did not wish to displease him, but it would not have been rational to give this idea much weight. Carried along as he then was by the loyal support of the whole nation, immersed in a thousand preoccupations of desperate urgency, news of my departure was not likely to give him more than a minute's flicker of displeasure. Even the estimate of a minute is perhaps too great. But what could only be a flicker of displeasure for him was a long heavy shadow for me. It was sad indeed to think that one had had these pre-war links with the greatest man of our age, and was deliberately severing them. I hardly saw Churchill at all after 1942, although he has occasionally sent me kindly letters and messages, and he went out of his way on several occasions to urge Conservative selection committees to adopt me as their parliamentary candidate.

By an unfortunate chapter of accidents my relations with

the Prof. and Churchill were destined to get worse before they got better.

★

After my return to Oxford I had a period of relative ease. I wrote a lengthy memorandum for the Royal Commission on Population and a short pamphlet on this subject which was published by the Oxford Press. I continued to do certain work for the Prof. on international economics, as already described, but naturally I was restive. I even went to Colonel Wilkinson to ask him if there was anything useful that I could do in connection with the Oxford University Corps.

Somehow Sir Frederick Ogilvie got to learn that I was in the market, and, on an inquiry by Admiral Boyd, a great man, then Fifth Sea Lord, mentioned my name. I went to see the Admiral and he explained that they needed someone of statistical experience, as they were getting into muddles in relation to the presentation of the requirements of the Fleet Air Arm to the Cabinet at home and to the Lend-Lease authorities in the United States. They had a professional statistician, a highly efficient one as I was to find, Mr. R. E. Beard of the Prudential Assurance Company. When asked some question on the telephone, such as how many new propellers were still needed for Swordfish aircraft, he could make calculations from complicated basic data by playing lightly on the calculating machine with one hand while he held the receiver with the other, and give the correct answer almost without any delay. But it was outside his province to draft the final versions of memoranda to the higher authorities. Well, I felt that there could be no one in the country better qualified than I for this particular task. The Fleet Air Arm was clearly a respectable institution ; it had had rather a raw deal owing to the priority given to the Royal Air Force in the early years of the war ; it had growing responsibilities and would have still greater tasks as the war against Japan developed. Here, it seemed, was a useful bit of work that I could do, and I accepted the offer. I took the precaution, however, of saying that I must continue with my work at Christ Church and that I could only take a half-time appointment with the Admiralty ; I was absolutely determined to avoid any further time-wasting, and I planned to tailor my attendance at the Admiralty to the real work for which I was needed there.

After I had taken up my position at my desk, I had a more intimate talk with the Fifth Sea Lord on the reasons why he had sought my assistance. There had been a Ministerial meeting, with Churchill and the Prof. both present. The Prof. had made a certain calculation from the figures furnished which went against the claim of the Admiralty, and Admiral Boyd had challenged his calculation as erroneous. Unfortunate, innocent Admiral ! Opinions may differ as to whether the Prof. was one of the great minds of our century, but no one has denied that he had an almost unrivalled gift of lightning calculation. The Prof. was highly incensed at being corrected by a mere Admiral and complained to the Prime Minister. There was in fact a 'stink' about it. This had caused the Fifth Sea Lord to decide that he must get someone to brief him better.

This did indeed make me feel the force of that hackneyed adage : 'What a small place the world is !' I had spent the early years of the war writing minutes on behalf of the Prof., and now I had been unwittingly engaged to write minutes against him ! There at once flashed into my mind the Prof.'s unforgiving attitude to anyone who ventured to correct him. Of course the Admiral had been proved quite wrong about the figures. I thought of my unfortunate colleague who had incurred a lifelong hostility by accusing the Prof. of 'guessing'.

I told the Prof. all about this, and he was much amused. He did not seem to mind ; but he would have been hardly human — and he was very human in such ways — if he did not mind at all. I told him that he must take a kindly view in regard to the Fleet Air Arm, owing to the heavy tasks that lay ahead, but I was much more concerned to describe Admiral Boyd in the most glowing terms, knowing how that correction would rankle in the Prof.'s mind, and might almost even lead him — this was indeed his central failing — to take a jaundiced view of all future claims by the Fleet Air Arm. Well, he contented himself with saying that he was all in favour of the Fleet Air Arm requirements being better presented under my guidance.

I had a very interesting time in the Admiralty. I learnt about aspects of our war effort that were fresh to me, and made the acquaintance of a number of delightful naval officers. I was twice sent to the United States for periods of three or four weeks to assist in negotiations about the allocation of naval type aircraft under Lend-Lease. During my spare time there I made contacts and had extensive discussions about Anglo-American plans for post-war reconstruction with such characters as Harry White, Adolph Berle, Dean Acheson, Eddie Bernstein and others. I knew in detail all about the latest phase of our negotiations which were to lead up to Bretton Woods. I endeavoured to put certain British points of view to these men, and also gave ideas of my own as a professional economist. After both visits I reported my impressions to the Prof. Thus the facilities arising out of my Admiralty appointment may have enabled me to have been of some help to him.

The plot was destined to thicken.

★

In the next few pages the reader's attention will be drawn away from the Prof. I venture to think that my campaign at Huddersfield, although an isolated political phenomenon, has a certain historical interest. This book affords a good context for putting it on the record. The Prof.'s reaction, which can be assessed rightly only against a rather detailed account of the event, was a striking example of his very peculiar combination of aloofness and possessiveness — or should I say 'and faithfulness' ?

*

During 1943 or 1944 I had an approach from Mr. Harcourt Johnstone (Crinks), then Secretary to the Department of Overseas Trade. He had been charged by Sir Archibald Sinclair, Leader of the Liberal Party, with the duty of following the progress of planning for post-war, both on the international and domestic sides, with a view to advising what attitude the Liberal Party, as such, ought to adopt to the various proposals. Could I help him in this ? I had had some acquaintance with Mr. Harcourt Johnstone over many years ; no doubt some common friend had suggested my name to him. When he approached me he had already very properly sought the consent of the Prof. I also consulted the Prof. about it. He was on excellent terms with Crinks ; the Liberal Party was then a part of the Coalition ; the Prof. was entirely agreeable to the plan. I pointed out that I should be advising Crinks on the same lines as I was advising the Prof. I may even on some occasions have sent identical memoranda to both.

In addition to obtaining my confidential advice, Crinks persuaded me to write a little book, which appeared anonymously under the title of *A Liberal Plan for Peace*, being sponsored by some committee of the Liberal Party and published by Victor Gollancz. It got little publicity. I believe that what happened was that the publishers supposed that the Liberal Party would look after the circulation of its own

publication, while the Liberal Party thought that, when one
had such a publisher as Victor Gollancz, one did not have to
bother about publicity. Thus, what with my work at Christ
Church and at the Admiralty, I had become quite busy again.

Crinks took me deeply into his confidence about the
political future. He attached immense importance to the
negotiations now proceeding with the Americans for securing
a freer flow of international trade after the war. He thought
that this new development should be brought into connection
with the age-old tradition of the Liberal Party in favour of
Free Trade. He told me that he was determined to make this
the principal plank in the platform of the Liberals at the next
General Election. He had been for a number of years quite
a key figure in the Liberal Party, and I supposed that he would
have considerable influence in determining its platform. He
took the view that our external problems would be of far
greater real importance than our domestic problems, when
the war was over, and success in our co-operation with the
Americans for greater freedom of trade would be a crucial
factor. I entirely concurred with the view that the external
problems would be more important than the internal problems. By good luck, from his point of view, the direction
of American thinking was entirely in line with the Liberal
doctrines of Free Trade. These were live and vital issues.
It was a unique opportunity for the Liberal Party to present
itself to the country as the proper champion of Anglo-American
co-operation on these lines. Critics were apt to say that Free
Trade was as dead as a door nail ; the Liberals would be able
to show that, so far from being dead, it was an immediate
and practical issue, and they would be able to substantiate
their claim by reference to what had been happening in these
very months in our negotiations with our great ally. I was
encouraged by his confidence that the Liberals would be able
to interest the voters in these developments.

I had initially some qualms. In the 'twenties I had seen a good deal of Francis Hirst. While I had a great admiration for his character and for his intrepid and untiring persistency in the advocacy of his special views — he is one of the few people I can think of as matching the Prof. for the 'courage of his convictions' — I found his doctrine quite unacceptable. He had failed to keep abreast of modern economic thought, and his criticisms of Keynes, although delightfully presented, were quite shallow ; he had little intellectual grip. I believe that there were still elements in the Liberal Party who thought with Francis Hirst on the lines of Cobdenite *laissez-faire*, and I wanted to make quite sure that Crinks was not of this way of thinking. I explained to him that I was a Keynesian economist. Although I was convinced that the more freedom of trade we had the better, I was by no means of the opinion that Free Trade would alone solve our economic problems. We had to work towards greater freedom of trade within a framework of positive policy, designed to ensure full employment and to promote investment, national and international. If I could not agree with Francis Hirst, I could not agree with Cordell Hull either. In our negotiations with the Americans we must be careful to make it quite plain to them that we by no means regarded the dismantling of trade barriers as sufficient to cure the economic ills of the world. Keynes had that in the forefront of his mind in the discussions that were proceeding. I was able to give a reassuring report, on the basis of the conversations that I had had when visiting America, that there were many important figures in the American Administration who were by no means of Cordell Hull's way of thinking. Our future depended on Keynes getting together with those of like mind in the United States, so that a sort of joint Anglo-American policy for full employment and high investment in the world could be implemented after the war. Within such a framework the Cordell Hull policy for greater freedom of trade would have an important place. What the Liberals should do was to revive the ancient British enthusiasm for Free Trade, but present it in a modern garb, namely as part of a wider Keynesian policy. Crinks often said that he regarded Free Trade as something which would itself make for a higher level of employment and standard of living ; I did not dissent from that.

As a result of numerous conversations I satisfied myself that Crinks was sound on these points. He was a highly intelligent man. There was a world of difference between the quality of his thinking and that of such a person as Francis Hirst. He assured me that the Liberal campaign would be conducted within the philosophy of the Keynesian outlook. I became quite enthusiastic for this Liberal campaign, as he sketched it out for me.

Then a more personal question came into our discussions. Why should I not stand for Parliament ? I pointed out that I had duties at Christ Church which I should have to retain. He did not think that this was an objection. They would arrange that I was not burdened with committee work in the House of Commons. Perhaps he, who had a touch of the *ancien régime* in many respects, was a little old-fashioned in his ideas about parliamentary duties. Where I could be useful to the Liberals would be in making an occasional speech, with my full authority as an economist, in debates on those vital questions of international economic co-operation.

Then one morning Crinks had a cerebral haemorrhage in his office and died within a few instants. He had had frightful premonitory headaches, and ought to have taken a long holiday. But he was deeply devoted to his work in the Department of Overseas Trade and no doubt felt it his duty during wartime to carry on through ill health. He may indeed be reckoned a war casualty in the fullest sense.

I continued to think after that of his plans for a General

Election. I had a certain feeling of piety. It seemed a shame that all those ideas of his should be wiped off the slate as though they had never existed. And so under the influence of his posthumous inspiration, I decided that I would stand. I offered myself to the Liberal authorities, and had some discussion with Sir Archibald Sinclair. I was finally adopted as candidate at Huddersfield.

I conducted my campaign at Huddersfield precisely on the lines sketched out by Crinks. I put Article 7 of the Mutual Aid Agreement and Bretton Woods in the forefront of my programme. But alas, Crinks was now dead, and I do not think that the Liberal campaign in other divisions proceeded much on those lines. Sir Archibald Sinclair did his best and made valuable references in his speeches. But he did not have a deep knowledge about the developments of the Anglo-American discussions in recent years, having been heavily preoccupied with his duties as Secretary of State for Air, which he had discharged with notable efficiency throughout the whole period of Churchill's Prime Minister-ship. He had been the Head of the Air Force which had won the Battle of Britain and had fought so gallantly and successfully for freedom over far-flung areas.

I was asked to make a speech to a meeting of candidates in London on this range of topics. None the less it struck me that in the country generally the Liberal campaign paid scant attention to these central problems. It fell somewhat under the spell of Lord Beveridge, who had done such excellent work in his plans for social welfare and full employment at home. The stress given in the Liberal campaign to domestic welfare questions was in diametrical opposition to the ideas of Crinks. Where the Liberal Party ought to differentiate itself from the other two parties, he held, was in its wide international outlook and in the stress that it laid on the pro-position, which was an absolutely true one, that the external problems in the economic field were far more important than the internal problems. Of course on the domestic side full support should be given to the Beveridge proposals, but these should not be unduly stressed. The other two parties would doubtless put forward similar proposals and, great as the name of Beveridge was at that time, the voters would not be convinced that the Liberals alone would have a care for the social problems. But they might be convinced, so Crinks thought, that the outlook of the Liberals was better adapted than those of the other two parties for coping with these far graver external economic problems. Accordingly, in campaigning, one should keep them constantly in the forefront.

Beveridge came to speak at Huddersfield, and attracted a vast audience, which was welcome to the candidate. As I knew that he would have much to say about his plans for insurance, I explained to him that I had been laying foremost stress on Article 7 of the Mutual Aid Agreement — a matter on which I judged that he knew almost nothing — and begged him to say a few words in his speech on that topic ; otherwise the voters of Huddersfield would think that I was a crank with a bee in my bonnet. He assured me that he would do so ; but when he became immersed in his speech on social insurance, he forgot all about it.

I was not overmuch perturbed in ploughing my rather lonely furrow at Huddersfield. I knew that Keynes warmly supported my efforts, and that was a great tonic. I knew that some of my friends in the Economic Section were of the same way of thinking. One was reported to me as having said : 'There is only one division in the whole country where the true issues are being put before the electorate, and that is Huddersfield'.

Afterwards I wrote down the main arguments that I used in my campaign and published them in a little booklet

entitled, *A Page of British Folly*.[1] I endeavoured to impart a
sense of urgency into what I said, stressing the danger to our
standard of living at home, should we drift apart from the
Americans in our ideas about international economics. We
depended on our exports and therefore on a prosperous world.
In fact we did drift apart after the war, and the international
institutions planned by the Americans and by Keynes seemed
to go for the time being into the doldrums. The American
and British modes of thinking about these matters diverged
rapidly and there was little mutual consultation. It must be
remembered that Keynes died shortly after his success in
securing a large loan from the Americans ; he had been the
essential link between the American and British points of
view. The Labour Party, then in power, concentrated largely
on its domestic reforms, and the kind of ideas inherent in the
Anglo-American planning had no great appeal to it at that
time. In discussions that I had with distinguished American
officials in the following years, they complained to me that,
once the war was over, the British had in fact seemed to show
little interest in the development of the wartime planning or
in the international institutions that had been set up. This,
they explained, had tended to have a bad effect on the American orientation ; the internationalists within their Administration had their own difficulties in Congress, and the fact that
the British seemed to take so little interest in these things
discouraged them from continuing to urge the importance
of these international arrangements ; they would get no
thanks at home for doing so. In Huddersfield I expressed
grave forebodings about what might happen to our country
should such a drift away from the Americans occur.

We did drift away from the Americans, and yet the worst
did not happen. To that extent my predictions were not
fulfilled. It seems clear, however, that this non-fulfilment

[1] Published by Macmillan.

was due to a development, which could not have been foreseen clearly in the summer of 1945, namely, the widening
gulf between Western Europe and Russia and the danger
that the Communist parties in the free countries of the
Continent would gain power if economic conditions there
continued to deteriorate. Out of these conditions arose the
great plan of Marshall Aid ; although there was no danger
of a Communist victory in Britain, we had serious difficulties
of our own, and, in view of our war record, could hardly
be left out of a scheme of aid for other countries in free
Europe. In 1945, before Communism had begun to look
really menacing, any such plan as Marshall Aid was entirely
out of the question. Accordingly it was correct to urge that
the only thing that could save this country from a period of
grave economic difficulties was active co-operation with the
Americans under Article 7.

After Huddersfield I entered into the inner counsels of
the Liberal Party and was even, for a time, a member of the
'Liberal Shadow Cabinet'. I could not work up any enthusiasm in it about the Article 7 aspect of things. Opinion
seemed to be as much divided as it was in the Conservative
Party. There was indeed a sector, surviving from the great
past, of Hirstian Free Trade ; but this struck me as pre-
Keynesian in outlook and therefore of little value. The
death of Crinks was probably of crucial importance ; he
might have succeeded in welding together the old and the
new. It was idle to pretend that there was any great difference
between the Liberals and the modern Conservative Party on
questions of social welfare. There was a left-wing element
within the Liberals, which struck me as somewhat Labourite
and dangerously complaisant of nationalization projects. The
Conservative Party under the leadership of men such as
Churchill, Eden, Butler and Macmillan was a very different
thing from that of Baldwin and Chamberlain. Accordingly

late in the 'forties I joined the Conservative Party and have since done much active campaigning on its behalf.

We had a lively contest at Huddersfield. I enjoyed electioneering. As the days proceeded, it became evident that Labour was the principal danger, and the greater part of my speaking was devoted to warning the electors against the nationalization of industry.

But it was a three-cornered fight. When I offered myself to Liberal Headquarters, I did not appreciate how widely the three parties would fall apart overnight after five long years of co-operation for the defeat of Hitler. Churchill and Sinclair had throughout been on excellent terms, but now in the twinkling of an eye all was changed ; the parties were warring against one another. It is only fair to say that Churchill himself gave a striking example on these lines. He threw himself into downright Conservative partisanship. He warned the voters that the Socialists could not run their system without having an inquisition into the private actions of citizens, which would amount to a sort of Gestapo ; some thought that even from a party political point of view, it was an error of judgement to go so far.

In Huddersfield I had to contend against a National-Liberal, who had held office under Churchill. The National-Liberals were, at that time, completely identified with the Conservatives, and no Conservative candidate stood. It was an essential part of my duty to warn voters against the dangers of a Conservative victory, as well as that of a Labour victory. In this matter I had a case which was absolutely truthful in substance, but I could not deploy it fully under the Official Secrets Act. I had to rely entirely upon the public statements of Conservatives, and they were extremely scanty, since on the morrow of V.E. day there had been little opportunity for public debate. The substantial point was that in fact there was already a division within the ranks of the Conservatives, which had led to a certain stalling in recent months in our negotiations with the Americans. There was a group of Conservatives who were entirely opposed to proceeding boldly on the lines of Article 7.

My line of argument was accordingly as follows. I was most scrupulous never to make any remark that constituted, directly or indirectly, a criticism of Churchill himself. I daresay that on the morrow of victory I should not have won any votes by doing so ; be that as it may, it was a matter of personal conscience with me. But I affirmed that there was grave danger in returning the Conservatives to power, since there was every likelihood that those Conservatives who opposed the programme of greater freedom of trade would get their way, and that all our prospects, which depended on a further pursuit of Anglo-American co-operation on the lines of Article 7, would be impeded and perhaps totally frustrated. Churchill, whose own ideas on these topics might be perfectly sound, would be a prisoner in the Conservative camp. This made the basis of a campaign which was entirely truthful in substance and by no means disloyal to Churchill.

Once one has got hold of one central theme, one works it hard. I summoned up all my resources of oratory. It does not serve to make under-statements in a General Election. Quite a wave of enthusiasm was generated in Huddersfield. At the big Beveridge meeting I returned to the charge, after Beveridge himself had departed for a neighbouring division. I was hotting things up, and my National-Liberal opponent, judging that I was making them too hot, appealed to Churchill to issue some contradictory statement. Churchill complied and told the voters of Huddersfield to pay no attention to my 'mischievous' allegations.

How far indeed had I drifted in the brief space of three years. Churchill's ardent supporter in Munich days and his faithful servant in S Branch, working away through the night in conditions not always congenial, as a member of a band of 'irregulars' specifically devoted to helping Churchill personally, I was now publicly rebuked by him for my mischievous statements. He was of course perfectly correct, in the conditions of a General Election, in coming to the aid of my National-Liberal opponent. But I could not help being saddened at having drifted so far away. The pattern of events had been unfortunate. Yet, as I looked back over them, I could not feel that I could blame myself, or accuse myself of disloyalty to Churchill. There had been the advice I had given to Crinks, his ideas of the nature of the General Election campaign and the proposal that I should stand ; I had been a lifelong Liberal, and it was quite appropriate that I should stand as a Liberal ; there was my enthusiasm for the Article 7 negotiations, the consilience of these with traditional Liberal policy, my earnest zeal on behalf of the work that Keynes was doing, and his encouragement ; then there had come the overnight cleavage between the parties, the sharp partisanship of the campaign in many phases, for which Churchill himself had some share of responsibility ; there was the solid truth behind my contention that a Conservative victory would be a danger, since Churchill might be dependent on the group opposed to close co-operation with the Americans on the lines of Article 7 ; the stalling by the Cabinet towards the end of the war had been a fact. I was not, of course, so carried away as to envisage that the Liberal Party would be returned to power ; what one rather thought was that, if the Conservatives were dependent on Liberal votes, that would tilt the balance in favour of Conservative supporters of Article 7 and give strength to Churchill's elbow in pursuing the correct policy. The fact remained that, from my own personal point of view, I could not but be saddened at having drifted so far from Churchill.

Some time afterwards I received a friendly letter from

him, saying that he did not take too seriously what might be said in the heat of a General Election.

And so what of my relations with the Prof.? He could not be expected to approve of this altercation with Churchill. It had been incumbent on me, of course, to make an immediate public riposte when Churchill intervened in the Huddersfield election. I am not normally addicted to embarrassment, but I do recall a shade of embarrassment on meeting the Prof. a few weeks afterwards in the Christ Church Common Room. Yet somehow everything seemed to pass off fairly smoothly. I believe that he said, 'Well, how are you getting along?' in a rather sarcastic voice. That was about the sum of his rebuke.

At that moment I felt that there was a certain bigness in the Prof., to which I had not yet done full justice. Despite his passionate possessiveness, his elephant doctrine, his long-sustained grudges for minor misdemeanours, his tendency to attribute evil motives, his violent partisanship, he seemed to appreciate that I had acted throughout with honourable intention. So far as the General Election was concerned, he seemed to be able, for once, to look at the pattern of events from my point of view.

He was deeply inscrutable, but on the surface our relations did not appear to be substantially impaired. Indeed we must have entered into friendly intercourse, for I remember his telling me a good story immediately on his return from Potsdam. To understand it one must bear clearly in mind the time sequence of events. First came the General Election; the count was postponed for about a month in order to give time for the votes of men serving overseas to be collected for it. It was in that interval, between the Election campaign culminating in polling day, and the count of the votes, that Churchill led the British delegation to Potsdam. Then he had to return to the count and face defeat, and after that

Attlee returned as Head of the British Government to Potsdam
for further proceedings. Churchill had taken the Prof. over,
and had had to introduce him to Stalin for the first time.
He had no ready formula for describing the Prof. He explained that he was a man who had been advising him about
a balanced use of our resources for the war effort, drawing
his attention to shortfalls, and generally keeping his eye on
the whole scene of government, to inform him if anything
was amiss ; in fact he had acted as a kind of Gestapo for him.
'Oh !' said Stalin immediately, 'I thought it was only Mr.
Attlee who had a Gestapo.'

*

In the following October we were all back at our muttons,
mingling together in the Common Room as though there
had been no war, nor General Election either. Soon after
that the Prof. beckoned to me one evening after dinner and
asked me if I had a little spare time. Would I go over to his
room ? When I arrived there, he handed me a large wad of
foolscap pages. This was the speech that he intended to
deliver in the House of Lords on economic problems. It
was the first of a long series of such occasions. It seemed
that he was anxious that I should return to him in the rôle
of 'adviser', and I was willing to do so.

On economic questions we were in substantial agreement
in that phase. I was strongly of the opinion that the Labour
Government was over-loading the economy with various
forms of outlay, in a way that would tend to cause inflation
and jeopardize our external position, by causing delivery
delays to our export markets. The Prof. cordially agreed.
I held that we were attempting to do too much 'investment',
particularly in the 'basic' industries, now being national-
ized, on which the Labour Government laid especial stress.
Investment should be confined to reconversion and the

provision of capacity in manufacturing industry, which could export its products. Expenditure on infrastructure could wait.

I also took the view that consumption should be increased. This was stressed in the title of a little book that I wrote at that time, *Are These Hardships Necessary ?* I held that if one wanted the people to work hard at their top level of efficiency, it was desirable to reduce 'austerity'. An early return towards the peacetime standard of living would give people a new hope and encourage them to do their best. It may occur to the reader that such ideas were in line with the philosophy of S Branch during the war. If its ideas were relevant in wartime, they were relevant in the peacetime period of reconstruction also, when it was incumbent upon us to work hard if we were to recapture our pre-war position in the world. It is the case that I was influenced at that time by what I had learnt in S Branch, ultimately by what I had learnt from Churchill. The Prof. was naturally in full sympathy. He used to mouth the word 'investment' in that tone of self-assured scorn that he had previously applied to army 'requirements'. As always, there was something delightfully encouraging about his lively disdain.

In very recent years the position has been entirely different. I have been keen to increase investment. I have also been more favourable than some of my economic colleagues to an expansion of consumption. My main reason for that is now different. I have wanted more consumption as the means of getting more investment ; in recent years the danger has been that we should get neither and that the economy would remain under-employed. Consumption and investment must expand together. But although this has been my main reason recently for wanting an expansion in consumption, my ideas still retain the colouring that they derived from S Branch. The idea that people will continue working strenuously on the basis of unchanging austerity, with a view to piling the investment of the country ever higher, is a psychological monstrosity.

The Prof. and I were in complete accord in deploring the devaluation of sterling in 1949.

When he took me into his confidence about his House of Lords speeches, it was borne in upon me that it was not really about economic problems that he sought my advice. He may have consulted me on some minor questions of fact ; I may have dotted some i's and crossed some t's. What he was much more concerned to know was whether his speeches were 'all right', *convenable*, suitable for the ears of their lordships. I appeared to have become for him an authority on decorum.

The speeches were not all right. They were full of appalling insults. Some of these were open and blatant, others tortuous in the manner that I have described earlier. On the latter I often had to get his explanations. I then entered into a process of bargaining. I allowed him to retain, even encouraged him to retain, some tortuous insult, feeling sure that it would not be understood, on condition that he erased a blatant one.

I believe that I vetted all the speeches that he made in the House of Lords during the period of Conservative opposition (1945-51). He was then the chief spokesman on the Conservative side on economic problems. This must not be taken to imply that I approved of all that was in the speeches ; I concentrated especially, as requested, on matters of decorum, but even there I cannot claim to have had complete success. I never heard him deliver a speech in the House of Lords. I should suppose that his delivery cannot have been good. In conversation it was his quiet tone that was effective, and even attractive ; but when he had to raise his voice, an unfortunate snarl entered into his intonation.

After the General Election of 1951, Churchill happily became Prime Minister again, and the Prof. entered the Cabinet. He was again without portfolio. He re-formed some kind of S Branch and MacDougall returned to his service ; it was also joined by my very able post-war pupil, Mr. J. S. Fforde. The University gave the Prof. leave of absence for one year from his professorial duties. At the end of a year he was still needed and the University gave him a further, and, as it proved, final year's leave. He wrote characteristically to the Comtesse de Pange :

1952 *December 25*

The University, in my view wrongly, not to say offensively, prolonged my leave of absence for another year. So I am still in the Cabinet and have to spend my time worrying over things remote from my proper sphere. It is quite a strain, having had no fixed duties except twenty-eight lectures a year, having to attend so many meetings and argue on such diverse topics.

'Not to say offensively' should be noted. During this period he came back to Oxford and paid his post-prandial visits to our Common Room as often as he could manage. He frequently spent the weekends, as he had done so much during the war, with the Churchills. He had his own sources of economic information now, and I do not recall being consulted.

His roots in Christ Church had become very deep by this time. For many years he had had no other home. I recall seeing his brother, Brigadier Lindemann, in the United States during this phase, and he expressed the anxious hope that his brother realized that his real allegiance was to Oxford and not to politics. It must have been a severe wrench for the Prof. to resign from Churchill's Cabinet at the end of the second year. But he was doubtless taken into frequent

consultation thereafter, and in a diminished way he continued
to play his old part.

★

In this final phase there occurred a distressing development.
During his period of office the Prof. acquired a rooted conviction that we should not return to sterling 'convertibility' ;
and subsequently he remained of the same opinion. I believe
that it will be found that he played a crucial part in dissuading
the Conservative Government from such a return. I, on the
contrary, held that the earliest possible return to convertibility
was very desirable. Having some slight inkling of what was
going on, I made some advances to him. He snubbed me
off rather rudely. He suggested that an economist who
proffered advice should show his credentials by having made
some money. I thought, 'You did not say that, you old Prof.,
when you were only too glad to learn your economics from
me in the 'twenties'. In the 'fifties I had more of value to
offer him. In voluminous, but widely scattered, writings I
had many predictions to my credit. If two parties give
alternative reasons for certain events, the reasons supplied by
the party that has predicted that the events will happen on
the basis of those very reasons, have a *prima facie* case for
being preferred to the reasons supplied *ex post* by the other
party which has not predicted the events at all. This criterion
of prediction would have been one that might have appealed
to the Prof. But I did not join forces with him.

In the old days I would have entered into strong combat
and battered him with my reasonings. But I did not do so
on this occasion. So far as the Prof. was concerned, I felt
exhausted ; I had worked out the vein. There was a long
history now. I had fought great battles on the side of the
Prof. and I had contended against him hotly on many occasions. Then there had been the experience in S Branch and

the embarrassment at leaving him, and the hurly-burly of Huddersfield, and then in due course those differences seemed to have been overcome and there were the six years in which he invited me to vet his speeches. I took it that our relations were re-established, but now we saw much less of each other. I just did not have the heart to enter into a great new campaign. I knew that it would be a more formidable undertaking, since he seemed to have become quite convinced on the other side.

Another motive actuated me. Grim though the prospect of entering into a new great debate with him was, I might have felt it my duty not to shirk the issue, had I conceived it to be really vital from a national point of view. But I was aware that there were many difficulties confronting a return to convertibility, and that the precise dating of it was a nice point. I felt quite confident that we should in fact return, and, if the Prof. succeeded in delaying it for a time, that would not be a national disaster.

My confidence was justified. What I had throughout desired was *de facto* convertibility, realizing that a premature return to formal convertibility might involve us in a tangle of irrelevant commitments. In February 1955 the Bank of England took the step of making transferable sterling *de facto* convertible subject only to a small discount. The Prof. was much opposed to this and mumbled his grumbles ; but as things were now going in the way that I wanted, I let him be.

Through all this period we avoided economic discussions. There was a sort of tacit agreement. I think that he felt, on his side, that he did not want to enter into the rough and tumble of a full encounter. But then it happened in a curious way that this agreement to differ seemed to cause a greater gulf between us than had ever been formed by my resignation from S Branch and the electoral contest at Huddersfield.

Ever since the days of the return to the gold standard in 1925, economic questions had been a frequent matter of discussion between us. It seemed unnatural, to me at least, not to be having such discussions with him. I felt somehow that he had retreated to a remote distance. He came regularly into the Common Room, and, if a bridge four was proceeding, liked to stand behind the table and watch the game. He had a standing complaint that I arranged my cards the wrong way round. Everything was very friendly and natural ; but I felt that our relations were much more distant than they had ever been before. I suppose that it is a dictum of wide application in personal affairs that he who seeks for the sake of peace to avoid a passionate contest can so achieve it only at the price of some estrangement.

Incidentally this difference about convertibility gives some support to the reasoning on which I resigned in 1942. Keynes had to make a definite commitment about convertibility in his negotiations for the American loan in December 1945. I do not know what the Prof.'s attitude would have been then, had Churchill still been in power.

*

Towards the end of his life the Prof. made a remark on more than one occasion with such an air of seriousness that he seemed to regard it as his testament of wisdom, and I accordingly feel it incumbent upon me to record it here, although not in perfect sympathy with it. 'Do you know' he asked, 'what the future historians will regard as the most important event of this age ?' Well, what was it ? 'It will not be Hitler and the Second World War, it will not be the release of nuclear energy, it will not be the menace of Communism.' These negatives seemed very comprehensive. He put on an expression of extreme severity and turned down the corners of his lips. 'It will be the abdication of the white man.' Then he nodded his head up and down several times to drive home his proposition.

This seemed to go against one's liberal sentiments. It occurred to me that this was but another example of the Prof.'s remoteness and lack of fellow feeling with the mass of mankind. In my own person I have never felt any colour bar. Many non-whites whom I have known have been most charming men, with whom the assumption of the status of equality could not possibly present a difficulty. Anyhow it was absurd of the Prof. to lump all non-whites together, when one knew that some had attained a high level of civilization, not readily to be dubbed inferior to our own, while others were delightful savages, about whom it was reasonable to reserve doubts on their viability in responsible and efficient self-government.

Yet one could not but feel, as the Prof. sat there gravely nodding, that, although his formulation was altogether too negative, it gave food for thought. For it was incumbent on one to counter his wide sweeping negative by some constructive philosophy. What was there to hand ? The formula of arithmetical democracy, whether within each nation or among the nations, would hardly do. At the very moment when this formula seemed to have some official acceptance, the world was in fact locked in a deadly embrace of power politics of an intensity never before known in human history — a situation remote indeed from the democratic ideal. I myself believe that in the future of the human race the various non-white peoples will have great parts to play in developing their own capacities and contributing to civilization. But the modes by which this happy development will in fact be achieved, whether in terms of power politics or in terms of political principles, are still totally obscure. There is still a political vacuum in many places ; a dense fog enshrouds the

future ; there is still great uncertainty about the innate capacities of various non-white peoples ; and, more alarming,
there is uncertainty about what their emotions or impulses
would be, should it come to be physically within their power
to enslave the white peoples. All these matters require deep
thought ; we require new principles ; Locke and Bentham
do not give us formulae for solving the real problems of
to-day, nor Marx either ; we need new precepts to give
guidance to men of goodwill in all nations, whether white
or non-white. One saw the Prof. sitting there with his
ageing brain, nodding his head up and down ; and behind
him unseen was Winston Churchill with his ageing brain.
What young men in their twenties, one wondered, were
there who were thinking deeply of these problems and producing new principles, related to current reality ? Was there
any young man in the world of comparable calibre to the
Prof., to whom one could say, 'Now, come along to Christ
Church Common Room and put your ideas before the Prof.,
so that we may see if you can give an adequate defence of
them'. Perhaps there really are such young men, and it is
only the gulf of years that leaves me unacquainted with their
profound thoughts.

In this connection the Prof. made an attack upon the
formula of arithmetical democracy in the House of Lords
(April 10th, 1957) which, although characteristically caustic,
and an overstatement, is worthy of attention.

There was another subject in that last year of the Prof.'s
life on which he felt very strongly. This time I was in
sympathy with him. He held that we should not agree to
suspend the tests of atomic and hydrogen bombs until we had
had as many tests as the Americans and the Russians. Not
to have tests was tantamount to not producing bombs at all.
He thought that one did not need to dwell for long on those
persons living deep in mines of unfathomable folly who held

we should make the bombs but suspend the tests. The project of spending many millions of pounds on making bombs that might be useless and would therefore have little deterrent power could only be dismissed, he held, with a shrug of the shoulders in despair at human stupidity.

Britain could not be a power for peace in the world unless she had these weapons. Did one, or did one not, believe that Britain was a power for peace and that she might have some part to play in the future in preventing war ? If she did not have the weapons, she could have no influence on the course of events. Would that be likely to make for world peace ? What was to be gained by suspending tests before Britain was quite sure that her own weapons were as good as those of the others ? The plea that the tests should be suspended was a mere parrot cry. If Britain had the bombs, that might be a real influence preventing the outbreak of a war, which could inflict untold misery and even jeopardize life on the planet. What arguments were there to set against this argument ? 'We ought to suspend the tests' seemed to be a bare form of words, the sound of which might sooth the nerves of some, but had no cerebral process behind it. That was the Prof.'s view ; I was inclined to agree with it.

There is one tiny little argument, only a featherweight in relation to the argument in favour of Britain having the atomic weapon (which meant, 1957, having more tests) and thus helping to prevent the ghastly horrors of an atomic war ; it is that the tests themselves might be injurious to human health. This suggestion put the Prof. into his most splendid form ; the idea that these experiments would make any appreciable difference to human health roused his most scathing contempt. I heard him argue the point a number of times ; to have done so makes it extremely depressing to read the comments on this topic in some of our 'well-informed weeklies'. It was a case where the arguments turn

THE BOWLER HAT GOES TO ADELAIDE, EN ROUTE FOR WOOMERA

essentially on orders of magnitude and for such cases the Prof. had a special aptitude ; my experience over thirty years had been that he was invariably right in that type of case ; I knew well how to distinguish occasions where he was speaking outside his range from those in which he was speaking from a conviction based on deep and careful thought ; this matter he had evidently considered in all its bearings, and accordingly I had confidence in his verdict. Furthermore I knew that he was inclined in discussion to overstate his arguments and my experience of him made me fully able to allow for that; as was so often the case with him, probing and cross-examination led him to state his case in a more reasonable and convincing way. I have no doubt that the contempt which he expressed for those who held the opposite view on this matter was genuinely felt. His arguments are set out in a speech delivered in the House of Lords on May 8th, 1957, and I need not repeat them here.

Shortly before delivering it he beckoned to me, and I was bidden to go over the typescript of the speech. This was a return to the old pattern of things, after our un-spoken estrangement over convertibility, which gave me pleasure in those last months. In the course of our discussion he made a very characteristic remark. After reading the speech I told him that he had not touched on a point which I thought was much in the minds of ordinary people. I said that I believed that they thought that radiation due to the explosions would have an adverse effect on the fecundity of the human race. 'Oh,' he said, 'I have never heard that.' 'Well,' I said, 'I do not suppose that the people think that there will be anything very rapid, but only that there may be a cumulative effect in due course.' 'You mean that they will cause people to have deformed children.' 'No,' I said, 'I do not mean that ; that is another point ; I mean that they think that it will actually tend to have some slight sterilizing effect on the human race, that it will impair its genetic powers.' 'Well,' he said, 'I have read all the literature on this subject and I have never heard that one before.' 'I have no doubt that people are profoundly ignorant on this subject,' I replied, 'but I do believe that that is what they actually think.' 'Are you sure they think that ? I have never heard it.' 'Well, I am not absolutely sure, but I believe it to be the case, and, I think you ought to put something into your speech to relieve anxieties.' 'Well,' he said, 'if you believe that they think that, I must call in at No. 10 and find out if they really do.'

What a beautiful idea ! Although the Prof. was no longer in the Cabinet, and although Churchill was no longer Prime Minister, apparently the private secretaries of the existing Prime Minister would not be surprised if the Prof. should come in and put such a question to them. There was almost an oriental touch in his concept of the way in which things should be done. One imagined a Celestial Majesty ; one imagined the Great Chamberlains of his palace, whose duty it was to know what was passing in the minds of his subjects. How wonderfully the Prof. had arranged his life to fit in with his own scheme of things. A Viscount, he could make a speech in the House of Lords on any subject that occurred to him, and then, if he was in doubt about what 'the masses' thought on any topic, he just called in at No. 10 Downing Street and asked the private secretaries for information on that point.

*

In the 'twenties he had informed us that he would never retire, and, to tease us, added that he intended to use modern scientific methods for his own rejuvenation in due course. He was one of the few surviving 'vested interests', having been appointed to his Chair before the new statutes of 1925, which laid down a retiring age. But now his temper had changed somewhat ; the passage of years renders one less sprightly.

He was already beyond the age at which he could, under the *later* statutes, have remained a professor without a special resolution of the Visitatorial Board. However, he had attracted some first-class physicists to the Clarendon Laboratory, who were in charge of the departments there. They did the active work. He was the titular head, and, being a great power in the land, could be of practical use. If strings had to be pulled in order to get grants or other advantages, who better qualified than he to pull them ? I took the precaution at this time of going in some detail into the position at the Clarendon Laboratory with one of the most prominent physicists there. My ancient concern with matters pertaining to the Clarendon and my continuing interest in the Prof.'s affairs impelled me to put the questions. The physicist assured me that things were running smoothly, and that the Prof. was not being tiresome ; it might be a chore to have to explain all that was proceeding to the Prof. at regular intervals — and he insisted on being kept informed — but this was worthwhile in view of the Prof.'s usefulness to them in many ways. Reassured by this conversation, I told the Prof. that I hoped that he had no intention of resigning.

Unfortunately this happy position could not be maintained indefinitely. Some time after my conversation one or two valued members of the Laboratory took higher appointments elsewhere, in which they would have even greater scope. This was a severe blow, undermining, as it did, the Prof.'s arrangements. I told him that he must replace these men. But he pointed out to me that it was impossible. No first-rate physicists would be attracted to Oxford without some security of tenure of the position offered. The Prof. was past the normal retiring age, and a new man would want an assurance about where he would stand under the Prof.'s successor. This was precisely what the Prof. himself could not give. For this reason, he explained, he could not continue to hold his own Chair for much longer.

When he finally retired, Christ Church paid him an unprecedented honour. The Senior Censor informed him that he could retain his rooms in College. This had never been done before within living memory. Even tutors, like Sidney Owen, who had devoted their whole lives to teaching Christ Church undergraduates and working in other ways for the College, were compelled, when the fatal day to retire came, to pack up their books and leave. After all, the College had to provide accommodation for a perennial stream of undergraduates and for the dons in active work. None the less everyone greatly welcomed this concession to the Prof. How far off were the days when normal seniority at High Table had only been granted him with great reluctance and under the threat of legal action. Before he died, machinery was set in motion for making him an Honorary Student. He knew this, but it proved too late to complete the formal election.

In his last year he was made a Viscount. I ventured to observe to him that this further promotion was satisfactory, since, Churchill no longer being Prime Minister, no one could say that it was due to his favouritism. The Prof. did not reply directly to this remark. Perhaps he was reflecting that he preferred the favouritism of Churchill to the impartial recognition of all the rest of the Conservatives put together. Instead he made a characteristic observation. In recent years quite a number of donnish figures had been finding their way into the House of Lords. He said that he was pleased with the Viscountcy, because it signalized that he was a cut above those.

When he was originally awarded his Barony he beckoned me into the corner to have a few words in confidence. He was intending to take the title of Cherwell, the Oxford river. Although the Derby provides a good analogy for its pronunciation, few people spontaneously pronounce his name correctly. I had suggested a title, which would have given still greater difficulty ; why not call himself by the name of the street in which Christ Church, where he had lived all his life, was placed ? It would sound quite dignified — Lord St. Aldates (pronounced St. Olds, as in old man). However, he had rejected that proposal. Now it seemed that he wanted to consult me about what 'the masses' thought about the Cherwell. It was quite analogous to his mission to 10 Downing Street many years later, to find out what ordinary people thought about the atomic fall-out. He would not like to take the name of Cherwell, if it was commonly associated in the jesting conversation of undergraduates with fornication. I was able to reassure him.

During his last years a great controversy broke out about the proposal for a road across the Christ Church Meadow. On this he had very strong feelings and joined eagerly in the campaign to save the Meadow. He had already formed a close friendship with my colleague, Mr. Robert Blake, and they co-operated on this matter. He had a very high regard for the qualities of Mr. Blake. Shortly after his retirement he was asked to make a speech at the 'Censors' Dinner'. This is an annual event at Christ Church of an intimate character. He observed in the course of his speech that 'what he liked about Robert Blake was that he never nailed his colours to the fence'. One could not have higher praise than that from the Prof.

In the same speech, having expressed appreciation of the action of Christ Church in allowing him to retain his rooms in College, he pointed out the corollary that we should have to devote some time to entertaining him with our conversation in Common Room. 'It may not be pleasant for you, but it is your duty.' The old, old refrain. How well I recognized those words, 'it may not be pleasant for you', from times long past. Did he, despite all his honours, still feel like that ? I fear that he may have done so, although I have no doubt that most members of his audience regarded the words merely as a polite trope.

He had no need to feel it. Almost all now delighted in his company. Round about 9.15 our eyes wandered to the door, hoping that he would appear. He was most expansive to all our guests, old or young, British or foreign. He talked about grave matters or told funny stories, or sometimes amused us with little puzzles or conundrums. One night Dundas had an undergraduate guest who was a most efficient bowler on behalf of the University. The Prof. had never been a cricketer, but he bent his mind to the interests of this guest by discussing how one put on a swerve ; he went into the scientific aspect, discussing the velocity of the perimeter relative to the velocity of the centre of gravity of the ball and such matters. I could not help adjuring him to stop talking like that, or he would make the unfortunate man too selfconscious ever to be able to bowl again.

I reflected that he had probably worked all this out himself in his great tennis-champion days. No doubt he had adjusted the twist of his wrist to nice calculations concerning the velocities of the different parts of the tennis ball. When talking of tennis he used to explain that one had to work out all possibilities three or four strokes ahead. I do not know if tennis champions usually do this. His lightning speed of thought may have assisted him to gain all those tennis trophies, since, although he was of good physique, he had the handicap of poor eyesight.

It was a year or so after the visit of the bowler that Prince Obolensky had a guest who was interested in tennis. I put him next to me in Common Room, being in the Chair myself — that Chair so much coveted by the Prof. thirty years earlier. It made no difference now, since, contrary to his forecast, he had resigned ; furthermore, for many years he had been having dinner in his own rooms, so that precedence did not affect him. In due course he appeared round the door, and I bade him come and sit between me and Prince Obolensky's guest. I directed the conversation to tennis, knowing how much the Prof. loved to discuss old times. He was able to give his assessment of the merits and faults of all the different players who had been notable between the wars. He also brought out some of his favourite stories about tennis in Germany before the First World War. There was one about Kaiser Wilhelm II. When a sycophantic player lobbed up a ball towards him and he had smashed it down, he remarked : '*Das war ein echt Hohernzollscher Schlag*'.[1] The Prof. seemed to be in good form that evening and in excellent spirits. He intended to take the Blakes in his car to Wimbledon during the following week.

I wandered back with him in the dark along the terrace of Tom Quad. There was a point where we usually parted, unless I was going back to his rooms. 'Good night, Roy,' he said. The last word he pronounced in an affectionate, almost sentimental, tone. I was surprised, as the Prof. was usually so very undemonstrative. I reflected, as I watched him slowly finding his way into the cloisters, that this seemed to say that his feelings were unimpaired, despite all our troubles about S Branch, convertibility and the rest.

I did not see him again.

One evening during the next week he took a walk with Robert Blake round Christ Church Meadow. They parted, after fixing details for the drive to Wimbledon a couple of days later. The Prof. felt unwell as he reached his rooms. A doctor was summoned. All his life he expressed the utmost reluctance to take the advice of doctors. It was thought fit that a cardiogram should be taken the next day. The Prof.

[1] 'That was a truly Hohenzollern-like stroke.'

moved quickly. He wished to get signatures for certain alterations to his will, and Christ Church had to be scoured, since it was the vacation and few were living in. When Harvey left him in bed, it was arranged that the Prof. would turn on the light if he felt the need of anything. The light never went on. It is thought that he died peacefully very soon afterwards.

He looked calm. I would not use of him the hackneyed term, 'serene'. His face was very placid, and yet I thought that my practised eye detected some lingering expression on his features. He seemed to be saying, 'I accept this', with that same marvellous imperturbability that I had seen on so many occasions when he received some news fatal to an enterprise on which he was engaged.

*

The next days were heavy with sadness. There was something unexpected in the strength of the feelings that assailed me. Over the many years his intense reserve had precluded mutual expressions such as may serve as the outward signs and adornments of a warm friendship. But everything relating to the Prof. had a certain depth of quality ; and he was in his own nature so entirely different from his fellow men, that one knew that no new friend could ever qualify in the smallest degree to fill the niche that he had left. One had been living in two worlds. There was the greater world of one's interests, economics, the twentieth century, one's various friends ; and then there was another quite different world which was the creation of the Prof.'s imagination. And now the insubstantial pageant of that second world had faded.

If one has to present the character of the Prof. to the reader, the three qualities that it would seem most incumbent

on one to describe are the depth and originality of his thinking, the humour that enlivened his conversation and a certain
lovable quality. But one has only to mention those three
for it to be apparent that by their very nature such qualities
are beyond description, and can be apprehended only by
direct confrontation. And so, instead, I have had to content
myself with gathering together a few anecdotes, episodes and
sayings, in the hope that these may convey something of his
flavour and that my knowledge of them may serve as my
credential for making far-reaching claims on his behalf.

I have had opportunities in one way or another of holding
discourse with a fair proportion of those who have acquired
a reputation in our age as distinguished intellectuals, even
sages. It would be invidious to mention names. Measuring
them against the yardstick of the Prof. I would say that they
were men of opinions, while the Prof. was a man of thought.
If you ask one of these others for the reason for his stated
opinion, he will no doubt give it you ; he may be able to
tell you his reason for the reason ; but if you proceed further
with the peeling of the onion, you usually come to a mushy
substance. With the Prof. the tendency was the other way ;
the reason for the reason tended to be better than the reason ;
the deeper you got, the firmer his thought seemed to be.
He had depth, he had quality ; he gave you a new standard
by which to compare, and, I fear, too often to find wanting,
the clever ones of this world.

Then, quite apart from this question of the quality of the
thought, there was something else that was truly remarkable
the continuousness of it. For him to live was to think. Cogito,
ergo sum. But by this criterion most of our friends exist
but for a few brief minutes of a morning or afternoon. The
Prof.'s mind was always working as he moved quietly from
Common Room to his rooms, as he sat in his car, as he sat
in his arm-chair.

The Prof. was a thinking reed, in the fullest sense an intellectual. But intellectuality was by no means the sum total of his peculiarity. He was a man of passion also. Encased, reserved, moving in a studied routine, heavily armoured against all encroachments, ensuing comfort, valeted, cosseted, quiet in his manners except when especially provoked, avoiding the possibility of predicaments and carefully prepared for dealing with those that might within a narrow range arise, avoiding contacts not previously sponsored, and, he hoped, guaranteed, by the Christ Church Common Room, the Clarendon Laboratory, Churchill, or rich hostesses, a bachelor, seeing him thus one might be tempted to prefix to 'intellectual' the word 'bloodless'. Not in the least degree. He was a person in whom the emotions normal to mankind seemed to be raised to a higher intensity. Devoted in friendship, fierce in enmity, revengeful in thought, sensitive, angry, scornful, courageous, resolute, obstinate, abounding in humour, he was all this to an extent not commonly to be met with. In himself he was every inch human, palpitating with life. I suppose that it was this very enhancement and exaggeration of those emotions that are man's heritage that had to be balanced by inhibitions, which were responsible for his reserved and encased exterior. He was consciously cautious, stepping carefully, and there were no doubt unconscious mechanisms keeping in check his own too heady feelings. The result was a personality full of conflicts and one not readily to be understood. At the right moment, when the combination of circumstances was propitious, these heightened qualities had the chance of producing a heightened effect, and one had something quite out of the ordinary, such as his learning to fly in order to do a spinning nose dive. I should suppose that the aura of Churchill's greatness constituted a medium of a special kind in which the conflicts between his exaggerated feelings and his over-strong inhibitions were resolved and a balance achieved, so that his personality could find an easy and natural self-expression.

I think of the Prof. as the type of person which has been responsible for human progress. Man has lived through the ages in grooves of settled routine. Then occasionally you got a shift. Nowadays, it is true, progress itself has become a sort of routine, owing to certain veins of scientific thinking ; we do not know how long it will be before those veins are exhausted. The essential ingredient required for the shift is thought ; man is, after all, *homo sapiens* ; with him it is the new idea that causes the movement forwards. The Prof. was assuredly a man of thought. But a thought may illuminate the mind and then die away. The thought must become a conviction. One needs also persistence, and courage in the face of obstacles. The Prof. had all those qualities in overflowing measure. One needs some fire and passion to carry one along, and the Prof. had those also.

The thought must be a little different ; otherwise it is just part of the routine. The Prof. had an intense originality ; he was quite unlike anyone else. Some people become dons and acquire recognizably donnish qualities ; some mingle in Bloomsbury and take on a Bloomsbury manner ; you go into Parliament and become like a politician ; in these days you may become an 'angry young man' and as such you must also conform to type. The Prof. was always the same, wherever you found him, wherever you placed him. No friend of his could ever imagine that the most strange circumstances could avail to make him one whit different. As his thought was deep, so his originality was deep ; right to his very core he was the same. He seemed to give meaning to the words, I am what I am.

And I believe that in those words may also lie the secret of the love that was felt for him. Oh, no doubt it was partly that under the heavy armour you got a glimpse of an unsatisfied

fund of affection ; there was an appeal there that you wanted
to meet. But that was not the whole story. There was
something genuine about the Prof. through and through ;
that in itself is an endearing quality. And he was constant
too ; time and circumstance could not change him ; thus if
you had some stake in him, you knew that you had a permanent possession.

★

I venture to repeat here the words that I used in my
telegram of condolence to Sir Winston Churchill : 'it was
like the Prof. to have managed this business so unobtrusively'.
In reply Churchill informed me, as I had confidently expected,
that he would be coming to the funeral. I got into touch
with his secretary. His plan was to drive over from Kent to
Oxford in the morning and return home immediately after
the service. As this seemed rather arduous for a man of
eighty-two, I suggested that he should go to my rooms in
Killcanon for rest and refreshment before his journey back.
She agreed that this would be a good plan.

I felt sure that, if past associations have any meaning in
this life, it was I who should conduct Churchill from his car
to his seat in church. We paused on the lawn of Tom Quad
and I explained our plan for a brief rest. 'But I must go to
the grave', he said. Lady Churchill asked him if he was sure
that he would want to do anything more after the funeral
service was over ; the cemetery was a couple of miles away.
'I must go to the grave', he reiterated firmly and simply.

As we came up the aisle of Christ Church Cathedral the
congregation rose spontaneously to their feet. After the
service he drove to the cemetery. He walked in the procession
up the cemetery path. He walked beyond the path, advancing
over the difficult tufts of grass, with unfaltering, but ageing,
steps, onward to the graveside of his dear old friend.

INDEX

277

INDEX

INDEX

THE END

PRINTED BY R. & R. CLARK, LTD., EDINBURGH